ESSENTIALS OF
SOCIAL WORK
PRACTICE

ESSENTIALS OF
SOCIAL WORK PRACTICE

A Concise Guide to Knowledge and Skill Development

KATHLEEN F. COX

California State University—Chico

cognella®
SAN DIEGO

Bassim Hamadeh, CEO and Publisher
Amy Smith, Project Editor
Alia Bales, Production Editor
Jess Estrella, Senior Graphic Designer
Sara Schennum, Licensing Associate
Natalie Piccotti, Director of Marketing
Kassie Graves, Vice President of Editorial
Jamie Giganti, Director of Academic Publishing

3970 Sorrento Valley Blvd., Ste. 500, San Diego, CA 92121

BRIEF CONTENTS

DETAILED CONTENTS

PREFACE

T HE PROFESSION OF social work is rapidly evolving as it rises to the demand for services that are effective, strength based, collaborative, and responsive to the values and beliefs of increasingly diverse communities. If students are to meet the challenges presented in the 21st century, they must have access to education that is current and relevant. In preparing for a social work career, undergraduate and graduate students need academic material that not only celebrates the historical traditions of the field but also highlights the value of new and innovative practice models that are tailored to the complex needs of clients in today's world. In keeping with this focus, this text is devoted to core concepts and essential skills that are vital to successful practice and desired by agencies that offer internships and employment to current or graduating students.

The purpose of this book is to provide a concisely written, engaging, and relatable resource for foundation-level social work students. Distinct from other direct practice texts, it seeks to clearly connect human behavior theories to various approaches to engagement, assessment, intervention, and evaluation. It also illustrates fluidity between micro, mezzo, and macro level activities. Consistent with the current emphasis on self-care in social work, each chapter provides suggestions for self-care as they pertain to commonly encountered stressors within differing domains of practice. Sections devoted to this topic include strategies for managing countertransference and exposure to client trauma as well as methods for promoting safety, risk management, cognitive coping, adaptive goal setting, self-compassion, and gratitude. Woven throughout the text are discussions of ethical dilemmas and decision-making. The final chapter offers a broad selection of resources that can be utilized to promote life-long learning in social work.

On a more personal note, writing this book has allowed me to consolidate and share lessons learned and insights acquired over 30+ years of experience as a social work practitioner, researcher, and educator. I am very grateful to all my mentors who have furthered my knowledge, skill, and professional identity, and to my students who have helped me appreciate their needs for clarity, inspiration, self-efficacy, and emotional sustenance as they lay the groundwork for a robust and rewarding career.

Pedagogically, the text offers a variety of aids to enhance learning. Narratives and dialogues provide detailed illustrations of the use of core skills and strategies with diverse populations. Images, tables, and boxed material provide added emphasis and detail for concepts covered; they also feature contemporary and cutting-edge programs that exemplify strength-based, ethically oriented, and culturally relevant practice. At the end of each chapter are questions that can be used for small group or full classroom discussions. Exercises are provided to further skill development, self-awareness, and familiarity with relevant videos, websites, and other online resources. These exercises can easily form the basis for individual or group assignments. Finally, key terms are set in bold type and listed at the end of every chapter.

Acknowledgments

I would like to extend my gratitude to several individuals, in particular, who have been central to my learning in social work. I would like to thank Steve Kaplan for taking a chance on a young, relatively unexperienced social worker to be part of a nationally recognized demonstration project devoted to the creation of mental health systems of care (SOC) in the 1980s. SOC was a novel concept at the time. Carmen Flores, Sharon Clark, and Nancy King further guided my understanding of systems of care as they meet the needs of youth in the juvenile justice system. Lyn Farr taught me invaluable lessons in the importance of offering voice and choice to families served by public and nonprofit organizations. Most of all, I would like to thank Sue Steiner for her guidance and unwavering support throughout my tenure at California State University, School of Social Work. She is an inspiration to all social workers who dedicate themselves to social justice, cultural humility, and being a kind and caring person.

This text could not have been completed without the guidance and support of Kassie Graves, Vice President of Editorial, and Amy Smith, Project Editor, at Cognella, Inc. I would like to thank them for their valuable feedback and on-going encouragement. I would also like to thank my reviewers: Their comments and suggestions are greatly appreciated.

CHAPTER 1

Introduction to Social Work

Once you choose hope, anything's possible.—CHRISTOPHER REEVE

W HAT DRIVES PEOPLE to enter the field of social work? The job requires years of education, training, and personal investment. The work is taxing at times, both mentally and emotionally. Yet, many strive to join this vital profession and devote themselves to years of human service. Why? Because they feel compelled to carry hope for those who struggle with despair, hardship, oppression, and discrimination. They are inspired by opportunities to ease human suffering, even when substantial barriers stand in the way. In short, budding social workers know that they can make a difference.

It is often a very personal decision to become a social worker, as is seen in the applications of many who seek acceptance into an undergraduate or graduate educational program. Aspiring students cite not only a desire to help people (a given amongst practitioners) but a longing to live up to the ideals of a social worker who had supported them in their past. They may be determined to leverage their own experience with hardship to aid others struggling with similar forms of adversity. Moreover, they may recognize a personal gift for unearthing the needs of the disenfranchised. Most feel drawn into battle against the injustices that have persisted over centuries throughout our society.

As a student enters a Bachelor of Social Work (BSW) or Master of Social Work (MSW) program, the complexity of the work becomes clear. They are required to learn theory as it relates to human behavior and utilize basic and specialized skills, while developing an appreciation for both applied research and social policies that impact practice. It is expected that they will acquire a sense of responsibility to carry out services that are timely, effective, ethical, and strength based. Investment in this educational endeavor is what transforms a helper into a professional who understands the purpose of social work and is prepared to tackle social issues with knowledge that has been acquired and adapted to evolving trends since the late 19th century. Furthermore, higher educational programs provide the foundation for a lifelong process of learning and growing as a social work practitioner.

What Makes Social Work Unique?

Historical Foundations

The social work profession enjoys a very rich history. It was born out of hardship that faced many individuals and families that relocated to urban areas following the Industrial Revolution. To address the impoverished conditions, numerous charity organizations were established in the United Kingdom and shortly thereafter in the United States. During the late 1800s, the settlement movement emerged, focused on bringing the middle class in contact with the poor in order to mitigate a variety of social problems. The most renowned of all settlement houses, Hull House, was founded in 1889 by Jane Addams, the first American woman to receive a Nobel Peace Prize.

a.

b.

FIGURE 1.1. Hull House.

Often referred to as the "mother of social work," Jane was well-educated and privileged yet devoted her life to understanding the poor and bridging the gap between the upper and lower classes. She was a gifted advocate, author, and speaker who refused to accept the prevailing view that poverty is synonymous with laziness and inevitable in a progressive society. Jane understood that this false belief only served to separate the rich from the poor. She argued that "many of difficulties in philanthropy come from an unconscious division of the world into philanthropists and those to be helped" (Addams, 1899, p. 168). Jane asserted that the upper classes and elites should exercise compassion without condescension and step into the world of those in need. Ahead of her time, she also confronted traditional gender expectations and gave voice to those who had little political influence. Her "intellect and her power as a theorist of democracy" has, over the last few decades, captured a great deal of interest by scholars across many fields of study (Fischer, Nackenoff, & Chmielewski, 2009, p. 1). Jane Addams left behind a legacy that is a source of pride and inspiration for many who continue to actualize her vision.

Another pioneer of social work, Mary Ellen Richmond, is credited with professionalizing the field. She developed the first set of guiding principles for casework and called upon schools to educate and train social workers. Her landmark book, *Social Diagnosis* (Richmond, 1917), reveals her vast knowledge of history, philosophy, law, psychology, psychiatry, and medical social work. Mary was the first social worker to formulate theory and methods for identifying societal problems (NASW Foundation, 2004), and her work was key in establishing credibility for the profession. By 1929, there were 10 university programs in social work, and graduates served in volunteer agencies, correctional settings, state hospitals, out-patient centers, and child welfare as well as public assistance programs.

Other notable social workers include Jeannette Rankin, who graduated from what is now the Columbia University School of Social Work. She was a strong advocate for the suffrage movement, and in 1916 became the first woman elected to U.S. Congress. Harry Hopkins was elected the president of NASW in 1923. He went on to become the eighth Secretary of Commerce and one of Franklin D. Roosevelt's most trusted advisors. In fact, Hopkins was a key player in drafting the New Deal. Edith Abbott, dean of the School of Social Work Administration at the University of Chicago was also a consultant for Roosevelt and helped write the Social Security Act of 1935. Dorothy Height completed postgraduate education at the now named Columbia University School of Social Work. Due to her advocacy for African American women, she was honored with the Presidential Medal of Freedom in 1994 and a Congressional Gold Medal in 2004. Dorothy has been referred to as the "unsung heroine of the civil rights era" (Fox, 2010). These individuals, and many more, deserve recognition for their significant contributions to national policies that have advanced civil rights and provided social and economic relief to many Americans.

In April of 1998, the National Association of Social Workers (NASW) sponsored a social work centennial commemorative celebration with the stated goal of raising visibility of the profession and improving the public perception of social work.

Purpose of Social Work

In clarifying the purpose of social work, this section begins by disputing commonly held myths about direct social work practitioners. First is the myth that social workers are "baby snatchers." Students often lament the fact that some people associate social workers with the removal of children from their home, even without cause. It's true that some are employed at agencies devoted to child protection, but it is also clear that their work is not about snatching children from their parents—these practitioners devote their time and talents to strengthening and preserving families in order to prevent the need for out-of-home placement of at-risk youth.

Another myth is that all social workers are stressed out. While some do experience burnout due to high caseloads and rigorous demands, most manage their stress well and do not suffer deleterious consequences as a result of working with troubled or traumatized clients. This point is supported in a study conducted by Bride (2007) in which he administered the Secondary Traumatic Stress Inventory (Bride, Robinson, Yegidis, & Figley, 2004) to 284 master's level social workers. Almost half of the social workers surveyed did not meet any of the three core criteria for secondary traumatic stress (intrusive thoughts/nightmares, avoidance of secondary trauma reminders, increased arousal). Only 15% reported having symptoms in the previous week that met criteria for secondary traumatic stress across all three of these symptom clusters. This research does not suggest that social work is stress free, but it does reveal that many social workers use self-care and other stress management tools quite effectively. Many of these tools will be provided throughout the upcoming chapters.

Next, the term *social worker* is not synonymous with "socialist" or "sociologist," as is sometimes presumed. Socialism is a political and economic ideology that favors an egalitarian distribution of wealth within a society. While many social workers advocate for greater economic equality, some work for private companies that depend upon profit made possible in a capitalist system. Yes, social work and sociology are closely related fields but sociologists are focused on the use of research to better understand social order, institutions, and change; social workers seek to intervene so as to address social problems.

Some view social workers as rescuers, meddlers, and enablers. This couldn't be further from the truth. The social work code of ethics makes clear that practitioners should work to enhance the capacity of people to address their own needs versus solving all their problems for them (National Association of Social Workers, 2017). They must also respect a client's right to self-determination unless doing so would pose imminent and serious risk of harm to the client or others. Thus, they are committed to helping clients identify and clarify their own goals versus imposing expectations upon them.

Finally, social workers specializing in clinical work are no less qualified than psychologists in the performance of psychotherapy. In fact, they go through a rigorous process to obtain licensure as a clinical social worker. In most states, they are required to earn a master's degree, perform at least 3,000 hours of clinical work under the supervision of a licensed therapist, and complete a written clinical examination. Many are trained to specialize in a variety of evidence-based models of therapy.

It should be noted, however, that while some social workers have an interest in clinical work, others specialize in areas of direct practice (e.g., case management, behavioral intervention, supportive counseling, discharge planning, program coordination) that do not require a license or a degree in psychology. In fact, many practitioners suggest that one of the most attractive aspects of the social work field is the wide variety of choices one has for serving.

HIGHLIGHT 1.1: Social Workers are NOT ...

- Baby Snatchers
- Stressed Out
- Socialists or Sociologists
- Rescuers, Meddlers, and Enablers
- Less Qualified Than Psychologists

In defining the true purpose of the profession, the national association that represents social work education provides some guidance. The Council on Social Work Education (CSWE) notes that the profession's primary purpose is to "promote human and community well-being" (Educational Policy and Accreditation, 2015, p. 5). How this is done varies by service setting and subfield of the profession. For example, medical social workers support the emotional and physical functioning of patients served by hospitals, convalescent homes, home-health agencies, and hospice programs. Social workers in the behavioral health field provide psychotherapy and/or case management services to further the recovery of consumers with mental health or substance abuse disorders. School-based social workers enhance the social, emotional, and academic functioning of children, adolescents, and college students. Practitioners in the corrections field perform suicide risk assessment in correctional facilities and/or engage youth and adult participants in restorative justice programs. Rehabilitation social workers promote the full inclusion of people with physical and/or cognitive disabilities, while adult and child protective workers investigate reports of suspected abuse and provide case management services to individuals and families at risk of abuse or neglect. Social workers in veterans' affairs support military families when the service person is deployed and when they return. They also help veterans cope with loss and/or trauma related to combat. Social workers in the field of gerontology assess the functioning of older adults and address their psychosocial needs. Community organizers empower people to act in the interest of their community and advocate for a more equal distribution of power and resources. Last but not least, international social workers promote the human rights and prosperity of people around the world, including war victims, refugees, orphaned children, and victims of trafficking. Within these subdisciplines, social workers carry out a variety of roles that require specialized knowledge and skill.

Direct Practice Roles

Social workers assume many roles that involve both direct and indirect practice responsibilities. Indirect roles include those pertaining to policy analysis, evaluation research, report writing, and other forms of documentation and administration. This text will focus on several of the most important roles carried out by social workers conducting direct practice with individuals, groups, families, and communities. Each is defined by its functions, responsibilities, and required skill sets.

The Role of Broker

As a broker of services, social workers connect clients with needed resources. Such resources may provide emotional support, information, socialization, or concrete goods, and services such as food, clothing, transportation, and child or elder care. In making referrals, it is important that the social worker determine that their client meets the eligibility requirements for the service. Also imperative is consideration of the cultural preferences clients have in the way of service providers. If the client is uneasy about accessing recommended resources, the social worker may help them resolve their fears or concerns.

The Role of Case Manager

The case manager role involves not only brokering services but ensuring that they are provided in a timely manner. Case managers maintain contact with clients and other service providers to confirm that the linkage between the person referred and the needed resource was successful. Due to the social worker's focus on strengths and assets, they often strive to enhance the natural supports of their clients, such as extended family members, friends, and neighbors. In some cases, they may coordinate the development of a team on behalf of their client, as is done with many team conferencing approaches. In addition, they may be asked to facilitate team meetings and oversee the implementation of a coordinated plan of care.

The Role of Client Advocate

In carrying out the role of client advocate, social workers challenge barriers that stand in the way of individuals, families, and communities accessing resources needed to overcome problems and sustain well-being. When clients are capable of advocating for themselves, this is encouraged and supported. There are times, however, when barriers are substantial and beyond the person's reach. In this case, with permission from the client, the practitioner may act on their behalf and negotiate or mediate, as needed. If legal action is necessary, the social worker should never give legal advice, as this is beyond their scope of practice. They may, however, encourage the client to seek legal representation.

The Role of Coach

Social workers are often called upon to coach clients in a variety of ways. As a coach, they assist people in adopting new behaviors, skills, or styles of communication so as to resolve interpersonal problems or otherwise reach their goals. Social workers serving as coach may also promote new patterns of thinking in clients about their strengths and challenges. When the social worker observes the client making steps needed change, the use of positive reinforcement through praise can be an important tool, as it increases the likelihood of behavior maintenance. Whenever possible, it is helpful to coach clients in their natural environment where the beliefs, behavior, or communication generally occurs.

The Role of Counselor/Clinician

When assuming the role of counselor, social workers conduct psychosocial assessments and develop treatment plans to help individuals, families, and groups cope with difficult life events and circumstances. They provide emotional support and validation for clients who are suffering from grief and loss or experiencing other significant stressors. Counselors also help individuals gain insight into their behaviors, along with a better understanding of their relationships with others. In many cases, they assist clients in recognizing their strengths and in developing solutions to their problems and difficulties.

Licensed social work clinicians (LCSWs) perform diagnostic assessment using the *Diagnostic and Statistical Manual of Mental Disorders* (*DSM*; American Psychiatric Association, 2013). They also provide psychotherapy using cognitive-behavioral, solution-focused, narrative, and/or psychodynamic approaches, among others. LCSWs must complete continuing education units each year in order to maintain their status as a licensed practitioner.

The Role of Evaluator/Researcher

Whether or not they have the formal title of "evaluator," social workers engage in a variety of functions aimed at evaluating practice. They conduct needs assessments in their community, assess the effectiveness of their own practice, and participate in data collection for purposes of program evaluation. It is also important that they stay abreast of the literature concerning best practices with the population they serve.

NARRATIVE APPLICATION: Social Work Roles

Emily was hesitant to leave her husband, Jason, even after he had given her a black eye while in a drunken rage. She loved him but had seen a long-term pattern of him becoming intoxicated and violent. Emily shared her situation with a friend, who encouraged her to "get out now" in order to protect herself and her 3-year-old son, who had begun having nightmares. Eventually, she took her friend's advice—packed her bags, put her son in the car, and drove to a domestic violence shelter in her community. She was welcomed by staff and residents at the shelter and settled in quickly.

Emily was seen weekly by a social worker, Sue, who had been assigned as her *counselor*. Sue seemed to understand Emily's mixed feelings about leaving Jason on a permanent basis and helped her think about the pros and cons of ending her 5-year-long marriage. Emily began to realize that she needed to break it off with Jason but was afraid of living alone and becoming a single parent. In her role as *broker*, Sue referred Emily to various agencies that would help her access housing and employment. However, Emily didn't follow through with the required paperwork for these programs, as it seemed too overwhelming.

As Emily's 3-month allotted time period in the shelter neared, Sue talked to her about next steps. Emily teared up, acknowledging that she hadn't pursued the resources provided and had nowhere to go. "Is there any way I can stay here a little longer and get things together?" she asked. Sue responded with hesitation, "I'm not sure. It's not usually allowed, but I will check with the program manager." In her role as *client advocate*, Sue approached the manager and requested more time for Emily in the shelter. The manager asked what would be different this time around if she authorized more time. "I will help her complete the requirements for housing and employment and continue to counsel her around her ambivalence about leaving her husband. If we don't get more time, I think she will return to her ex and that would be bad news." The manager agreed to a 2-month extension.

During that time, Sue stepped up her role as *counselor* and devoted time to helping Emily process her grief related to ending her marriage. She also assumed the role of *coach* by assisting her in completing job and rental applications and practicing for interviews. As a result, Emily was successful in landing a small apartment and a job working with developmentally disabled adults. She left the shelter but was able to continue seeing Sue for a few weeks. During that time, she and Sue discussed her needs for long-term counseling. Emily agreed to see a therapist but wanted Sue to make the arrangements, as she knew little about how to access therapy through her insurance. Sue agreed and assumed the role of *case manager* by obtaining a list of therapists for Emily to review. With a written consent, she contacted the therapist Emily selected and coordinated a transition session that would include all three of them. In so doing, she ensured that her linkage and brokerage of therapeutic services was successful. Finally, at the close of their last meeting together, Sue asked Emily to fill out an outcome assessment and anonymous client satisfaction survey, thereby serving as *evaluator*.

TABLE 1.1. Social Work Roles

Role	Responsibilities
Broker	Determine client eligibility for needed resources; link client to services; resolve concerns about accessing services
Case Manager	Broker services and confirm linkages are established; enhance natural supports of clients; facilitate team meetings aimed at developing plan of care
Client Advocate	Challenge barriers that interfere with client access to resources; negotiate or mediate with service providers as needed
Coach	Assist clients in adopting new behaviors and skills; promote new patterns of thinking; positively reinforce client progress
Counselor/Clinician	Perform psychosocial assessments; develop treatment plans; provide emotional support and validation; promote client insight
Evaluator/Researcher	Conduct needs assessment; assess effectiveness of services; participate in program evaluation; stay current on research

Person-in-Environment Focus

A central aspect of social work that makes it unique is its focus on person-in-environment. Distinct from other human service disciplines that stress biological and psychological factors in understanding behavior, social work appreciates the reciprocal influence between individuals and their physical and social environments. This emphasis is rooted in *ecological* systems theory, an over-arching conceptual framework that unites both ecological theory and systems theory. Ecological theory originated in the subfield of biology that was concerned with the study of organisms within the context of their habitat. As applied to humans, ecological theory offers some important concepts that drive direct social work practice. The first is that of the **social niche**. As defined by Brower (1988), the social niche is "the unique place in which one 'fits' into the environment, the workplace, or community. It is a special place where one feels comfortable" (p. 412). Taylor (1997) suggests that not all niches are conducive to growth, however. He argues that settings or relationships that stigmatize people can be thought of as *entrapping niches*, while those that offer ample resources and growth-enhancing opportunities are *enabling niches* (p. 193). Social work services may be directed toward minimizing the negative impact of entrapping niches and promoting the development of enabling ones (Cox, 2008).

NARRATIVE APPLICATION: Building an Enabling Niche

Alicia had moved with her mother to her new neighborhood 6 months ago and was feeling more and more uncomfortable attending her middle school. She believed that the other kids didn't like her and thought she was weird. This belief had followed her from her previous school, where she had been bullied. Her symptoms of anxiety included chronic worrying, panic attacks, and insomnia. When the school social worker, Mr. Richards, met with her, he asked about her troubles and what would make her feel better about coming to school. Alicia said that she stays up late at night ruminating over what the other students think about her—she wanted them to like her. Mr. Richards began exploring her interests and talents. She had difficulty naming any but then disclosed that she knew how to crochet; her aunt had taught her several years back. The social worker asked Alicia if she would be willing to start a crocheting club at school, and she agreed to try. He made the arrangements quickly, and announcements went out that the club would be starting the following week. To Alicia's surprise, several girls began attending the meetings regularly and seemed to enjoy learning a new skill from her. She started to feel like she fit in and spent less time worrying while at home. She continued to suffer panic attacks, but much less often. When the school principal, Ms. Hayes, heard about the club, she proposed a project. A local hospital was in need of warm hats for the children in the cancer ward. When Ms. Hayes asked the club members if they would be willing to crochet hats for the children, they eagerly took on the project. Several months later, Alicia and the club were recognized at an assembly for the generous work they had done.

Another focus derived from ecological theory is the alignment of individual needs and goals with environmental strengths. It is important that social workers not only identify their client's personal strengths but also their environmental assets that can be accessed to support goal attainment. Rather than assuming a "cookie cutter" approach in which all clients are referred to the same programs, this effort involves matching individuals' needs and preferences to community resources. A useful tool in this process is referred to as the **community assets map**, developed by Kretzmann and McKnight (2005). It provides a template for assessing community supports, including faith-based centers, clubs, educational and recreational programs, cultural groups, and self-help support groups, along with formal social service organizations.

Early work in formulating **systems theory** occurred in the field of cybernetics, which was concerned with the communication of both living systems and machines. A special emphasis was placed on a system's ability to receive feedback in order to exercise control. Social scientists adapted systems theory to study the mutual influence individuals have on the various social systems with which they interact (family, school, workplace, peers, neighborhood, etc.). Family systems theory recognizes that families are systems defined by **boundaries** that determine the extent to which members engage with outsiders and are open to new

Associations

Animal Care Groups
Anti Crime Groups
Block Clubs
Business Organizations
Charitable Groups
Civic Events Groups
Cultural Groups
Disability/Special Needs Groups
Education Groups
Elderly Groups
Environmental Groups
Family Support Groups
Health Advocacy and Fitness
Heritage Groups
Hobby and Collectors Groups
Men's Groups
Mentoring Groups
Mutual Support Groups
Neighborhood Groups
Political Organizations
Recreation Groups
Religious Groups
Service Clubs
Social Groups
Union Groups
Veteran's Groups
Women's Groups
Youth Groups

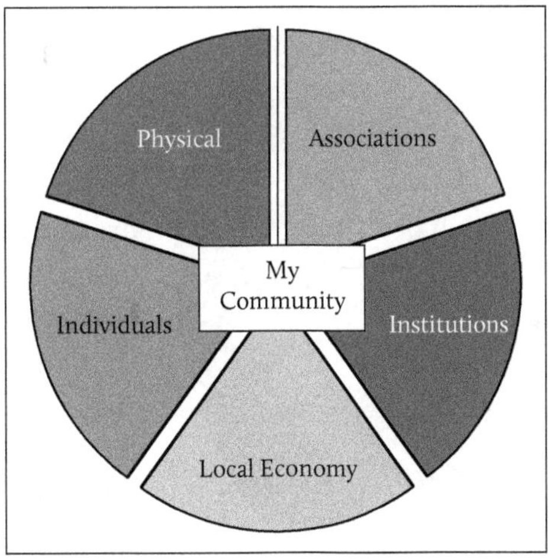

Physical Space

Gardens
Parks
Playgrounds
Parking lots
Bike Paths
Walking Paths
Forest/Forest Preserves
Picnic areas
Campsites
Fishing spots
Duck ponds
Zoos
Wildlife center
Natural Habitats - coastal, marine, amphibian
Bird Watching Sites
Star Gazing Sites
Housing
Vacant Land & Buildings
Transit stops and facilities
Streets

My Community

Physical
Associations
Individuals
Institutions
Local Economy

Institutions

Schools
Universities
Community Colleges
Police Departments
Hospitals
Libraries
Social Service Agencies
Non Profits
Museums
Fire Departments
Media
Foundations

Individuals

Gifts, Skills, Capacities, Knowledge and Traits of:

Youth
Older Adults
Artists
Welfare Recipients
People with Disabilities
Students
Parents
Entrepreneurs
Activists
Veterans
Ex-offenders

Local Economy

For-Profit Businesses
Consumer Expenditures
Merchants
Chamber of Commerce
Business Associations
Banks
Credit Unions
Foundations
Institutional - purchasing power and personnel
Barter and Exchange
CDCs
Corporations & branches

FIGURE 1.2. Sample Community Assets Map.

information and input. It also makes clear that change in one member of the family unit is likely to have an impact on others. Another key concept from family systems theory is that of **homeostasis**, which is defined as the balance that families seek to maintain on an on-going basis. If the family is upset, efforts will be made to bring it back into equilibrium. Social work assessment and intervention with families is frequently rooted in this theoretical model.

Urie Bronfenbrenner is a well-known psychologist who developed an ecological-systems framework for explaining human development. He conceived of the ecological environment as a "set of nested structures, each inside the next, like a set of Russian dolls" (Bronfenbrenner, 1979, p. 3). At the center is the individual

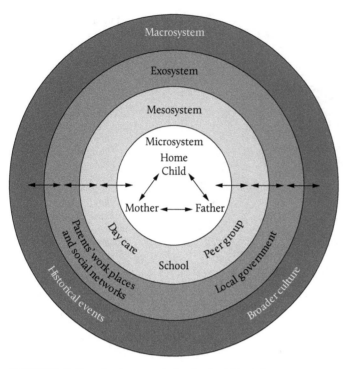

FIGURE 1.3. Bronfenbrenner's Ecological Model.

and his or her immediate setting, typically home and family; Bronfenbrenner referred to this as the microsystem. The next layer is the mesosystem that he defined as "a set of interrelations between two or more settings in which the developing person becomes a participant" (p. 209). Examples are the relations between school, home, and peer group for a developing child. The exosystem is viewed as a broader sphere that impacts the individual, even though they are not included as an active participant. An example is the indirect impact of a parent's workplace on his or her family members. Finally, the macrosystem includes the larger sociocultural context in which the other systems operate; this context embodies meanings, values, and institutions that are embraced by members of a society. Bronfenbrenner's model provides a visual representation that is extremely useful in furthering understanding of a person-in-environment orientation to practice.

Levels of Practice

The social work profession has borrowed terms from Bronfenbrenner's model in delineating the three primary levels or domains of practice: *micro*, *mezzo*, and *macro*. Micro practice involves working with individuals and/or families to help them resolve problems and improve functioning. It is considered the most common level of practice in the field, with ample employment opportunities falling into this direct service realm.

The term *mezzo practice* is commonly *used* when referring to group work aimed at building mutual support among people with common challenges or concerns. Examples include facilitating a support group for veterans or a treatment group for depressed individuals. Mezzo practice is also thought to include work with schools or other local organizations. This text adopts a slightly broader interpretation of mezzo-level practice, one that is consistent with Bronfenbrenner's view of the mesosystem. As noted above, he described this system as one that includes the relationships between two or more settings in which the individual is a participant. By assuming this perspective, it becomes clear that when a social worker is conducting micro-level practice with an individual and intervenes on their behalf to improve relationships between settings in which they participate, they are also carrying out mezzo-level work. Examples include activities aimed at increasing collaboration between agencies serving a family or efforts to improve the connection between a child's parents and his or her school. Upcoming chapters will provide additional illustrations of the fluidity that occurs between micro and mezzo levels of practice as social workers tackle the complex and multilevel needs of client populations.

The third domain of practice occurs at the macro level and includes work aimed at making changes on a wide scale through research, grant writing, advocacy for policy change, coalition building, and community organization. As with the micro/mezzo distinction, fluidity occurs between micro-level practice and macro-level efforts. In fact, the argument has been made that social workers should not view micro and macro practice as a dichotomy (Pearlmutter, 2002; Vodde & Gallant, 2002; Moya-Salas, Sen, & Segal, 2010). The most meaningful social work practice "entails assisting individuals in getting their needs met and in altering conditions that create oppression" (Moya-Salas, Sen, & Segal, 2010, p. 94).

Diversity, Social Justice, and Oppression

The emphases on embracing diversity, enhancing social and economic justice, and challenging oppression are hallmarks of the social work profession. Social justice means "fairness and access to opportunities for social mobility and improved potential for individuals and society—a better life for all people" (Bisman, 2014, p. 66). Direct social work practitioners advance this ideal by treating their clients with respect and dignity as they assist them in meeting basic needs for food, housing, safety, education, and healthcare. They also aid individuals and families in overcoming various hardships that have prevented them from achieving their potential. Social workers have a particular interest in serving oppressed populations, defined as those who are vulnerable and at-risk of poverty, discrimination, or hate-related violence. Practitioners also appreciate the challenges faced by people who are stigmatized due to addiction, mental illness, or disability. In addition, they are keenly aware of the rejection their clients face due to advancing age, gender identity, sexual orientation, culture, and physical attributes. They promote tolerance for diversity and compassionate care and treatment for all.

HIGHLIGHT 1.2: Enriching the Lives of LGBT Seniors

A model social work program created by the Los Angeles LGBT Center in 2008 is devoted to reversing discrimination faced by gay, lesbian, bisexual, and transgender older adults.

The Center's Seniors Services Department provides educational workshops to local social services agencies to support their efforts at becoming "LGBT welcoming." Once this training has been completed, the organization is eligible to receive referrals from LGBT Center case managers. The Seniors Services Department also operates the largest affordable housing complex for LGBT older adults (50+) and offers a wide range of events to aid LGBT seniors in connecting with their social environment:

- Health and wellness programs (exercise, stretching and conditioning, chair yoga, etc.)
- Enrichment classes (computer, writing, art, dancing, acting, photography, etc.)
- Monthly dinners and social networking opportunities
- Cultural excursions (theater, opera, museums, etc.)
- Educational seminars and workshops
- Senior-Youth Photo Project
- Senior-Youth Dinner
- Men's activities
- Women's activities
- Communidad Latina

The overarching goal of this program is to help LGBT seniors successfully age in place (Gratwick, Jihanian, Holloway, Sanchez, & Sullivan, 2014). Visit the LGBT Center website at https://lalgbtcenter.org/social-service-and-housing/
senior for further information.

What Qualifies Social Work as a Profession?

Not all occupations have achieved professional status. Social work, however, is one that has evolved over
the last century, developing features that allow it to meet the criteria for a profession. Theorists who
operationalize the term *profession* generally agree that to qualify, an occupation must have the following
attributes: a systematic body of theory and knowledge, public recognition, a regulatory code of ethics,
and a professional culture supported by professional associations (Weiss & Welbourne, 2007). Each of
these characteristics will now be discussed as they relate to social work.

Systematic Body of Theory and Knowledge

Social work draws from the knowledge base produced by a wide variety of fields, including sociology, psychology, child development, psychiatry, political science, and gerontology, as well as women and gender
studies. Social workers access conceptual models and research from these fields of study to assist them
in identifying risk and protective factors for populations served. Knowledge of the behavioral and social
sciences also prepares social workers to adopt various strategies for changing policies, creating viable
community resources, addressing substance abuse and mental health challenges, and otherwise meeting
the needs of marginalized, vulnerable populations, including immigrants, LGBTQ clients, older adults,
or at-risk children and families.

Social work has its own unique knowledge base as well. In fact, many scholarly works devoted to the
profession are published each year in **peer-reviewed journals**. These publications require an article to
be reviewed and accepted by experts in the field to ensure that they meet quality standards. The widest
read peer-reviewed social work journals include the following:

- *Social Work* is the official journal of the National Association of Social Workers (NASW) and is
  provided to members on a quarterly basis. Its primary focus is on improving practice and addressing
  critical social policy issues.
- *Journal of Social Work* offers a forum for scholars and practitioners to debate key concepts as well
  as the implications of research. It has an international editing board, which broadens its appeal.
  This journal strives to advance theory, inform practice, and shape policies relevant to social work.
- *Clinical Social Work Journal* publishes book reviews and articles related to evidence-based and
  clinically-oriented practice with individuals, families, and groups.
- *Journal of Family Social Work* features articles concerning policy, theory building, clinical practice,
  and research as it pertains to social work with couples and families. It aims is to blend practice,
  wisdom, and innovation with academic excellence.
- *Journal of Gerontological Social Work* publishes articles devoted to theory, research, clinical intervention, systematic reviews, and policy analysis related to gerontological social work.

- *Health and Social Work* includes scholarly work related to aging, long-term care, depression, maternal health, and other topics related to medical social work.
- *Journal of Social Work Values and Ethics* is an online journal that examines the impact of ethics and value issues on social work practice and research. It also provides a historical perspective on the development of social work values and ethical decision-making.
- *Social Work Research* publishes rigorous research that informs social work practice. It also includes theoretical articles pertaining to research and analytical reviews of evaluation studies.
- *Journal of the Society for Social Work & Research* seeks to advance the rigor of social work research by publishing empirical findings and studies using innovative research methods to examine social problems, policies, and programs. An emphasis is placed on studies of the effectiveness of social and health services.
- *Journal of Social Work Education* offers a forum for the exchange of information on trends and issues pertaining to education at the BSW and MSW levels.
- *Journal of Baccalaureate Social Work* publishes articles that promote the continued development of BSW educational programs.

Public Recognition

When an occupation is recognized publicly, efforts are made to ensure that the those entering the field are qualified to perform assigned duties. In the United States, public credentialing of social workers began in 1934, with a focus on certification or registration. Today, most states offer title protection, meaning that one must have completed an accredited social work education program to call themselves a social worker. Undergraduate- and graduate-level programs are accredited by the Council of Social Work Education (CSWE). In addition, all 50 states have some form of licensing but eligibility requirements vary; some states only license social workers with an MSW-level education while others license those at the BSW and MSW level. Licensed clinical social workers (LCSWs) have a great deal of flexibility in their careers and are permitted to open their own private practice.

Regulatory Code of Ethics

All social work students, interns, and employees are expected to abide by the NASW Code of Ethics (National Association of Social Workers, 2017), which provides a set of values, principles, and standards aimed at regulating professional conduct. Most importantly, it guides them in ethical decision-making, a process that is not always straightforward. Social workers often encounter situations in which ethical responsibilities clash, creating confusion and uncertainty as to the proper course of action. The code is a useful reference in this regard as it identifies "relevant considerations when professional obligations conflict" (NASW, 2017, p. 2). An example is when a commitment to client confidentiality clashes with the need to prevent harm to another individual. This dilemma occurs when a client reveals incidents of serious child abuse that have been occurring in his or her home. The code is beneficial here in that it makes clear that the principle of confidentiality does not apply "when disclosure is necessary to prevent serious foreseeable, and imminent harm to a client or other identifiable individual" (p. 12). Thus, the social worker is required to file a suspected child abuse report. Chapter 2 will cover social work values and ethics in depth, and subsequent chapters will offer illustrations of ethical issues frequently encountered in various domains of direct practice.

Professional Culture and Associations

The culture of professional social work honors diversity, cultural humility, and an emphasis on strengths and assets versus deficits in carrying out all components of practice. These values and norms are promoted by various professional social work associations, the largest of which is the National Association of Social Work (NASW). This organization was founded in 1955, and over the last half century its membership has grown to 130,000. NASW sponsors continuing education, conferences, and national awards. The association also offers legislative alerts and updates, while coordinating a delegate assembly that develops a collective stance on policy issues. All 50 states have a chapter that is an extension of the national organization.

An important tradition of the social work profession is the celebration of Social Work Month every March, as sponsored by NASW chapters in the United States. World Social Work Day (WSWD), as launched by the International Federation of Social Work (IFSW) in 1983, is celebrated on the 3rd Tuesday in March. On this day, social workers across the world highlight the contributions of the profession and promote their international solidarity. WSWD events have been held at the United Nations in New York since 1983, in Geneva since 2012, and in Bangkok since 2017. For further information about these celebrations, see the IFSW website (https://www.ifsw.org).

To explore the historical roots of social work, one can visit the Jane Adams Hull House Museum in Chicago. It serves as both a memorial to Jane Addams and a preservation of the original Hull House site. The museum offers guided tours and exhibitions, and houses a collection of over 5,500 artifacts from the early settlement period, including textiles, drawings, pottery, furnishings, and oral histories of residents and neighbors. Roughly 30,000 people visit each year to learn about democratic ideals, women's history, immigration, and the settlement movement.

Overview of the Helping Process

The process of direct social work practice includes several phases—engagement, assessment, goal setting, intervention, transition/termination, and evaluation. However, these phases should not be viewed as entirely distinct in that the activities in each overlap with those of the others. For instance, the process of engaging clients and building rapport is central in the first phase of work but continues throughout service delivery. Assessment also begins early on, but continues as new information emerges during the intervention stage. Termination, while the primary focus at the end of care, should be discussed as goals are set in order to make clear the likely duration of services, along with the circumstances that will indicate that the need for services has come to a close. Evaluation is done both during and post service completion. For ease of explanation, however, each phase will be discussed consecutively, and one chapter will be devoted to each later in this text. The singular term *client* will be used in referring to the recipient of services, with the understanding that social workers are often working with couples, families, groups, and communities.

Engagement is the process through which the foundation is set for practice. Here, the practitioner places a strong emphasis on establishing rapport with the client and understanding their perspective regarding the need for services. Trust is built by validating the client's concerns and recognizing the ways in which they have struggled and survived pain. Motivation is enhanced by exploring the change the client would like to see happen in the near and distant future.

Assessment is both a product and a process. The *product* is the written or electronic document produced by the practitioner that includes information gathered about the client's strengths and needs across a variety of domains of functioning—biophysical, psychological, social, cultural, and spiritual. It provides a holistic and multidimensional account of the person within the context of their environment. The assessment *process* is the manner through which the practitioner creates safety in the helping relationship as they explore topics that may provoke discomfort in their client. It is often helpful for the social worker to explain the importance of the information gathered for the development of a well-informed plan for services.

Goal Setting is the translation of presenting problems and client strengths into objectives that are to be accomplished over the course of service delivery. Short- and long-term goals should be stated in terms that emphasize growth versus the elimination of deficits. They should be established collaboratively with the client and significant others that the client has chosen to be involved. It is also important that specific tasks and actions are identified that will be taken toward short-term goal attainment.

Intervention is activity aimed at managing crisis or risk and creating change toward goals and objectives. It can be carried out with individuals, families, groups, and/or communities, sometimes referred to as the *units of service*. Whenever possible, it is best to utilize evidence-based models of intervention—those with ample research demonstrating effectiveness. It's also important to use interventions that provide a good fit with the cultural beliefs and practices of the client. This text will review some of the most commonly used change-oriented strategies in social work as well as ways they may be adapted for differing cultural groups.

Transition/Termination refers to the client's graduation from services. It ideally involves a review of progress made, skills learned, and assets developed. Sometimes a gradual step-down process is used to lessen the frequency of meetings before final termination occurs. Different forms of termination and transition, both planned and unplanned, will be discussed in this text.

Evaluation involves gathering information about the benefits and limitations of the services that were provided. It can focus on client satisfaction with various aspects of the service delivery process. Evaluation also captures information about client outcomes attained as well as those that were not fulfilled. It is important that practitioners embrace the evaluation process and reflect upon the feedback it provides as to the strengths of services delivered as well as areas for needed improvement. Formal and informal methods for evaluation will be covered in an upcoming chapter.

Sustaining Social Work Practice Through Self-Care

It is increasingly understood that self-care among practitioners is vital for sustaining high-quality services. When work-related stress is not managed effectively, it can pile up and, in some cases, lead to burnout, secondary traumatic stress, or vicarious trauma. These conditions are distinct yet can occur simultaneously. **Secondary traumatic stress** (STS), or compassion fatigue, is a syndrome that results from exposure to client trauma and manifests in symptoms similar to that of post-traumatic stress disorder (PTSD), including intrusive thoughts, nightmares, high arousal, and avoidance of reminders of the traumatized person. Exposure to client trauma can involve reading accounts of horrific abuse or listening to clients describe disturbing and frightening events. Social workers with their own trauma histories are most susceptible to STS (Figley, 1995), as encounters with client trauma can trigger memories of the practitioner's own unresolved conflicts around traumatic experiences. Thus, it is advisable that trauma survivors complete their own healing and recovery before attempting to provide service to individuals who have experienced similar traumatic events.

Continual exposure to traumatic material can lead to **vicarious trauma (VT)**, conceptualized as an altered worldview that results in pessimism, mistrust of others, and jaded attitudes (Pryce, Shackelford, & Pryce, 2007). To illustrate this mental state, Gold (1998) offers comments provided by child welfare workers who were interviewed so as to shed light on the positive and negative impacts of the work. One stated, "I don't see the world with any normalcy any more. I only see it through the eyes of child abuse" (p. 712). Like STS, VT is more common among trauma survivors (Pearlman & Saakvitne, 1995).

Burnout is a fairly frequent outcome of chronic stress and has been linked to high turnover in social work (Mor Barak, Nissly, & Levin, 2001). Its source differs from that of the above two conditions, however. Burnout occurs when a person is employed in a work environment that demands a great deal yet provides limited supports, rewards, and personal satisfaction. To illustrate this condition, one can think of a new social worker who is initially "on fire" and enthusiastic about their assigned responsibilities; over time, their flame is extinguished (Schaufeli, Leiter, & Maslach, 2009), and they become physically, mentally, and emotionally exhausted.

Thankfully, these conditions can be prevented or remedied if they begin to take hold. **Self-care** is frequently prescribed as an antidote and, although practiced by individuals, it should be supported by supervisors and administrators. However, the meaning of self-care is not well understood and varies among authors, researchers, and practitioners. According to Cox and Steiner (2013), the literature promotes the use of strategies that entail *lifestyle choices* and *workplace adaptions*. The former category includes efforts to improve diet, sleep, exercise, recreation, and home/work balance, while the latter may involve taking breaks in the workday and accessing supervisory or co-worker support. These authors recommend an additional self-care strategy, that of *cognitive coping*. After conducting focus groups with practitioners across a range of socials service settings, they concluded that through the use of positive reappraisal, or cognitive reframing, social workers shift their thinking from harm done to opportunities provided by challenging or distressing events. Examples of the use of cognitive coping and other self-care strategies will be woven through the upcoming chapters. It is hoped that they will stimulate creative thinking about additional tools that might be used to manage the stress of social work.

SUMMARY

This chapter provides an introduction to social work that highlights its status as a uniquely qualified helping profession, one with deep historical roots and a strong theoretical foundation. The primary levels of practice (micro, mezzo, and macro) were presented with an emphasis placed on their interplay and integration. An outline of the helping process was offered that guides the organization of upcoming material on engagement, assessment, goal setting, intervention, transition/termination, and evaluation. This chapter concluded with a discussion of self-care as a means of sustaining ethical and effective social work service. These themes will be furthered developed and illustrated throughout this text.

KEY TERMS

Assessment	Evaluation	Secondary traumatic stress
Boundaries	Goal setting	Self-care
Burnout	Homeostasis	Social niche
Community assets map	Intervention	Systems theory
Ecological theory	Micro, meso, macro, exosystems	Transition/Termination
Engagement	Peer-review journals	Vicarious trauma

DISCUSSION QUESTIONS

1. In what ways is it a personal decision for you to enter the field of social work?

2. In reviewing the narrative application on page 6 consider the seamless way in which Sue assumed a variety of roles with one client. Which role(s) do you think were most important and why?

3. Review the discussion of social niches on page 8. What are some examples of entrapping and enabling niches? What makes them either enabling or entrapping?

SKILL DEVELOPMENT ACTIVITIES

1. Find the website for the NASW Chapter in your state. Explore upcoming events and opportunities for networking. Consider attending one and reporting back to your class.

2. Go to the website for the International Federation of Social Work (https://www.ifsw.org). Click on the tab titled "Global Agenda." Explore what is being done to advance the IFSW agenda.

3. Go to a campus library or online database and find one of the social work journals listed on page 12. Select an article to read, and write a brief summary of its main points.

REFERENCES

Addams, J. (1899, February). The subtle problems of charity. *Atlantic Monthly, 84*, 168–178.

American Psychiatric Association. (2013). *Diagnostic and statistical manual of mental disorders* (5th ed.). Washington, DC: Author.

Bisman, C. (2014). *Social work: Value guided practice for a global society.* New York, NY: Columbia University Press.

Bride, B. (2007). Prevalence of secondary traumatic stress among social workers. *Social Work, 52*, 63–70.

Bride, B. E., Robinson, M, M., Yegidis, B., & Figley, C. R. (2004). Development and validation of the Secondary Traumatic Stress Scale. *Research on Social Work Practice, 14*, 27–35.

Bronfenbrenner, U. (1979). *The ecology of human development.* Cambridge, MA: Harvard University Press.

Brower, A. M. (1988). Can the ecological model guide social work practice? *Social Service Review, 62*, 411–429.

Cox, K. (2008). Tools for building on youth strengths. *Reclaiming Children and Youth: The Journal of Strength-based Interventions, 16*(4), 19–24.

Cox, K., & Steiner, S. (2013). *Self-care in social work: A guide for practitioners, supervisors, and administrators.* Washington, DC: NASW Press.

Educational Policy and Accreditation Standards for Baccalaureate and Masters Social Work Programs (2015). Council on Social Work Education.

Figley, C. R. (1995). *Compassion fatigue: Coping with secondary traumatic stress disorder in those who treat the traumatized.* New York, NY: Brunner-Routledge.

Fischer, M., Nackenoff, C., & Chmielewski, W. (Eds.) (2009). *Jane Addams and the practice of democracy.* Champaign, IL: University of Illinois Press.

Fox, M. (2010, April 21). Dorothy Height, largely unsung giant of the civil rights era dies at 98. *The New York Times*, p. A25.

Gold, N. (1998). Using participatory research to help promote the physical and mental health of female social workers in child welfare. *Child Welfare, 77*, 701–724.

Gratwick, S., Jihanian, I. J., Holloway, I. W., Sanchez, M., & Sullivan, S. (2014). Social work practice with LGBT seniors. *Journal of Gerontological Social Work, 57*, 889–907.

Kretzmann, J. P., & McKnight, J. L. (2005). *Discovering community power: A guide to mobilizing local assets and your organization's capacity.* Evanston, IL: Northwestern University, Asset-Based Community Development Institute.

Mor Barak, M. E., Nissly, J. A., & Levin, A. (2001). Antecedents to retention and turnover among child welfare, social work, and other human service employees: What can we learn from past research? A review and metanalysis. *Social Service Review, 75*, 625–637.

Moya-Salas, L., Sen, S., & Segal. E. (2010). Critical theory: Pathway from dichotomous to integrated social work practice. *Families in Society: The Journal of Contemporary Social Services, 91*, 91–96.

NASW Foundation (2004). *NASW social work pioneers.* Washington, DC: Author.

National Association of Social Workers (2017). *Code of ethics of the National Association of Social Workers.* Washington, DC: NASW Press.

Pearlmann, L. A., & Saakvitne, K. W. (1995). Treating therapists with vicarious traumatization and secondary traumatic stress. In C. R. Figley (Ed.), *Compassion fatigue: Coping with secondary traumatic stress disorder in those who treat the traumatized* (pp. 150–177). New York, NY: Brunner-Routledge.

Pearlmutter, S. (2002). Achieving political practice: Integrating individual need and social action. *Journal of Progressive Human Services, 13*(1), 31–51.

Pryce, J. G., Shackelford, K. K., & Pryce, D. H. (2007). *Secondary traumatic stress and the child welfare professional.* Chicago, IL: Lyceum.

Richmond, M. (1917). *Social diagnosis.* New York, NY: Russell Sage Foundation.

Schaufeli, W. B., Leiter, M. P., & Maslach, D. (2009). Burnout: 35 years of research and practice. *Career Development Journal, 14*, 204–220.

Taylor, J. A. (1997). Niches and practice: Extending the ecological perspective. In S. Saleebey (Ed.), *The strengths perspective in social work practice* (pp. 217–226). New York, NY: Longman.

Vodde, R., & Gallant, J. P. (2002). Bridging the gap between micro and macro practice: Largescale change and a unified model of narrative-deconstructive practice. *Journal of Social Work Education, 38*(3), 439–458.

Weiss, I., & Welbourne (Eds.). (2007) *Social work as a profession: A comparative cross-national perspective.* Birmingham, UK: Venture Press.

CREDITS

CHAPTER 2

Social Work Values and Ethics

The time is always right to do what is right. —MARTIN LUTHER KING, JR.

W HAT DOES IT mean to master social work values and ethics? One can easily memorize the six values advanced by the National Association of Social Workers (2017): service, social justice, dignity and worth of the individual, importance of human relationships, integrity, and competence. The principles and standards listed in the National Association of Social Workers (NASW) Code of Ethics can also be the focus of study and review. Yet, such exercises don't ensure that a social worker will practice in a manner that is consistent with the moral core of the profession. This chapter will not only name the values and ethical codes of social work, but will also explore ways that direct service practitioners can appreciate their intent and champion their application, thereby demonstrating moral leadership across all of their roles and responsibilities.

To begin knowledge building as it concerns social work values and ethics, it is important that practitioners understand the difference between absolutism and relativism. Moral absolutism suggests that certain actions are inherently good or bad, that one must always abide by the rules and laws, no matter the consequences. In contrast, relativism argues that there are occasions in which it is appropriate to violate rules when doing so will lead to a greater good for all concerned. A relativistic judgement is sometimes needed when applying ethical principles in direct social work practice. The Code of Ethics provides clear guidelines for professional conduct, yet there are circumstances in which the social worker may do significant harm to self or others by following them to the letter of the law. In fact, any value or principal, when taken to an extreme, can be problematic. A balanced and well-reasoned approach to ethical decision-making is needed and will be illustrated in the sections below.

Professional Social Work Values

Professional values reflect what is deemed important by those who set standards for an occupation. As individuals are socialized into their field, they are taught ways of thinking and doing that embody these values. In social work, students, interns, and new employees are exposed to a multitude of ways that they may serve, pursue social justice, preserve the dignity of others, promote human relationships, and demonstrate integrity as well as competence. However, some entry-level practitioners also observe instances in which the ideals of the profession are not fulfilled in practice. This is true in most, if not all professions, as the **espoused values** of employees and organizations do not always line up with the values implied by their activities (Argyris & Schon, 1974). Ultimately, it is up to every social worker to devise their own moral compass that will guide them in upholding the purpose and mission of the profession. The development of critical thinking about how to conduct oneself in ways that are consistent with social work values is an important aspect of social work education.

Service

Social work is a human service occupation that is focused on helping individuals, families, groups, organizations, and communities to access needed resources, resolve problems, and achieve optimal functioning. As a practitioner, one is expected to make service their primary objective. In fact, the NASW Code of Ethics states that social workers are expected "to elevate service to others above their own self-interest" (National Association of Social Workers, 2017, p. 5). This principle should not be misinterpreted as a call for social workers to relinquish all of their own needs in the name of service. Clearly there are times when practitioners must set limits on service requests in order to preserve their own safety as well as their physical and emotional security. Yet the fundamental focus needs to be on helping clients and serving their needs versus exploiting them so as to further the worker's own personal gain. Direct service practitioners are also expected to participate in activities that address broad social issues such as poverty, oppression, and discrimination.

Social Justice

Social workers have a responsibility to advocate for fair and equal access to resources and opportunities for all people, particularly those who are vulnerable, oppressed, and disadvantaged. Every subfield of the profession provides ample opportunities for direct service professionals to uphold this ideal and combat various forms of injustice. Social workers may advocate for individual clients to receive the resources they need and deserve, or provide outreach to populations that have limited access to services. Practitioners may also propose programs that enhance opportunities for vulnerable groups and support policies aimed at improving the human condition. Because social and economic inequities shift over time, it is important that service providers stay current on the primary issues plaguing the people in their community.

In an effort to prioritize the social justice issues of this decade, the American Academy of Social Work and Social Welfare kicked off the Grand Challenges of Social Work Initiative, as discussed by Richard Barth and colleagues (2014). In January of 2016, this group of 72 prominent scholars and practitioners released a list of 12 primary challenges for the field, all of which require collective action and focused attention in upcoming years. Four of the challenges relate to individual and family well-being: ensuring healthy development for all youth, closing the health gap, eliminating family violence, and advancing long and productive lives. Several more are aimed at creating a stronger social fabric: eradicating social isolation, ending homelessness, providing a social response to a changing environment, and harnessing technology for the social good. The final four are focused on furthering a just society by promoting smart decarceration, building financial capability for all, reducing extreme economic inequality, and achieving equal opportunity and social justice. All of these ambitions clearly require broad systemic change, yet every social worker can do their part by educating the public about their importance. Direct practitioners can also take concrete steps toward the fulfillment of one or more of these challenges, as applicable to their subfield of social work. Go to the Grand Challenges Initiative at http://grandchallengesforsocialwork.org/grand-challenges-initiative/12-challenges/

TABLE 2.1. Social Work's Grand Challenges

Three Organizing Areas	12 Grand Challenges
Individual and family well-being	1. Ensure healthy development for all youth 2. Close the health gap 3. Stop family violence 4. Advance long and productive lives
Stronger social fabric	5. Eradicate social isolation 6. End homelessness 7. Create social responses to a changing environment 8. Harness technology for social good
Just society	9. Promote smart decarceration 10. Build financial capability for all 11. Reduce extreme economic inequality 12. Achieve equal opportunity and justice

Note. With permission of the National Association of Social Workers. Table found in Bent-Goodley editorial in *Social Work,* *61*(3), 197–198.

Dignity and Worth of the Person

When a social worker truly values the dignity and worth of a client, they not only offer them genuine respect but make it a priority to discover their unique gifts. This requires a core belief that all people have strengths, even if they are buried amongst the fallout from years of degradation, abuse, self-sabotage, or stigmatization. Upholding this value requires that social workers get past labels and stereotypes (e.g., "welfare mom," "drug addict," "abuser," "illegal alien," "redneck") and see into their client's hopes, dreams, and aspirations for a better life. This is not to say that social workers should agree with and condone behavior or attitudes that are harmful or destructive. It does mean that they should seek to understand why a person feels, thinks, and behaves the way they do, given their circumstances. When this type of validation is communicated, the dignity of the client is preserved and the foundation for trust building is established.

For some social workers, it is relatively easy to embody this value in their interactions with clients but much harder in their communication with co-workers and colleagues. Here again, social workers benefit by getting past labels (e.g., "lazy," "nasty," "burned out," "toxic") and appreciating the needs that underlie their co-worker's behavior. For example, if a colleague is irritable and makes a rude remark, one could take the time to consider the stress or insecurity that drives their demeanor rather than rush to judgment. This is not to excuse bad behavior, but to encourage tolerance and sensitivity versus retaliation. When practitioners assume good will and preserve the dignity and worth of their colleagues, they contribute to a positive workplace culture that supports high-quality service delivery to clients.

Human Relationships

Interpersonal relationships are valued by social workers due to their power in promoting wellness and well-being. Yet, practitioners understand that not all relationships are created equal with respect to the benefits they offer. Relationships that serve as a source of emotional and concrete support reduce the negative impact of stress on physical and mental health (Thoits, 2010). High-quality, close personal connections are linked to happiness (Demir, 2013). On the other hand, conflicted and abusive relationships result in a wide range of physiological and psychological problems (Antle, Karam, Christensen, Barbee, & Sarr, 2011). Thus, social workers place an emphasis on developing and promoting healthy relationships.

Practitioners may define **healthy relationships** for their clients as those characterized by mutual support and respect, clear boundaries, congruent communication, and negotiation in response to conflict (Eckstein, 2004). Social workers may also teach skills in nonviolent and compassionate communication that have been found to improve empathy and relationships with others (Beck, 2005; Sears, 2013). It's essential that they also attend to their own professional relationships with clients, co-workers, and supervisors, and strive toward healthy communication, partnership, and collaboration in their role as direct service provider.

Integrity

Practicing social work from a place of integrity means being reliable, accountable, and willing to assume responsibility for one's actions. It also means fulfilling one's obligations, providing coherent accounts of events and circumstances, and demonstrating a commitment to quality practice. A social worker who values integrity can be trusted to speak honestly and follow through with their assigned responsibilities. Specific actions that uphold the value of integrity include the following:

- Accurately representing one's credentials; being clear with clients if one is a social work student or intern
- Providing an honest account of one's training or areas of expertise
- Serving within one's scope of practice
- Attending appointments made on a timely and consistent basis
- Admitting to mistakes versus denying responsibility or making excuses
- Documenting and billing for services provided in an honest and accurate manner

Competence

Direct social work practitioners must commit to an on-going process of knowledge and skill development. This commitment can be fulfilled through supervision as well as face-to-face or online educational programs and workshops. The highest level of competency is obtained by seeking out and utilizing feedback from supervisors, field instructors, or trainers who have observed the practitioner in action, either in-person or via audio or video recordings. Participation in this type of supervision and training can be stressful, as it requires the social worker to become vulnerable and accept constructive criticism about their style and use of skill.

In managing the stress and anxiety that arises when one is receiving performance-related feedback, the practitioner may choose to draw on the insights of renowned speaker, author, and social work professor Brene Brown. In her landmark book, *The Gifts of Imperfection* (2010), she discusses the "gauntlet of gremlins" that can get in the way of us finding our gifts and cultivating meaningful work. These gremlins feed our insecurities and self-doubt by telling us that we have to be perfect and prove ourselves in order to be accepted. She encourages us to embrace vulnerability and take the journey toward whole-hearted living, defined as follows:

> Whole-hearted living is about engaging in our lives from a place of worthiness. It means cultivating the courage, compassion, and connection to wake up in the morning and think, *No matter what gets done and how much is left undone, I am enough.* It's going to bed at night thinking, *Yes, I am imperfect and vulnerable and sometimes afraid, but that doesn't change the truth that I am also brave and worthy of love and belonging.* (p. 1)

TABLE 2.2. Translating Social Work Values into Action

Value	Ethical Principle	Knowledge, Skill, Practice Behaviors
Service	Social workers' primary goal is to help people in need and to address social problems	Ability to assess and address client needs, provide linkage to appropriate resources, recognize potential conflicts of interest
Social Justice	Social workers challenge social injustice	Alertness to forms of oppression, ability to advocate for vulnerable populations
Dignity and Worth of the Person	Social workers respect the inherent dignity and worth of the person	Ability to convey genuine respect, continually discover client strengths and aspirations, empower and validate clients and colleagues
Importance of Human Relationships	Social workers recognize the central importance of human relationships	Awareness of the importance of healthy human relationships, ability to model the use of healthy communication for clients and co-workers
Integrity	Social workers behave in a trustworthy manner	Honest communication, accountability, reliability, willingness to admit to mistakes
Competence	Social workers practice within their areas of competence and develop and enhance their professional expertise	Ability to utilize continuing educational opportunities, supervision, and performance-based feedback

Ethical Standards in Social Work

Imagine what it would be like be a social worker if there were no laws or ethical standards to guide practice. It's a frightening thought—a world in which practitioners made their own rules and decided how best to conduct themselves in any given situation. Chaos would inevitably rule the day, and the field would have little, if any, credibility. Fortunately, the NASW Delegate Assembly approved a Code of Ethics in 1960. It has been revised several times, most recently in 2017. The aim of the code extends beyond establishing the means for adjudication when a social worker violates professional expectations; it also provides guidance to social workers on how to conduct themselves in a manner that is ethically responsible and likely to minimize harm to clients, colleagues, self, and others.

The NASW ethical standards cover the social worker's responsibilities to clients, colleagues, and practice settings, as professionals, and to the profession and broader society. This chapter will highlight those most relevant to direct practice and will summarize several others.

Commitment to Clients and Confidentiality

Every social worker is expected to devote their work efforts to the promotion of client welfare and well-being. In doing so, they are required to safeguard their client's privacy and protect the confidentiality of all information obtained over the course of service delivery. Most of the time, the commitment to clients, loyalty to their interests, and the preservation of confidentiality are fairly straightforward. However, there are occasions in which these standards are superseded by the practitioner's responsibility to protect clients or others from serious harm.

One example of the limits on confidentiality occurs if a client discloses a serious intent to do bodily harm to another individual. In this event, the social worker may have a legal responsibility to warn the intended victim and notify law enforcement. The **duty to protect** laws came about in response to a California court case, *Tarasoff v. Regents of the University of California* (1976). The case began as a civil suit launched by the parents of a college student, Tatiana Tarasoff, who had been murdered by another student at the university. The offender had disclosed his plan for killing Tatiana to his UC Berkeley psychologist and, although the therapist notified campus police, Tatiana remained unaware of the threat. When the Supreme Court of California reviewed the case, they ruled that when a client threatens to do bodily harm to another person, the mental health professional who was witness to the threat has a duty to notify the intended victim. In the record of proceedings, Justice Matthew O. Tobriner commented that the "protective privilege ends where public peril begins" (*Tarasoff v. Regents*, p. 442). Since this ruling, most states have passed laws requiring social workers to warn intended victims of a client's threat to do serious harm.

Another limit on confidentiality comes up when a client discloses a clear and imminent intent to take their own life. In this case, the social worker may disclose this information to the client's significant others in order to create a safety plan. If the danger to self cannot be managed through family and social support or safety planning, further steps must be taken. This could include contacting law enforcement and/or arranging transport for the client to a crisis unit where it will be determined if they require psychiatric hospitalization. Guidelines for suicide risk assessment will be covered at length in Chapter 6.

Similar to the limits on confidentiality discussed above, when a client reveals child or elder abuse or neglect, practitioners are mandated to make a suspected abuse report to the local protective services agency. In determining whether a report needs to be made, social workers must be familiar with state laws that define various forms of abuse, including physical, sexual, and emotional. You may go the Child Welfare Information Gateway at https://www.childwelfare.gov/topics/systemwide/laws-policies/state/ to explore your state statutes.

When making a suspected abuse report, the social worker must limit their disclosure to information that is pertinent to the suspected abuse or neglect. They also need to exercise good judgment in deciding if the client should be informed of the report prior to it being completed. In many cases, it is prudent to inform the client of one's obligation to report the information shared, as this may minimize feelings of betrayal if a protective services investigation occurs.

There may be situations in which a client gives a social worker permission to share confidential information that otherwise would be considered **privileged communication**. For example, if the client is starting services with another professional, that new worker may request information about assessment and intervention provided previously, with the stated approval of the client. When this occurs, the practitioner receiving the request should always obtain a written consent for release of information that has been signed by the client. Other circumstances in which a client may waive their privilege is in a court of law when it is to their advantage to have the social worker testify about their reasons for seeking services or some other aspect of service delivery. Records can also be subpoenaed by the court, in which case the social worker should consult with an agency supervisor or attorney about how to proceed.

Respecting Self-Determination

Most social workers have instances in which they grapple with the principle of self-determination. This ethical standard requires that helping professionals respect the client's right to choose how they want to live their lives. Sometimes client choices are understandable; other times they are very hard to comprehend, given their harsh consequences. Yet, ultimately, the decision is theirs and should be respected; interference with self-determination should occur only under rare and life-threatening circumstances.

What social workers can do is offer support and an appreciation for the fear and discomfort that comes with change. They can use various strategies to increase a client's motivation, while helping them understand the consequences of harmful behavior. They can cheer them on as they take steps forward in their change process. What social workers can't do is control the outcome of these efforts.

Embracing the principle of self-determination can be difficult because it requires humility and recognition of the fact that, even though helping professionals think they know what is best for others, they may not have all the facts. It also necessitates appreciation for the reality that clients are sometimes not ready to change in the ways that practitioners would like; there are limits on one's influence as a change agent. Finally, there are likely to be occasions in which the social worker will experience the sadness that comes with knowing that their client has continued along a self-defeating path. The consolation is knowing that the practitioner did their best, and perhaps even succeeded in reducing the damage that might have been done.

Obtaining Informed Consent

When obtaining informed consent, the social worker should be clear with their client about the purpose of services to be provided as well as the "risks related to the services, limits to services because of the requirement of a third-party payer, relevant costs, reasonable alternatives, clients' right to refuse or withdraw consent, and the time frame covered by the consent" (National Association of Social Workers, 2017, p. 8). It is also important that they explain mandated reporting laws and other limits to privacy and confidentiality discussed above. In carrying out the informed consent process, the practitioner should use interpreters or translators, as needed, and provide an opportunity for the client to ask questions. The informed consent standard is not met by merely asking the client to sign a consent for treatment form.

Social work students frequently ask how to obtain informed consent from a client who is mandated by the court to receive services. There are a variety of ways this can be handled, most of which involve validating the client's concerns about being ordered to participate in services, making clear the client's right to refuse services, discussing their options for responding to court mandates and the consequences of each, and working with their desire to gain control over their lives.

Other challenges arise when obtaining informed consent for services with a child, or with an adult who lacks the capacity to provide such consent. In most cases, the parents or legal guardians of a minor child provide consent for them to receive services. State laws vary as to the circumstances that may allow for a minor to consent for mental health-related services. An adolescent's right to consent to treatment may depend upon their age, type of services requested, maturity level, and their status with regard to emancipation or parenthood. In obtaining consent to serve adults who are incapable of doing so for themselves, the practitioner should protect their interests by "seeking permission from an appropriate third party, informing clients consistent with client's level of understanding" (National Association of Social Workers, 2017, p. 8).

Preserving Professional Boundaries

The professional relationship that a social worker has with their clients differs in critical ways from the one that they have with friends and family. Clearly, there are certain actions practitioners should never take with a client that they might with a friend, partner, neighbor, family member, or co-worker. **Professional boundaries** draw the line between worker and client, not to establish hierarchy but to mark off territory a social worker should avoid in order to preserve a healthy and ethical helping relationship.

The Code of Ethics makes crystal clear that, under no circumstances, should a practitioner engage in sexual contact with a client. It also states that social workers should not provide services to individuals with whom they have had a prior sexual relationship, as this could harm the client and limit the practitioner's ability to serve in a professional and unbiased manner. Physical contact with clients must be avoided when there is "a possibility of psychological harm to the client as a result of the contact" (National Association of Social Workers, 2017, p. 15). Social workers should never take advantage of a client or exploit them to further their own personal, professional, or financial interests. In fact, they should be alert to and avoid any conflicts of interest.

Dual or **multiple relationships** with a client are to be avoided, to the extent possible; these develop when the social worker becomes involved with a client across more than one type of transaction or alliance (i.e., professional, social, business). For example, if a practitioner were to hire a client as a babysitter, this would be considered a dual relationship that presents with a host of potential problems. Similarly, if a social worker began socializing with their client, they would be muddying the waters between friend and professional helper. These types of dual relationships should be prevented in that they can easily result in harm to the client and the therapeutic relationship. However, there are times when the line between professional and social connections becomes blurred in ways that can be successfully managed. When this occurs, the practitioner should make clear to the client that the professional relationship is their primary focus, and privacy as well as confidentiality will be maintained across all other contacts (see narrative application below). Any time boundary issues arise, it is advised that the social worker discuss the situation with their supervisor and document the reasoning behind decisions that are made.

The use of self-disclosure by social workers is another boundary issue that frequently causes uneasiness or uncertainty, especially in those new to the field. Clearly, overuse of self-disclosure can complicate the therapeutic relationship and create the impression that the social worker is more like a friend than a professional partner vis-a-vis their client. However, *strategic use of self-disclosure* can, in many cases, be a valuable, therapeutic tool. When a worker shares limited information that communicates understanding of the client's plight, trust and rapport may be strengthened. Key is the management of self-disclosure, a process that should involve consideration of the content, intimacy level, and duration of the divulgence of personal information (Reamer, 2013). Certain intimate topics (e.g., worker's marital or relationship struggles) would not be appropriate to disclose. On-going and continuous self-disclosure can result in blurred boundaries and ethics violations. However, modest and occasional disclosures pertaining to appropriate, service-related topics may be beneficial when, and only when, they are motivated by a desire to meet client needs versus the worker's own needs for emotional connection.

NARRATIVE APPLICATION: Dual Relationships

Justine had been providing clinical social work services to Anna for three months to help her resolve her anger toward her ex-husband and parent her 10-year-old son, Trenton. Over the last month, counseling focused on setting limits with Trenton, who had become increasingly oppositional with his mother and fourth-grade teacher. During a recent session, Anna mentioned that she was disenrolling Trenton from his current school and enrolling him into the same elementary school that Justine's daughter attended. Justine didn't say anything to Anna about her daughter attending that same school and merely held out hope that it wouldn't present as a boundary concern. At the next PTA meeting, Justine saw Anna walk into the cafeteria where the proceedings were set to begin. She avoided eye contact with Anna and left the meeting early. The next day, Justine spoke with her supervisor about the situation and how to proceed. They agreed that the dual relationship that existed (social worker and PTA member) could be problematic, so they explored Justine's options and the challenges connected with each. Justine could discontinue attendance at PTA meetings, but she really didn't care for this option, and it wouldn't prevent contact with Anna at other school events. She could refer Anna to another counselor, but she was reluctant to terminate services prematurely—good progress was being made. They decided that Justine should discuss the issue with Anna and get her thoughts on how to best handle the situation.

At their next session, Justine asked Anna if she had seen her at the PTA meeting and Anna admitted that she had. Justine connected with Anna about the value of PTA participation and the benefits of becoming involved in school-based decision-making. She then talked to her about dual relationships and the discomfort they can bring, along with fears about the professional helper disclosing private information. Justine assured Anna that she would not reveal any information to other parents or teachers about their work together in counseling. Anna seemed relieved to have had this conversation and agreed that they could make it work to have them both attend meetings in the future. They established a clear boundary; while at the school, they would only acknowledge each other as parents, and during counseling, they would avoid conversation about PTA issues.

HIGHLIGHT 2.1: Protecting Professional Boundaries in the Age of Social Media

The use of online social networks and other social media tools by human service professionals can result in a collision of their personal and professional lives in ways that can have unintended consequences. The NASW Code of Ethics (National Association of Social Workers, 2017) notes that social workers should be aware that posting personal information on a website that is available to the public can cause "boundary confusion, inappropriate dual relationships, or harm to clients" (p. 11). To address this concern, authors Kimball and Kim (2013) advocate for the use of **virtual boundaries**, defined as the limits professional social workers should place on their use of social media.

They recommend that the practitioner carefully consider the following questions prior to posting information on social media sites:

- What information do you want to share? Is it relevant, protected, potentially harmful?
- What are the benefits and expected outcomes from sharing it?
- Who needs to see this information? Will clients have access to it?
- Where is the best place to share the information?
- How does the NASW Code of Ethics guide its sharing?

These questions provide a good starting point for evaluating the likely impact of social media use on the reputation of the professional and their social work organization.

Cultural Awareness and Social Diversity

The Code of Ethics states that social workers should strive toward cultural awareness and an evolving appreciation for the nature of social diversity. It further suggests that practitioners should have an adequate knowledge base as it concerns their clients' cultures. This standard should not be taken to mean that practitioners should know everything about every cultural group in their community. However, a lifelong interest in understanding the layers of cultural identity is vital and a virtue to which every professional social worker should aspire. This can be cultivated by developing a genuine desire to learn about the cultural groups with which one's clients identify—groups that may be based on ethnicity, national origin, gender identification and expression, age, sexual orientation, religion, political beliefs, and/or rural versus urban place of residence. More specifically, practitioners should consider the ways in which their clients define problems, as well as the intervention options that are appropriate, given their culturally based beliefs, customs, and roles. It's particularly important that cultural strengths are understood and embraced and that client experiences with oppression and discrimination are recognized and validated.

NARRATIVE APPLICATION: Cultural Awareness

Mai lived in an urban community in Northern California. At 15 years of age, her behavior changed dramatically. She seemed to be seeing and hearing things that others didn't and, on a daily basis, drank small amounts of toxic chemicals, such as bleach and laundry detergent. Mai was also physically aggressive with her mother and father and, on one occasion, threatened to kill them with an axe. Because she was at high risk of out-of-home placement, the County Department of Mental Health asked a team of behavior specialists to intervene in the hopes that they could help the family get her behavior under control.

The behavior specialists began seeing Mai and her parents in the home and made use of an interpreter, as Mai's mother and father were monolingual Hmong speakers. As was typical with their approach to behavior management, they established a safety plan and set up a system of positive reinforcement in which the parents were asked to reward her with stickers and other tokens when she behaved in a safe and respectful manner. However, the parents didn't follow through with the system and insisted that Mai was of age to be married and cared for by a husband who could provide her with the structure she needed.

After several weeks of limited success, the team sought out the assistance of a Hmong-speaking psychiatric consultant who met with Mai, her mother, and her sister-in-law to gain their perspectives. He then debriefed with the behavior specialists to help them understand why they had been making little headway with the family. First, he shared that even though Mai spoke English, she much preferred speaking in Hmong, as she had greater comprehension when using her native language. Second, he informed them that the parents understood Mai's high-risk behavior to be an indication that she was being visited by spirits and called into the role of a shaman. They didn't want to curtail her problematic behavior entirely, but did want to keep her safe and free from serious harm as the spiritual evolution took hold. Finally, he clarified that the specialists should never enter the home when a cluster of green leaves was hanging on the front door; this was an indication that a spiritual cleansing was taking place.

Based on these new insights, the team made an increased effort to recognize and appreciate the family's preferences, beliefs, and traditions. They expressed an interest in learning about shamanism from Mai and her family; this resulted in the family being more receptive to team member visits. The cultural consultant encouraged the parents to use the therapeutic tools that were being offered by the team, thus granting the family permission to accept help from outside of their cultural community. As collaboration took place, Mai's behavior improved and she was able to remain in the home. When services were ending, the family thanked the team for not giving up on them or their daughter and expressed appreciation for the help that was provided. The team valued the lessons learned about the importance of cultural awareness.

Note. Based on case study in Cox, K., Sullivan, N., Reiman, J., & Vang, C. (2009). Highlighting the role of cross-cultural competence in ethically sound practice. *The Journal of Social Work Values and Ethics*, 6(1). *

Responsibilities to Colleagues

The Code of Ethics offers a clear expectation that social workers treat their colleagues with respect. Thus, they should abstain from making demeaning remarks about a co-worker's attributes or level of competence and should avoid "unwarranted negative criticism of colleagues in verbal, written, and electronic communications with clients or other professionals" (National Association of Social Workers, 2017, p. 18).

The question then arises as to how one should handle conflicts with co-workers. In considering this query, it can be helpful to recognize that conflict per se is inevitable in the workplace, and not always negative. Weinbach and Taylor (2015) note that conflict in social work settings can help staff members become more involved and less apathetic; it can "spotlight issues and areas of legitimate professional disagreement" (p. 216). Successful management of conflict is important, however, and can be accomplished through honest, open, and respectful discussion pertaining to areas of dispute. Resolution is furthered when workers seek to understand the perspective of others with whom they disagree. The recognition of common goals and interests with colleagues is another means through which conflict can be successfully managed.

Social workers who are members of interdisciplinary teams are expected to draw on the values of the profession when contributing to decisions that affect the well-being of clients. Collaboration with colleagues from other disciplines is also critical in furthering the effectiveness of team-oriented programs. In the field of child services, interagency collaboration is defined as the process of "agencies joining together for the purpose of interdependent problem solving which focuses on improving services to children and families" (Hodges,

---

* Adapted from Kathleen Cox, et al., "Highlighting the Role of Cross-Cultural Competence in Ethically Sound Practice," The Journal of Social Work Values and Ethics, vol. 6, no. 1. Copyright © 2009 by White Hat Communications.

Hernandez, & Nesman, 2003, p. 292). Within the medical field, interprofessional collaboration involves providers from differing professional disciplines working together toward common goals and improved patient outcomes. The elements of strong collaborative practice are said to include shared decision-making, mutual trust, respect, cooperative communication, and accountability (Bridges, Davidson, Soule-Odegard, Maki, & Kowiak, 2011).

An additional area of responsibility to colleagues concerns the rare occasion in which a social worker has knowledge of another social worker's unethical conduct or an impairment that interferes with their practice. When feasible, the first step in addressing such concerns is to consult with the colleague and encourage them to take remedial action. If this is not likely to be productive, the social worker should take action through the appropriate channels provided by their agency, NASW, or licensing and regulatory bodies.

Responsibilities in Practice Settings

Direct service providers are responsible for documenting services in an ethical manner. Assessment and service delivery plans should be timely; case notes and billing must accurately reflect the nature and extent of services delivered. Social workers are advised to limit their documentation to information that is relevant to service-oriented issues; case records should be maintained for the period of time required by contracts or state statutes.

Social workers are also expected to adhere to the commitments made to their employer. The Code of Ethics indicates that they should make efforts to improve the efficiency and effectiveness of social work services and to support the elimination of case assignments or hiring practices that are discriminatory. In fact, they are expected to educate their agency, as needed, on the ethical obligations of social workers. If they are responsible for distributing funds, practitioners should become "diligent stewards" of those financial resources by "wisely conserving them where appropriate and never misappropriating funds or using them for unintended purposes" (National Association of Social Workers, 2017, p. 24).

Responsibilities as Professionals

To qualify as a competent, professional social worker, one must stay current with the literature and participate in continuing education, particularly as it relates to empirically based knowledge of client conditions and evidence-based models of practice. If the social worker speaks on behalf of a professional social work organization, it is imperative that they accurately represent the official positions of the organization. They must also "take steps to correct any inaccuracies or misrepresentations of their credentials by others" (National Association of Social Workers, 2017, p. 26). For example, if a client refers to a BSW- or MSW-level practitioner as "doctor" or "psychologist," that social worker is obliged to correct that assumption. Because clients are vulnerable to undue influence, practitioners should avoid soliciting them for recommendations or donations to charitable causes.

Most importantly, practicing social workers should not allow their personal problems to interfere with their ability to carry out their professional responsibilities. If a social worker's distress related to legal issues, interpersonal conflict, substance abuse, or mental health difficulties begins to threaten their judgment or performance, it is critically important that they seek professional help and consult with their supervisor regarding needed accommodations (time off, reduced caseload, etc.). In severe instances of impairment, the direct service practitioner may need to terminate practice in order to protect clients and others in the workplace.

Responsibilities to the Social Work Profession

A primary aim of all social workers should be to uphold the integrity of the profession. This can be achieved by participating in critical thinking and constructive discussion as it relates to professional challenges and innovations. Practitioners are encouraged to contribute time and expertise to activities that promote respect for the social work profession. Ideally, they are inspired to share their practice knowledge in the literature and at professional meetings and conferences. The advancement of effective social work practice depends upon on the insights accumulated by direct service professionals as they encounter and overcome various practice-related challenges.

It is also expected that practitioners participate in the evaluation of their programs and practice interventions. When they are involved in the design of evaluation research protocols, they must ensure that participants provide voluntary, informed consent. In fact, social workers are required to support the protection of anonymity and/or confidentiality of research participants and report the findings of their research in an accurate and unbiased manner. Furthermore, they should stay abreast of the findings of other evaluation research projects, as they concern their subfield of practice.

Responsibilities to the Broader Society

Professional social workers are responsible for promoting the general welfare of people throughout society. This entails advocating for living conditions that meet basic human needs as well as opportunities for all to access education, employment, social services, and medical or mental health care. Direct service practitioners are also expected to offer their assistance in public emergencies, whenever possible. It is assumed that they will engage in political action intended to increase social justice and improve social conditions.

Social workers should assume a leadership role in private and in public by speaking out against oppression, discrimination, exploitation, and stigma directed toward vulnerable groups. They should support policies and legislation that promote the inclusion of diverse individuals in our communities. Finally, they have an obligation to model respect toward all people, regardless of their age, ethnicity, national origin, immigration status, religion, gender identity or expression, sexual orientation, political beliefs, or mental or physical disability.

Ethical Decision-Making

It is not uncommon for social workers to encounter a variety of conundrums or difficult questions about how to approach practice in an ethical manner. These dilemmas arise when one or more of a practitioner's ethical obligations conflict. An example given earlier is when the standard of confidentiality conflicts with the need to protect another person from serious harm. This is just one of many circumstances in which social workers may face difficult choices. Thankfully, there has been a great deal of attention focused on the process of ethical decision-making in the human services over the last few decades.

Frederick Reamer, a leading scholar in the field of social work, provides guidance in his book *Social Work Values and Ethics* (2013). Here he offers a framework that outlines the steps a direct service practitioner should take in making an ethically sound decision:

1. Identify the ethical issues, including the social work values and duties that conflict.

2. Identify the individuals, groups, and organizations likely to be affected by the ethical decision.

3. Tentatively identify all viable courses of action and the participants involved in each, along with the potential benefits and risks of each.

4. Thoroughly examine the reasons in favor of and against each course of action, considering relevant

   a. Codes of ethics and legal principles
   b. Ethical theories, principles, and guidelines
   c. Social work practice theory and principles
   d. Personal values, particularly those that conflict with one's own

5. Consult with colleagues and appropriate experts

6. Make the decision and document the decision-making process

7. Monitor, evaluate, and document the decision (p. 78)

The next few narrative applications will illustrate the application of primary portions of Reamer's framework in managing ethical dilemmas. Each is designed to show that what may seem like a simple choice on the surface has deeper lying ramifications that need to be carefully considered.

NARRATIVE APPLICATION: Gift Giving by Clients

Marilyn was providing individual and group counseling to 14-year-old Jeremey, as well as nine other youth in a juvenile corrections facility. There was an on-site school that all the youth attended Monday through Friday morning. One afternoon, Jeremy presented Marilyn with a ceramic owl that he had created in art class. "This is for you," he boasted. "Do you like it?" Marilyn praised his work and thanked him for honoring her with such a well-crafted clay bird. She took the ceramic owl into her office and mulled over what to do about this dilemma. She knew that there was a program policy that staff were not to accept gifts from the residents. Yet, she didn't want to hurt Jeremy's feelings by rejecting his gift. She approached her supervisor about her quandary and they discussed her options.

They acknowledged those who might be affected by her decision included Jeremey, the other residents, and the corrections staff as well as administrators of the program. Jeremey was a sensitive youth who was prone to anger outbursts when he felt disrespected by others. Several of the other residents in the program had been on the receiving end of his aggression. A few of the staff members were frustrated with him, as he had broken rules then side-stepped consequences by claiming ignorance. Marilyn wanted to account for everyone's reaction to her choice about how to handle this situation.

She, along with her supervisor, outlined the ethical issues, her possible courses of action, and the benefits and risks of each.

1. **Ethical Issues:** The NASW Code of Ethics does not provide a standard specific to the situation of gift giving by a client. However, there are several values and principles that relate to this dilemma. The standard of commitment to the client and the value of self-determination were at play in that Marilyn had a responsibility to further Jeremy's well-being and show respect for his decisions. Yet, she was also obliged to avoid the conflict of interest that would arise if she were to give the impression of favoritism. In addition, she had a responsibility to follow the policies and procedures of her practice setting.

2. **Possible Courses of Action:**
   - Marilyn could accept the gift, place it on the bookshelf in her office, and hope no one else noticed. This would please Jeremy, who would take pride in the display of his work. He might also feel that he had a special relationship with Marilyn and call attention to that with the other residents. The other youth on her

caseload might become concerned that she favored Jeremy over others. They might also feel compelled to give her gifts as well. Other staff may learn of this situation and complain that Marilyn was in violation of facility rules.

- She could explain to Jeremey that she was not permitted to accept gifts from any resident and return the ceramic owl. This would allow her to avoid breaking facility rules and to eliminate perceptions of favoritism toward Jeremey. He, however, might suffer from feelings of rejection and embarrassment that might negatively impact his behavior in the program.

3. **Other Considerations:** Marilyn's approach to practice was solution focused and strength based. She had been working with Jeremy to identify his skills and talents, and he had recently begun to recognize his artistic ability. His feelings of self-worth had been improving slowly.

4. **Decision:** In addition to consulting her supervisor, Marilyn spoke with the facility manager. They agreed that Marilyn could place Jeremy's ceramic owl, along with other student submissions, in a display cabinet in the common area. Marilyn explained to Jeremy that she wanted to allow as many people as possible to enjoy his work, that—it deserved to be featured in a public forum. Based on this compromise, the interests of all were served.

NARRATIVE APPLICATION: Indigenous Healing Practices

Angela was hired to perform psychosocial assessments with patients served by a home-health agency. She was assigned to visit Mr. Harrak, who had recently been released from the hospital following a hip replacement. He and his wife had immigrated from Morocco several years ago at the request of their daughter. Mr. Harrak had limited English speaking ability, although his wife was fairly fluent in English, her second language.

At Angela's first visit with Mr. Harrak, he was alert and resting comfortably on the sofa; the home appeared clean and orderly. His wife said that his pain was being managed successfully and he had been eating reasonably well, but his sleep was often disrupted due to stress. Since their move to the United States, Mr. Harrak had been having difficulties adjusting to the culture, and he missed his family back home. When Angela approached Mr. Harrak to offer support, she observed several round, inflamed, bruise-like patches on his neck. Angela pointed them out with concern and was told by Mrs. Harrak that they were the result of wet-cupping procedures that she performed on her husband to help him relax and to support his healing. This treatment, she explained, was recommended by the Islamic prophet, Muhammad, and has been used in her home country ever since. Mr. Harrak nodded with a smile as his wife spoke and translated the conversation for him. Angela then concluded her visit and left the home.

As she drove back to the office, Angela wondered if she should file a report with Adult Protective Services (APS). She was concerned about Mr. Harrak receiving what appeared to be harmful treatments at the hands of his wife. Yet, Angela had no knowledge of cupping and needed to learn more. She also knew that she needed to consult with the nursing supervisor about next steps. Her decision had implications for Mr. Harrak, herself, and her organization.

In preparing for this consult, Angela considered the ethical issues, possible courses of action, and benefits, as well as risks, for each.

1. **Ethical Issues:** The primary ethical standards that conflicted in this case are commitment to clients, self-determination, confidentiality, and cultural competence. Angela knew that she had a commitment to Mr. Harrak's welfare and a responsibility to do what she could to prevent harm that might come to him due to the cupping procedures. Yet, it appeared that Mr. Harrak was in support of these practices, in which case self-determination and privacy protection came into play. Angela also had a responsibility to understand her client's culture and conduct herself in a way that is sensitive to her client's cultural preferences.

2. **Possible Courses of Action:**
   - Marilyn could file a suspected abuse report with APS in order to ensure that he was safe and to prevent liability for herself and her home health agency. This would, however, involve the disclosure of confidential information. Furthermore, it would fail to support Mr. Harrak's free choice concerning the use of indigenous healing practices. It could also add to his stress if APS were to conduct an investigation.
   - She could ignore the matter, which would minimize current stressors for Mr. and Mrs. Harrak and support their use of culturally valued treatments. However, it could also put her credentials and her agency at risk if Mr. Harrak were seriously harmed by these procedures.

3. **Other Considerations:** Marilyn did some research and learned more about cupping. She discovered that it is a generally safe treatment used in many Asian and Muslim countries to remedy a variety of conditions, including headaches, hypertension, and musculoskeletal pain. Marilyn also found that the use of cupping is commonly misdiagnosed as physical abuse.

4. **Decision:** Marilyn met with the nursing supervisor to share her dilemma and the information she had gathered. The supervisor told her that the nursing staff at the agency had encountered cupping in the past and had decided that APS reporting was not necessary. The nurses merely clean the wound, as needed, to prevent infection. Based on this consult, as well as her research, Marilyn decided that an APS report was not necessary. She documented the reasoning behind her decision in her case notes.

NARRATIVE APPLICATION: Confidentiality with Minors

Richard was providing outpatient counseling to Rachel, age 16 years, who had been discharged from the psychiatric hospital a week ago; she had been admitted for a short time due to depression, self-harming behavior, and thoughts of suicide. Rachel was placed on antidepressant medication and her mood had improved quite dramatically. She was making good use of counseling to discuss her social anxiety and sadness related to moving from a neighborhood and school she loved to a place where she had no friends. Richard discussed various coping strategies that Rachel might use when lonely or stressed. Rachel was receptive but said that, if all else failed, she could cut herself to relieve emotional pressure. Richard then asked her how she would go about cutting if she felt the need, and Rachel replied that there were razor blades in her bedroom that she had hidden before she went into the hospital. Then a panicked look came over the girl's face, and she asked, "You aren't going to tell my parents, are you?"

Richard was caught off guard and wasn't sure how to respond. He didn't want to agitate his client any further, or risk losing her trust. Yet, he worried that Rachel could do serious harm to herself if she started cutting again. "Let's think this through, Rachel" he said in the calmest tone he could muster. "Who could be affected by the decision about whether or not I should tell your parents?"

"Me," she said with intensity. "They will search my room, find the blades, then lose trust in me. They will watch me like a hawk."

"Yes, that could happen," Richard replied. "Could you handle it if it did?"

"I don't know. Maybe. It would suck, though."

"Who else could be affected, let's say, if you do cut and injure yourself pretty badly?"

"Me, my parents …"

"Yes, and it would upset me too, having known about the blades, not telling anyone, and then finding out that you were seriously hurt. I don't want to get you in trouble, but I do want to keep you safe."

Based on their conversation, Rachel agreed to tell her mother about the hidden blades in a family session that was to be held later that afternoon. During the meeting, Rachel told her mother that the cutting instruments were in a drawer in her bedroom. Richard suggested to Rachel's mother that it was a good sign that her daughter was willing to bring this information forward. Rachel's mother agreed and made a plan to help Rachel dispose of the blades that evening.

In reflecting back on this dilemma, Richard considered the ethical standards that had been challenged. The protection of confidentiality conflicted with his responsibility to prevent foreseeable and imminent harm to his client. To make matters cloudier, his client was a minor, and the rights of minors to informed consent and confidentiality are limited based on a variety of factors, including maturity level, judgement, and decision-making ability. Parents, or legal guardians, often assume the privacy privilege. Thus, Richard's strategy for engaging Rachel in her own disclosure process was wise and effective. When working with youth and families, it is important to reach agreement at the onset of service delivery regarding minors' rights to privacy and the limits on confidentiality.

Self-Care: Share the Risk

All the above scenarios demonstrate that ethical decision-making is complicated.

It can be challenging for any practitioner who must analyze a variety of ethical concerns and settle on a decision, even when no perfect, risk-free solution exists. Thus, it is strongly recommended that social workers "share the risk" when ethical dilemmas arise. The concept of risk sharing is commonly used in the field of economics and refers to the process of dispersing the gains and losses from a financial investment across stakeholders. As applied to social work, it entails sharing responsibility for decisions made that could cause harm. Intelligent risk management offers protection to social workers during circumstances that involve a high degree of uncertainty (MacDonald & MacDonald, 2010).

Direct service providers can manage risk by discussing ethical dilemmas with their supervisor or another person in a lead position within their agency. The consultation process should ideally involve discussion of the likely benefits and risks for each possible course of action and documentation of the thinking process that occurred. By virtue of this consult, liability is shared. No one should have to stand alone in making complex ethical decisions that have consequences for the client, practitioner, and/or service providing agency. Supervisory and collegial support is critical in supporting ethical decisions across programs, organizations, and the profession. It is also an essential component of self-care for practicing social workers.

SUMMARY

The aim of this chapter is to bring alive information concerning social work values and ethics, material that can often be seen as dry, burdensome, and even onerous. Toward the fulfillment of this objective, the chapter offered specific ways in which social workers can embody professional values. It also discussed professional standards, along with difficulties that can arise in their application. A process for ethical decision-making was introduced and used in several narrative applications. The author's hope is that social work students will not only learn the values and ethical standards outlined in the NASW Code of Ethics but embrace an on-going process of owning them.

KEY TERMS

Dual or multiple relationships	Healthy relationships	Virtual boundaries
Duty to protect	Privileged communication	
Espoused values	Professional boundaries	

DISCUSSION QUESTIONS

1. What does it mean to you to value the dignity and worth of the person? How do you express this value?

2. Review the meaning of self-determination. What client choices might be hardest for you to honor and respect? How might you overcome this challenge?

3. Why is it important for social workers to establish "virtual boundaries"?

SKILL DEVELOPMENT ACTIVITIES

1. Visit http://grandchallengesforsocialwork.org/grand-challenges-initiative/12-challenges/ to explore the Grand Challenges Initiative. Which of the 12 challenges speaks to your primary interest as an advocate for social justice? How so?

2. Interview a social worker and ask about situations in which their professional boundaries have been tested. Learn about how they managed these boundary issues.

3. Write a paragraph about how you might explain informed consent to a client. Include the limits of confidentiality.

REFERENCES

Antle, B. F., Karam, E., Christensen, D. N., Barbee, A. P., & Sar, B. K. (2011). An evaluation of healthy relationship education to reduce intimate partner violence. *Social Work, 14,* 387–406.

Argyris, C., & Schon, D. (1974). *Theory in practice: Increasing professional effectiveness.* San Francisco: Jossey Bass.

Barth, R. P., Gimore, G. C., Flynn, M. S., Fraser, M. W., & Brekke, J. S. (2014). The American Academy of Social Work and Social Welfare: History and grand challenges. *Research on Social Work Practice, 24,* 495–500.

Beck, R. S. (2005). Developing nonviolent communication: An integral approach. (Unpublished master's dissertation). University of Victoria, British Columbia, Canada.

Bent-Goodley, T. B. (2016). Social work's grand challenges: Mobilizing the profession. *Social Work,* 61 (3), 197–198.

Bridges, D. R., Davidson, R. A., Soule Odegard, P., Maki, I. V., Kowiak, T. (2011). Interprofessional collaboration: Three best practice models of interprofessional education. *Medical Education Online, 16*(1).

Brown, B. (2010). *The gifts of imperfection.* Center City, MN: Hazelden.

Demir, M. (2013). Introduction to relationships and happiness. In S. A. David, I. Boniwell, & A. C. Ayers (Eds.), *Oxford book of happiness* (pp. 817–820). Oxford, England: Oxford University Press.

Eckstein, D. (2004). The A's and H's of healthy and unhealthy relationships: Three relationship renewal activities. *The Family Journal: Counseling and Therapy for Couples and Families, 12,* 414–418.

Hodges, S., Hernandez, M., & Nesman, T. (2003). A developmental framework for collaboration in child-serving agencies. *Journal of Child and Family Studies, 12*(3), 291–305.

Kimball, E., & Kim J. R. (2013). Virtual boundaries: Ethical considerations for the use of social media in social work. *Social Work, 58*(2), 185–188.

MacDonald, G., & MacDonald, K. (2010). Safeguarding: A case for intelligent risk management. *British Journal of Social Work, 40,* 1174–1191.

National Association of Social Workers (2017). *Code of Ethics of the National Association of Social Workers.* Washington, DC: NASW Press.

Reamer, F. G. (2013). *Social work values and ethics.* New York, NY: Columbia University Press.

Sears, M. W. (2013). Nonviolent communication: Application to healthcare. (Unpublished doctoral dissertation). University of Hawaii Maui College, Kahjlui, Hawaii.

Tarasoff v. Regents of the University of California, 17 Cal.3d 425 (Supreme Court of California July 1, 1976).

Thoits, P.A. (2010). Stress and health: Major findings and policy implications. *Journal of Health and Social Behavior, 51*(S) S41–S53.

Weinbach, R. W., & Taylor, L. M. (2015). *The social worker as manager: A practical guide to success.* Boston, MA: Pearson.

CREDITS

CHAPTER 3

Engagement

The curious paradox is that when I accept myself just as I am, then I can change. —CARL ROGERS

ONSIDER TIMES WHEN you sought out assistance from someone who was said to have expertise in an area where you needed help. Perhaps a friend or family member suggested that you see this person to access their services. What did you think about in determining if the helper could truly help? Did they seem trustworthy? Did they appear to have a genuine interest in understanding your needs? Did they come across as competent and dependable? Chances are you weren't able to answer these questions immediately; you most likely took some time to evaluate your service provider's true motives and decide if they had what it takes to serve you successfully. A similar questioning process takes place when a client meets their social worker for the first time. They may be uneasy about the partnership and uncertain about whether the social worker can be trusted. The client may doubt the practitioner's ability to understand their unique circumstances and provide help that is truly helpful. They may even recall negative, past experiences with social workers that contribute to their anxiety about starting a new helping relationship. Thus, the practitioner's approach to engagement is vitally important; it sets the tone for the entire process of service delivery to follow. A number of terms are used to describe the activities aimed at engagement—establishing trust, building rapport, developing a therapeutic alliance. These concepts have roots in humanistic theory, which assumes that acceptance by significant others is needed in order for individuals to change and grow. Engagement strategies, as utilized by the social worker, are focused on conveying genuine acceptance of the client with the goal of furthering their self-worth, an important vehicle for needed change. This chapter will begin by discussing the elements of humanistic theory that guide the engagement process. It will proceed with an examination of a variety of skills that may be used to establish a strong, therapeutic connection.

Humanistic Psychological Theory

As advanced by Carl Rogers and Abraham Maslow, the theory of humanistic psychology became very popular in the 1970s as a framework for understanding human nature. It was embraced as an alternative to behaviorist and psychoanalytic theories that had dominated psychological thought in preceding decades. Rogers and Maslow, along with other humanistic psychologists, viewed behaviorism and psychoanalysis as dehumanizing and deterministic. They argued that the focus of psychology should not be on behavior or the unconscious mind, but on the way individuals perceive and interpret events.

The humanistic approach recognizes the personal worth of the individual and their capacity for overcoming hardship and suffering. It understands that all humans have a desire for growth and self-actualization, a tendency that is fulfilled when the social environment offers empathy, genuineness, and acceptance. Consistent with this assumption, Rogers (1959) asserted that for a therapist to be effective, they need to offer "empathic understanding and his *unconditional positive regard* [emphasis added] to the client" (p. 213). When the client perceives themselves as worthy of the clinician's positive regard, favorable self-regard is established.

Maslow's work clarifies the importance of addressing the primary needs of the client while striving to enhance engagement. He believed that human needs can be viewed as a hierarchy, with deficiency needs at the base and growth needs higher up on the pyramid (Maslow, 1943, 1954). Deficiency

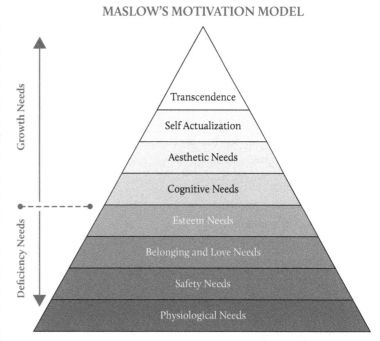

MASLOW'S MOTIVATION MODEL

FIGURE 3.1. Hierarchy of Human Needs.

needs (D needs) are defined as those that arise when individuals are deprived of food, shelter, safety, belonging, and esteem; they motivate people when they are unmet. Growth, or being, needs (B needs), become the motivating force only after deficiency needs are somewhat satisfied. Maslow initially focused on self-actualization as the primary B need, but in later years he added several more to that section of the hierarchy—cognitive and aesthetic needs, as well as the need for transcendence, which he placed at the pinnacle of the pyramid. This capstone need is thought to motivate people to connect with a force beyond the self; it may be met through mystical or spiritual endeavors and/or service to others (Maslow, 1970a, 1970b).

Maslow's model has implications for the social worker's approach to rapport building. For example, if a client is worried about being evicted from their home and the practitioner focuses on issues related to self-fulfillment, the opportunity for successful engagement may be lost. Once the client achieves a relative amount of safety and security, they may be more open to working on a plan toward meeting needs for self-worth, mental stimulation, creative expression, or self-actualization. This may seem obvious, but it is not uncommon for practitioners to miss the mark when attempting to tap client motivation for change. The humanistic orientation prompts the professional to create space for clients to be who they are and share what is important to them (Rogers, 1946). The social worker then meets them there.

Clearly, humanistic theory holds true to the values of the social work profession. It emphasizes human potential as opposed to psychopathology and seeks to preserve the dignity and worth of the person. Furthermore, it guides the engagement process by encouraging unconditional positive regard, understanding of the client's frame of reference, and validation of their primary needs and inherent strengths.

Use of Self

Max Siporin was a prominent author, clinician, and social work professor in the late 20th century. Ahead of his time, he conceptualized social work practice as a form of art through which understanding, deep relating, creating, and changing occur. He regarded the practitioner's **use of self** as a critical component of this artistry (Siporin, 2009). Through use of self, the social worker is able to express their human qualities, including their personality and beliefs about life's meanings. This, he argued, is what makes them believable.

Further elaborating on this concept, Siporin suggested that a variety of capacities are applied by the practitioner though use of self:

- Intelligence
- Imagination and creativity
- Intuition and wisdom
- Self-awareness
- Self-discipline
- Openness to new perspectives
- Empathy, caring, compassion
- Emotional expression
- Sense of humor
- Ability to handle emotionally stressful situations
- Ethical commitment to humanistic values (p. 22)

Many of the competencies listed above appear in recent comments made by clinical social workers regarding their use of self. In a qualitative study, Reupert (2007) interviewed seven practitioners and asked about the "self" they bring to their practice. Results suggest that practitioners integrate more than their professional persona into their work with clients. Along with knowledge, they bring "personality, history, philosophical beliefs, practice wisdom, baggage, and bias" (p. 110). Several of the study respondents noted inadvertent aspects of their presence during service delivery, including appearance, voice, scent, and office décor. Most acknowledged that they carry out purposeful or conscious use of self to establish rapport and initiate change. Examples include injecting humor (appropriately) to relieve tension, role modelling functional behavior, and making selective use of self-disclosure to normalize stressors, enhance credibility, demonstrate empathy, and educate. One reported that he self-discloses by proxy by sharing things about himself while referring to "someone I once knew" (p. 111). Some also spoke to the need for selectivity in their use of self and the importance of containing certain impulses or emotions that would be counterproductive to the engagement process. These insights may benefit new social workers seeking to develop and hone their own professional style.

Cultural Humility

Engagement with clients from diverse backgrounds is enhanced through the development of cultural humility. This capacity moves beyond cultural competence, as it requires that the practitioner make "a life-long commitment to self-evaluation and self-critique" (Tervalon & Murray-Garcia, 1998, p. 117). According to Ortega and Coulbourn-Faller (2011), cultural humility draws on three dimensions of the helping professional's evolving insight:

1. Understanding of self, including one's culturally based beliefs, attitudes, biases, and stereotypes that shape world view

2. Openness to the client's multicultural identity; willingness to learn from the client about their culture

3. Transcendence, or awareness of something greater than oneself; appreciation for the complex and dynamic nature of cultural identity

Cultural humility should be seen as a process as opposed to an outcome or end point (Waters & Asbill, 2013). Social workers who embrace this process are focused on understanding their own as well as their clients' multiple identities that may be based on "religious beliefs, race and ethnicity, socioeconomic class, age, ability, gender identity, or sexual orientation" (Ortega & Coulbourn-Faller, 2011, p. 32). They appreciate the role of intersecting group memberships, as they impact the individual's expectations of themselves and others. Rather than assuming the role of expert on the client's culture, they tap the client's expertise on this topic while establishing rapport. Finally, they acknowledge and address the power imbalances that exist in client-provider relationships (Fisher-Borne, Cain, & Martin, 2015).

NARRATIVE APPLICATION: Self-Awareness and Culture

Cherie was a social work student who took her studies seriously and maintained very good grades. She was struggling, however, with an assignment given in her cultural diversity course. A five-page paper was due in which students were asked to discuss their own culture. They were told to consider the multiple groups with which they identify, based on gender, age, religion, ethnicity, nationality, and sexual orientation. In addition, they were required to examine the culturally based values, beliefs, and traditions that comprised their early family culture. Finally, they were asked to discuss the ways in which their cultural identity might impact their work with clients who affiliate with a different cultural group.

Cherie was clear that she identified as a heterosexual, Caucasian American female belonging to Generation Y (having been born in the mid-1990s). She knew a bit about her ancestry—her great-great-great-grandparents immigrated to the United States from Scotland and Germany. Beyond that, she was stuck. She brought up her struggle in class, and the instructor suggested that the students explore the values, norms, and customs with which they were raised. The following questions were offered to stimulate thought:

1. What was valued in your family or families of origin?
2. What was feared?
3. What was rejected?
4. What events were celebrated and how?
5. How were emotions expressed or conflicts resolved?

Cherie thought about her experience growing up in a two-parent home. She was aware of the value that her parents placed on hard work and education and knew that they feared financial ruin, having both been raised by parents who grew up in the Great Depression. Her parents were also extremely frugal. Everyone was expected to work hard and save as much money as possible. Her family rejected organized religion but considered themselves Protestant. They celebrated birthdays within the nuclear family by giving gifts and eating birthday cake. Easter, Thanksgiving, and Christmas were celebrated in secular ways, usually with small extended family gatherings. Emotions were suppressed and conflicts were often swept under the rug in order to maintain the appearance of a well-functioning, happy family.

After reflecting on these tendencies, Cherie then researched the Protestant work ethic, and it fit her family's values and beliefs perfectly. She now had words to describe her family culture.

In considering the impact of her cultural roots on her approach to practice, Cherie had a revelation. In her family, the achievement of individuals was prized, and young adults were expected to strike out on their own to make their way in the world. This was not the case in the Hispanic families she served in her internship. The elders in these families expected the young adults to remain in their homes and help out after they came of age. Cherie understood at once that she should not impose her own cultural expectations of young adults on her clients. She must honor and respect the customs, roles, and worldview of the individuals and families with whom she works.

Effective Listening

Effective listening is a powerful tool that enhances client growth and motivation for change. It differs from casual or inattentive listening and requires a great deal of discipline on the part of the direct services practitioner. Carl Rogers (Rogers & Farson, 1979) used the term *active listening* in referring to this skill and suggested that it encompasses the following:

- Attending to content and underlying emotions of the expression
- Responding to or reflecting the emotional message
- Observing nonverbal communication

When social workers listen actively, they communicate interest in the client's point of view and respect for their thoughts and feelings. They focus on discovering the client's potential and avoid prodding, judging, scolding, or advice giving aimed at convincing the client to see things their way. The emphasis is on conveying in-depth understanding of the client's emotions and attitudes, given the experiences they have had with hardship.

The term *deep listening* has been used in recent years in religious and psychological circles by those speaking about this communication capacity. Deep listening is described as a practice that must be cultivated on an on-going basis (Miller, 2015). It requires curiosity and concentration that is fixed on the client's speech, the present moment, and the social worker's own internal response to what they are hearing. Yet, the practitioner must "refrain from getting caught up in their own inner dialogue" in order to listen to the other with "fresh ears" (p. 18). When listening deeply and with compassion, the listener is able to connect with the value and uniqueness of the speaker.

NARRATIVE APPLICATION: Effective Listening

Jennifer was overwhelmed with parenting her 14-year-old daughter, Kim. Her teenage daughter was staying out late and skipping school more days than not. When Jennifer tried to talk to her about her behavior, Kim became defensive, reminding Jennifer that she was no saint herself. Jennifer had a history of drug use, and at one point last year, Kim was taken into foster care for several months while Jennifer was in a clean and sober living facility. Jennifer felt guilty about her past and was at a loss as to how to control her daughter. She started seeing a clinical social worker who was on the list of therapists provided to her by child protective services. This was a hard choice, however, as Jennifer was very uncomfortable with social workers; she had several difficult interactions with them in the past. Yet, she decided to try, as there were no other options available. She was pleasantly surprised by the therapist's approach.

This social worker, Cynthia, was warm and accepting. While in session, Jennifer sensed that she was fully present, listening carefully and relating to her challenges staying sober and parenting Kim. What Jennifer appreciated most is that Cynthia didn't pass judgement or tell her what she needed to do in order to improve her situation. She heard Jennifer out and seemed to understand her struggles. This resulted in Jennifer feeling a sense of worth that had escaped her in the past. After several weeks of weekly sessions, she was ready to try some new strategies to gain control of herself and her daughter.

Nonverbal Engagement

Most of what a social worker communicates is not transmitted through the words they speak but via a variety of nonverbal channels. In fact, estimates suggest that nonverbal expressions are five times more influential than verbal components of communication (Argyle, 1988). Thus, it stands to reason that clients pick up on much more than the content of their social worker's speech. They form an impression that is based, to a great extent, on the practitioners facial and body movements, posture, gaze, and intonations. An example of the power of intonation is seen in the change in meaning that is communicated by altering tone in the following:

"You are feeling anxious today."
"You are feeling anxious today?"

Either phrase might be appropriate, yet they do send different messages: "It's clear you are feeling anxious" versus "Are you feeling anxious today?"

Illustrations of body movement are foot tapping or fidgetiness that may communicate unease on the part of the social worker. On the other hand, an open and relaxed body posture transmits confidence, interest, and openness. Empathy is relayed through "moderate head nodding and gesturing, a steady gaze and the minimum of activity or body movement" (Kacperek, 1997, p. 277).

Research has recognized the importance of nonverbal communication in clinical settings. In a systematic review of the literature on this topic, Henry and colleagues (2012) found that observable warmth and listening on the part of clinicians was associated with greater patient satisfaction. A large online study highlighted specific nonverbal behaviors that are positively correlated with perceptions of clinician warmth and competence. Those include open posture, eye contact, equal eye level, concerned facial expression, and the elimination of a physical barrier between practitioner and patient (Kraft-Todd et al., 2017).

It has been recommended by Hepworth and colleagues (2010) that early career social workers monitor their use of nonverbal communication. They suggest practice in the use of physical attending behaviors, such as facing the client squarely, leaning forward, maintaining eye contact, and using a relaxed demeanor. These authors also offer an important caveat by reminding their readers that "cultural groups ascribe different meanings to nonverbal behaviors" (p. 156). Likewise, Lorie and her co-authors emphasize the role that culture plays in the meaning conveyed by some nonverbal behaviors within the context of clinical work. Their research showed that while open body posture, smile, and warmth of facial expression appear to be universally valued as an expression of empathy, the length and directness of eye contact and use of hand gestures relay different meanings across cultures. They encourage practitioners to learn the norms for nonverbal communication of the cultural groups that they are serving.

HIGHLIGHT 3.1: Nonverbal Communicators of Interest and Empathy

- Open and relaxed posture
- Leaning forward
- Equal eye level
- Steady gaze
- Moderate head nodding
- Warm facial expression
- Minimum activity or body movement
- Elimination of physical barrier between practitioner and client

---

Balanced Use of Empathy

One of the social worker's greatest assets is their ability to empathize with their clients. Hepworth and colleagues (2010) stress that the direct services practitioner needs to be "empathically attuned" to their client's surface and underlying emotions. They argue that empathy plays an important role in building and maintaining the helping relationship. According to Raines (1990), empathic practitioners are those who let their defenses down and "feel the client's feelings reverberate within [their] own being" in order to appreciate their experience and offer genuine acceptance (p. 70). Clearly, empathy is an important tool in social work.

Overuse of this tool may be problematic, however. Consider the practitioner who has inadequate control over their use of empathy—they take on their client's suffering, as if they were a sponge soaking up a toxic solution. This worker may be at risk of becoming overinvolved with their client and vicariously traumatized themselves. For this reason, Cox and Steiner (2013) advocate for balanced use of empathy: They suggest that social workers cultivate the ability to empathize with their clients while also "standing apart from their pain" (p. 72). These authors offer the following Hindu myth to illustrate the tension between standing with and apart from another person.

> Legend holds that Shiva [Hindu God of Dance and Death] was a strict yogi who lived in the mountains of India. He had renounced worldly pleasures until lured into marriage by Parvati, a beautiful young maiden. The relationship that evolved between Shiva and his wife is thought to represent the tension between the ascetic of spiritual ideal and domestic life that includes marriages, sex, and children. Lord Shiva learned to do the dance between both worlds—he became both a part of and apart from the domestic world with his family. (p. 73)

Cox and Steiner go on to argue that a similar and delicate dance occurs for the social worker, who must establish an empathic connection while also standing apart from the pain and suffering that is part of their client's experience. It is a dance that takes practice in order to reach proficiency.

Exploring

Open-Ended Versus Closed-Ended Questions

In exploring the client's needs and strengths, two primary types of questions are utilized: closed-ended and open-ended. **Closed-ended questions** limit the response options to a few words, such as "yes," "no," or "maybe." They may require the respondent to select from various options or answer with a concrete piece of information, such as a date or number. When factual information is needed, these questions can be useful, but overuse of them in a client interview can come across as rigid and robotic. Below are some examples of closed-ended questions that might be used sporadically in social work.

- "Are you living alone?"
- "Do you feel depressed when you are alone?"
- "When was your first hospitalization?"

Open-ended questions have the advantage when it comes to eliciting in-depth information. They invite the person to express what they consider to be important or relevant. Often, they are used to prompt the client to elaborate on a previous response and provide more detail. Here are a few examples of open-ended questions and prompts:

- "Tell me about your living situation."
- "What is it like for you when you are home alone?"
- "What led up to your first hospitalization?"

It is not uncommon for novice social workers to rely primarily on closed-ended questions. An area for skill development often involves learning how to reformulate these questions into open-ended ones. One of the exercises at the end of this chapter is aimed at furthering this skill.

Clarifying Prompts and Questions

Understanding of client concerns is furthered through the use of clarifying prompts and questions. They allow practitioners to make certain that they have heard the client's words in a way that is consistent with the intended meaning. For example, the practitioner might **paraphrase** what they understood the client to be saying. This involves restating the client's message using the social worker's own words, not "parroting" their exact statement back to them. When paraphrasing, it is important that the professional remain receptive to correction if it becomes clear that they have misunderstood the client's message.

Understanding is also enhanced by questions aimed at *eliciting further details* about the client's experience, including events, thoughts, and emotions. This ideally prompts the client to explore topics in more depth and gain greater self-awareness. When they move off topic, it may be helpful to refocus the client in order to fully examine an issue of importance. Sometimes **refocusing** can best be accomplished by tying the client's thoughts together while summarizing content covered. The following dialogue serves as an example of the use of clarifying prompts and questions:

Client: "It was really hard to see my father in pain during my visit. I can't stop crying."

Social Worker: "You've been feeling sad since seeing your father suffer?"

Client: "Yes, and I can't understand my mother's lack of sensitivity to him."

Social Worker: "What does she do that is insensitive?"

Client: "She asks him to do things he is not capable of doing because he is in pain and has lost hearing and vision."

Social Worker: "How does he respond when she does this?"

Client: "He gets frustrated and teary-eyed and then I get upset. I try to explain to my mother that he is not able to do things he once did and that it upsets him when she asks him to do them anyway. She can't seem to stop herself. She is very self-centered and doesn't listen to reason. She told my sister-in-law that she doesn't like it when my dad opens up to her."

Social Worker: "It sounds as though your whole family is having a hard time adjusting to loss."

Client: "Yes, we all are."

Social Worker: "It's impressive how sensitive you are to your dad's needs, but your mother is not so sensitive and she hasn't been receptive to your feedback. I understand how upsetting that must be. When is she most open to your thoughts and ideas?"

Here the social worker begins by paraphrasing the client's initial statement. She then asks some clarifying questions to learn more about the client's perceptions. She refocuses the client onto the issue of loss for the family, communicates understanding of the client's experience, and begins to explore options for improving family communication. What began as a vague statement of emotional pain becomes a more clearly focused problem around which a solution may be built.

Socratic Questions

Socrates was a classical Greek philosopher and educator who taught by drawing out insights and answers from his students, thereby advancing their critical thinking about universal truths. Over the last century, his method has been adopted by prominent cognitive behavioral therapists, including Aaron Beck and Albert Ellis, as a technique for promoting change and growth. Its purpose in clinical work is to help clients recognize and dispute incomplete or distorted thinking (Bishop & Fish, 1999). When utilizing this method, practitioners ask a series of questions that guide clients in evaluating the accuracy of their beliefs and perceptions while expanding their understanding of their problems and strengths. **Socratic questions** often help people acknowledge various aspects of events or circumstances that have been hidden from conscious awareness.

According to Overholser (1993), there are seven types of Socratic questions, some of which may be very useful during the engagement process:

- Memory Question: asks the client to recall specific facts and details

  Example: "When did this problem begin?"

- Translation Question: requires that the client shape their perception into a different but parallel form

  Example: "How do you make sense of this situation?"

- Interpretation Question: helps the client identify relationships between facts or circumstances

  Example: "How are these two conflicts similar?"

- Application Question: asks the client to apply concepts or skills to a particular problem

  Example: "How will you address this issue?"

- Analysis Question: asks the client to use logic or deductive reasoning and support their beliefs with evidence

    Example: "How will you know if you are right or wrong?"

- Synthesis Question: asks the client to explore alternative views

    Example: "What's another way you can look at this problem?"

- Evaluation Question: asks the client to make a value judgment

    Example: "What is important to you in a relationship?"

The use of such questions can support client autonomy, reduce their resistance, and help them "realize the answers that they already possess" (p. 72).

Rolling with Resistance

When clients see a social worker, they are not always prepared to acknowledge certain problems, much less commit to working toward their solution. They may be seeking services involuntarily, required to attend by a law enforcement body or concerned family member. When this is the case, it is important that the social worker understand and appreciate the client's resistance.

Consider what is at the root of the resistance that most, if not all, people have when they are told that they must change a behavior or activity. Many develop concern that they are not able to do what is being asked of them. They may not know how to fulfill a legitimate need that was met by the behavior of concern. Some may be apprehensive about losing a person or activity that is familiar to them, even if it is accompanied by unpleasant consequences. Thus, at its core, resistance is about fear of change, failure, loss, and the unknown.

During the engagement process with a client who is unprepared for change, the technique of **rolling with resistance** (Polcin, 2002) is extremely useful. It is a strategy used in motivational interviewing, a practice model that will be discussed in depth in Chapter 7. For purposes of rapport building, rolling with resistance involves meeting it with acceptance versus opposition as the practitioner communicates understanding of the ways in which change can be hard. Clients tend to drop their defensiveness with someone who is open to understanding how altering behavior can be very difficult. Then, the door opens for exploring reasons to change and steps can be taken to reduce barriers that stand in the way of progress. The following dialogue illustrates rolling with resistance with a young man who struggles with alcohol abuse.

Social Worker: "What brings you here today?"

Client: "My wife says I need to go to counseling and quit drinking."

Social Worker: "What do you think about that?"

Client: "I hate being forced into counseling."

Social Worker: "Yes, it is hard to be forced into doing things you don't want to do, counseling especially."

Client: "Yea, and I don't think I can stop drinking. My job is stressful, and I don't see the problem with a few drinks after work."

Social Worker: "Drinking has helped you deal with stress?"

Client: "Yes, it has, especially over the last few months."

Social Worker: "What has been so stressful for you over the last few months?"

Client: "My boss is on me all the time and calling me out in front of the other staff."

Social Worker: "Yes, that does sound hard."

Here, the social worker resists the temptation to confront the client about his apparent denial or ask for information supporting his wife's concerns. Before exploring reasons for change, she connects with him around the difficulties he is facing. Rolling with resistance in this manner can further engagement with individual clients, groups, and families, and other professionals.

Creative Connections: Merging Micro- and Mezzo-Level Practice

When working with clients who are served by a variety of professionals, skill in collaboration is of upmost importance. Rapport building with the individual client is the micro aspect of this endeavor, while engagement of other professionals can be thought of mezzo-level work, as was discussed in Chapter 1. Team-based models for service delivery have become increasingly popular in recent decades, and they require that social workers understand and embrace the perspective of team members from other disciplines, including nursing, probation, law enforcement, education, child welfare, behavioral health, and disability services.

Few would doubt, however, that interagency or interdisciplinary collaboration can be challenging. Studies have shown that collaboration is impeded by a variety of factors that exist both within the organizations and among the professionals involved. Barriers that exist within organizations include negative work climate due to high caseloads and turnover, limited resources, and lack of guidelines for collaboration (Lee, Benson, Klein, & Franke, 2015). Hindrances at the individual level are narrow vision, role insecurity, poor communication, defensiveness, and a negative attitude toward service integration (Hornby & Atkins, 2008). These obstacles can be overcome, however, with concerted effort.

For the direct service practitioner, the aim is to learn how to best connect with colleagues who have very different backgrounds and educational experiences. This entails the recognition that every member of the interagency or interdisciplinary team belongs to a profession that has its own culture that embodies a mission, values, and preferred modes of communication. Every discipline has carved out an identity, a scope of practice, and roles that are assumed during service delivery. According to Hall (2005), this has led to each operating in a silo to preserve the values, common experiences, language, and expertise of its members. She suggests that in order to "bring down the walls of the professional silos," team members need opportunities to spend time together, recognize their common goals, and become familiar with the differing ways each has been socialized into their respective discipline (p. 193).

Theory of Role Socialization

The theory of role socialization in organizations was introduced by Katz and Kahn (1978). It suggests that, as social systems, organizations are sustained through psychological bonds and control mechanisms that allow the component parts to work together in an interdependent manner. Roles are viewed as the building blocks of the system. Employees learn to embrace roles through a process of socialization in which they are taught beliefs, values, attitudes, and norms of the profession. What follows is a summary of the role socialization that occurs in just a few of the professions that intersect with social work.

Community Probation: Officers are expected to uphold the mission to protect the public. They must monitor criminal offenders to ensure that they are in compliance with court orders to abstain from illegal or high-risk activity, seek or maintain employment, and participate in counseling or other services. Their communication style ranges from conversational to compliance-authority oriented, but probation officers typically spend less time processing their cases than a social worker might. In recent decades that may have been supported by a political and governmental shift toward "getting tough on crime." Research has shown that despite this shift, many probation officers place a high value on rehabilitation and recognize the role of poverty and substance abuse in contributing to crime (Forbes, 2010).

Nursing/Medical Care: Nurses are trained to provide and monitor patient care, educate patients and family members about medical conditions, and administer medication. They need to balance support for wellness and prevention with a focus on treating existing conditions. The medical system is a hierarchical one, with the physician typically in the role of leader. Nurses are considered the hub of interdisciplinary communication—they must interpret information between physicians, patients, family members, and interdisciplinary providers. Effective communication and compassion are considered the hallmarks of effective nursing.

Teaching/Education: Teachers must have knowledge of the subject matter taught combined with the ability to create a positive classroom environment. The latter requires leadership, behavior management, and conflict resolution skills. Often, teachers must navigate difficult situations in which the needs of an individual student may conflict with the needs of the classroom as a whole. The best educators adapt their teaching methods for students with special needs, embrace professional growth and lifelong learning, and appreciate the importance of a healthy home environment and parental support in the learning process.

The above summaries show that, in relation to social work, these professions do differ, but they share common features, as well. For example, social workers and probation officers both promote the consistent use of rehabilitation-oriented counseling services by criminal offenders and substance-abusing individuals. Nurses and social workers alike value compassionate care, strive toward symptom reduction, and must balance needs for prevention and intervention. Teachers, as well as social workers, focus on professional growth and on developing various strategies aimed at changing client/student behavior. In addition, they both understand the importance of family support for the educational process.

Appreciation for the commonalities and overlapping skills across disciplines is an important key to interprofessional collaboration. Barr (as cited by the Interprofessional Education Collaborative Expert Panel, 2011) makes this point as he delineates several types of competencies needed in interdisciplinary work. First, *common competencies* are those required of most health and human services professionals (e.g., clear communication, role clarity). Second, *complementary competencies* are those that enhance the value of other professionals on the team. For example, social workers can focus on increasing client motivation to comply with the terms and conditions of probation and/or classroom rules. Probation officers utilize accountability when requiring clients to attend meetings with social workers on a regular basis. Teachers can clarify concepts that supplement those utilized in counseling with social workers (e.g., assertiveness, mindfulness). Finally, Barr discusses *collaborative competencies* that professionals need in order to work

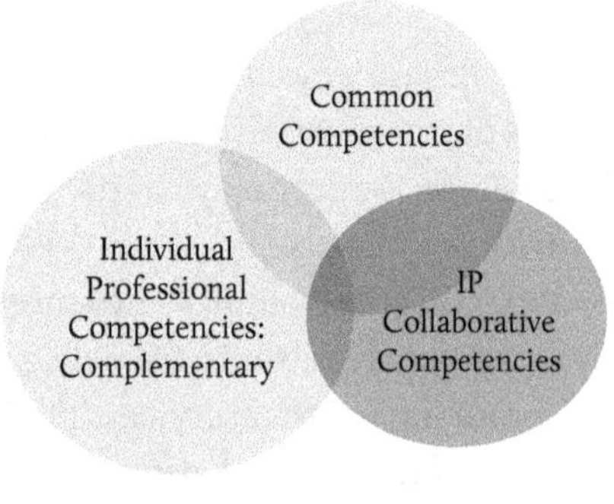

FIGURE 3.2. Barr's Three Types of Interprofessional Competencies.

effectively with other disciplines. The following are several of the most important collaborative competencies as identified in a recent report produced by the Interprofessional Education Collaborative (Interprofessional Education Collaborative Expert Panel, 2011):

- Respect for the unique culture of other professions represented on the team
- Recognition of one's limitations in skills and abilities
- Ability to explain the roles of other providers and how team members work together
- Use of active listening with interdisciplinary team members
- Receptivity to ideas and opinions of team members
- Use of common language for team communication that is free of discipline specific- jargon or terminology.

Once social workers develop these collaborative competencies, they are better prepared to offer leadership in the movement toward increased interdisciplinary collaboration.

Creative Connections: Merging Micro- and Macro-Levels Practice

The direct services professional is often presented with opportunities to intervene at a macro level to address adverse conditions experienced by groups, organizations, or communities. Observing through the lens of social justice, the social worker might discover that their agency's resources are not adequately distributed to a particular demographic in the community. For instance, a counselor serving victims of intimate partner violence may find that while younger women readily access services, older victims are less likely to do so. In response, they might advocate for outreach efforts at older adult communities or senior centers, in addition to those performed at high schools and community colleges. They may also suggest that the agency website include images of older women in addition to those of younger ones. Another example of the adoption of a macro lens pertains to an agency that serves adolescents with mental health problems. Upon learning that a high percentage of teens present with trauma-related symptoms, a practitioner might advocate for agency-based training in models devoted to trauma therapy. These are just a few instances in which macro-level activities become important supplements to micro-level work.

Ethics of Engagement

A variety of ethical considerations are important during the engagement process. In setting the stage for service delivery, practitioners are expected to clarify its purpose, related risks, limits to confidentiality, and payment/insurance-related issues while also establishing rapport. Furthermore, they must maintain professional boundaries as they inquire into personal problems and painful circumstances. Even when clients are hostile and defensive, the social worker needs to convey respect for the dignity and worth of the person. When other professionals are involved with the client, respect must be shown toward them, as well. What follows is a narrative application that illustrates the challenge that social workers sometimes face in fulfilling the latter standard.

NARRATIVE APPLICATION: Responsibilities to Interagency Colleagues

Upon graduating from her BSW program, Sharon was offered a job coordinating a multidisciplinary team serving at-risk youth. She enjoyed her work conducting assessment with families, setting up team meetings, and facilitating the development of service plans. Her main challenge, however, was in involving a child protective services (CPS) worker who was assigned to several of her cases. Sharon had made many unsuccessful attempts to contact this worker by phone to gain her perspective and schedule team meetings that she could attend. She began to resent the amount of time she was spending trying to contact her, along with the awkwardness that occurred when CPS wasn't represented at her meetings. She didn't want her anger to become obvious to the families, so she discussed her frustration with her supervisor. He suggested that she go to the worker's office early in the morning when she was likely to be there. Sharon followed this advice and reached the out to the CPS worker in person.

When she met her CPS colleague, Sharon was surprised to find her quite welcoming.

"Hi Sharon. How can I help you?"

"Well, I am new to my job and want to make sure that I get to know you since you are working with so many of my families," she offered.

"Oh, that's great. I saw from the notes that I missed some of the team meetings."

"Yes, I tried to keep you in the loop but couldn't reach you when I called."

"Oh, no wonder. Email is the best way to reach me. I have a hard time keeping up with phone calls."

"Oh, that's good to know. I'll email next time."

The two colleagues continued to visit and Sharon learned about some stressors that CPS was facing due to some negative press following a child's death. She acknowledged how hard that must be for those who work so hard to keep children safe and protected. The two also shared common experiences with one of the parents they were both serving. From that point on, Sharon and this worker had a very constructive working relationship.

Self-Care

The engagement process frequently brings the social worker face to face with case material that is disturbing. Practitioners may learn of severe hardship and suffering experienced by clients who have been victimized by poverty, discrimination, or bullying. They are likely, at some point, to hear accounts of traumatic experiences that have overwhelmed the client's ability to cope—violence observed in the home or community, incidents involving sexual abuse or assault, or memories of combat in a foreign country. Consequently, self-care is needed in order to prevent the practitioner from becoming overly distressed or even secondarily traumatized.

According to Cox and Steiner (2013), self-care begins with self-awareness, particularly as it relates to signs of stress that can be manifested physically, emotionally, behaviorally, and/or mentally (see Highlight 3.2). Physical signs include tension in the body, headaches, digestion difficulties, tremors or twitches, and skin conditions. Emotional cues are anxiety, depression, angry moods, excessive worry, and feelings of hopelessness. When a social worker exhibits behavioral signs of stress, they may become irritable, impatient, withdrawn, or judgmental. Mental signs include poor concentration, reduced organization, forgetfulness, and cynicism. The authors suggest that the key to spotting such signs of stress is "noticing irregularities in our bodily functions, mental aptitudes and attitudes, moods and emotions, and in our behavior" (p. 48).

Once identified, stress that is related to client trauma can be managed in a variety of ways. The social worker might utilize a workplace adjustment by interspersing trauma-ridden casework with lighter, less emotionally charged activities. They might talk with a trusted co-worker or supervisor about a case or situation that they find troubling. Furthermore, they may focus on creating a better balance between work and home life responsibilities. It is also recommended that they spend some time "catching their cognitions" as it relates to the trauma they have uncovered (Cox & Steiner, 2013, p. 55).

The cognitive approach to self-care is an antidote to thinking patterns that focus, almost exclusively, on harm done to clients and threats posed by traumatic events. It also guards against vicarious trauma (VT) that can cause the practitioner to become mistrustful, cynical, and alienated from others. This approach to coping encourages the social worker to cognitively reframe case related material with an eye toward opportunities for growth presented by painful and difficult circumstances. An example is finding the benefits for the client who has been seriously injured by their partner but is now ready to leave the relationship and begin the healing process. The following narrative application illustrates the cognitive coping process.

NARRATIVE APPLICATION: Coping with Client Trauma

Corrie was a group home counselor who had just begun seeing one of the residents, 15-year-old Jessica. Over the last few weeks, she had been meeting with Jessica weekly to establish rapport and gain her trust. The young teen had been placed in the group home by CPS, and Corrie knew that she had a troubled early life, having been removed from her mother's care at the age of nine. Jessica had then bounced from home to home in the foster care system before requiring the higher level of care that the program offered. By all accounts, Jessica had adjusted well to the schedule and routine at the group home, but seemed anxious and depressed. When Corrie inquired into her memories of her mother, Jessica was initially avoidant. Finally, she seemed to trust Corrie enough to share her story.

Jessica told Corrie that her most vivid memory of her mother was also the most upsetting. As a young girl, she had entered the motel room where she stayed with her mother and sister, seven-year-old Kasey. There, she saw her mother's boyfriend naked on the bed, on top of her younger sister. Kasey was crying as he proceeded to rape her. Jessica looked over to the corner of the room where she saw her mother slumped over and unconscious, with a needle in her arm. As she described the event, Jessica gazed off into the distance. Her lips trembled as she shared her regret that she hadn't done anything to help her little sister. Instead, she had raced out of the room and never returned. Then Jessica said something that really puzzled Corrie—she wanted to search for her mother who was now living on the streets. She was clearly confused by this impulse and was unable to articulate what she would say to her mother even if she did find her.

Corrie felt sadness for her client but remained calm as she thanked her for her openness and honesty. When she got home from work that evening, the first thing Corrie did was take a hot shower. She scrubbed her body as though she was washing off the grime and filthiness of the memory that Jessica had shared. Corrie was then able to relax somewhat but had an interrupted sleep that night. When she woke up in the morning, her first thoughts were of her teenage client. She wondered how a mother could allow such abuse to occur and how Jessica would ever recover from such a trauma-filled past. Corrie knew she was struggling to make sense of it all, so she contacted her clinical supervisor and requested a meeting for that day.

During her supervision meeting, Corrie shared the content of her last session with Jessica. It felt good to unload the sadness and anger she had been holding over the last 24 hours. Her supervisor validated her distress, then helped her explore her reactions to Jessica's trauma, along with the meaning she was making of the harm that had been done to her client.

"I didn't know how to help her feel better," Corrie confided.

"Well, maybe that's not what she needs right now. Maybe she needs someone to listen without passing judgement."

"That makes sense, but I feel so angry at her mother for allowing this to happen. How could someone be so neglectful?"

"Clearly, her mother's addiction was in charge."

"Yes, but what if Jessica finds her mother? There's no reason to think she is sober now."

"I think you are right about that. The good news is that Jessica now appears ready to process issues that have troubled her for many years, and she trusts you enough to let you into her world of hurt. Hopefully, you can help her cope with her trauma so that she is less inclined to resort to drug abuse. Break the cycle, so to speak."

"Yes, that will be my goal!" Corrie asserted.

In the above dialogue, we see Corrie struggling with the stress posed by exposure to traumatic material. She is being helped to verbalize her focus on harm done to her client and the threat posed to her future well-being. The supervisor is skilled in assisting Corrie with the cognitive coping process. She is now clearer on the opportunities presented by Jessica's disclosure; this allows her to manage her own stress that was triggered as she was establishing a therapeutic relationship.

HIGHLIGHT 3.2: What are Your Signs of Stress?

Review the following list of signs and symptoms of stress, and identify those that you have experienced in recent weeks or months.

Physical Signs

- Headaches
- Tension or pain in neck, back, or stomach
- Digestion difficulties, constipation, diarrhea
- Stuttering or stammering
- Excessive sweating
- Tremors or twitches
- Increased or decreased appetite
- Insomnia or hypersomnia
- Cravings for certain foods
- Skin conditions (acne, eczema, psoriasis)
- Dry mouth
- Hair loss

Mental Signs

- Poor concentration
- Forgetfulness
- Memory loss
- Lack of organization
- Difficulty making decisions
- Rumination about details
- Suspicious or hostile attitudes
- Nightmares

Emotional Signs

- Anxious moods
- Depressed moods
- Angry moods
- Excessive worrying
- Irrational fears
- Feelings of hopelessness

Behavioral Signs

- Irritability
- Impatience

- Defensiveness
- Blaming, judging others

- Nervous habits
- Reduced motivation

Source: Cox & Steiner (2013), *Self-Care in Social Work,* NASW Press.

SUMMARY

The foundation for this chapter is humanistic theory as it supports the social worker during the engagement process. Toward furthering knowledge of rapport building, critical skills are reviewed including conscious use of self, cultural humility, effective listening, nonverbal engagement, balanced use of empathy, exploration, and rolling with resistance. The link between micro, mezzo, and macro practice is made through discussions of interprofessional collaboration and outreach to underserved clients. Lastly, strategies for self-care are explored, as applicable to occasions in which the practitioner is exposed to client trauma. The importance of cognitive coping is stressed as a means of sustaining social workers who work with oppressed and/or traumatized individuals. By working on themselves, social workers are better able to follow through with the commitment established during their engagement with individuals, groups, and families.

KEY TERMS

Closed-ended questions

Open-ended questions

Paraphrase

Refocusing

Rolling with resistance

Socratic questions

Use of self

DISCUSSION QUESTIONS

1. Review the ways in which practitioners make conscious use of self. What aspects of your "self" do you bring to practice?

2. What does "deep listening" mean to you?

3. Pay attention to your nonverbal communication when you are listening to a client or friend share personal information. Which of the behaviors listed in Highlight 3.1 come easily to you? How might you further your nonverbal communication of interest and empathy?

SKILL DEVELOPMENT ACTIVITIES

1. Observe a colleague during a client interview. What nonverbal behaviors did you notice? What do you think they communicated?

2. Record either an interview you are having with a client (with their permission) or a role play in which you are the social worker. Review the recording and note the number of open-ended and closed-ended questions that you used. How might you transform some of your closed-ended questions to open-ended ones?

3. Interview a professional who works in an interdisciplinary program that includes social workers. How do they describe the differences in culture across professions? What do they see as the benefits and challenges associated with interprofessional collaboration?

REFERENCES

Argyle, M. (1988). *Bodily Communication* (2nd ed.) New York, NY: Methuen.

Bishop, W., & Fish, J.M. (1999). Questions as interventions: Perceptions of Socratic, solution-focused, and diagnostic questioning styles. *Journal of Rational-Emotive & Cognitive-Behavior Therapy, 17,* 115–140.

Cox, K., & Steiner, S. (2013). *Self-care in social work: A guide for practitioners, supervisors, and administrators.* Washington, DC: NASW Press.

Fisher-Borne, M., Cain, J. M., & Martin, S. L. (2015). From mastery to accountability: Cultural humility as an alternative to cultural competence. *Social Work Education, 34,* 165–181.

Forbes, D. (2010). Probation in transition: A study of the experiences of newly qualified probation officers. *Journal of Social Work Practice, 24,* 75–88.

Hall, P. (2005). Interprofessional teamwork: Professional cultures as barriers. *Journal of Interprofessional Care, 1,* 188–196.

Henry, S. G., Fuhrel-Forbis, A., Rogers, M., & Eggly, S. (2012). Association between nonverbal communication during clinical interactions and outcomes: A systematic review and meta-analysis. *Patient Education and Counseling, 86,* 297–315.

Hepworth, D. H., Rooney, R. H., Rooney, G. D., Strom-Gottfried, K., & Larsen, J. (2010). *Direct social work practice: Theory and skills.* Belmont, CA: Brooks/Cole, Cengage Learning.

Hornby, S., & Atkins, J. (2008). *Collaborative care: Interprofessional, interagency, and interpersonal.* Hoboken, NY: Wiley & Sons.

Interprofessional Education Collaborative Expert Panel. (2011). Core competencies for interprofessional collaborative practice: Report of an expert panel. Washington, DC: Interprofessional Education Collaborative.

Kacperek, L. (1997). Non-verbal communication: The importance of listening. *British Journal of Nursing, 6,* 275–279.

Katz, D., & Kahn, R. (1978). *The social psychology of organizations* (2nd ed.). New York, NY: John Wiley & Sons.

Kraft-Todd, G. T., Reinero, D. A., Kelley, J. M., Heberlein, A. S., Baer, L., & Riess, H. (2017). *Empathic nonverbal behavior increases ratings of both warmth and competence in a medical context. PLoS ONE, 12*(5): e0177758.

Lee, S. Y., Benson, S. M., Klein, S. M., & Franke, T. M. (2015). Accessing quality early care and education for children in child welfare: Stakeholders' perspectives on barriers and opportunities for interagency collaboration. *Children and Youth Services Review, 55,* 170–181.

Lorie, A., Reinero, D. A., Phillips, M., Zhang, I., & Riess, H. (2017). Culture and nonverbal expressions of empathy in clinical settings: A systematic review. *Patient Education and Counseling, 100,* 411–424.

Maslow, A. H. (1943). A theory of human motivation. *Psychological Review, 50*(4), 370–396.

Maslow, A. H. (1954). *Motivation and personality.* New York, NY: Harper and Row.

Maslow, A. H. (1970a). *Motivation and personality.* New York, NY: Harper & Row.

Maslow, A. H. (1970b). *Religions, values, and peak experiences.* New York, NY: Penguin.

Miller, W. B. (2015). Like an elephant pricked by a thorn: Buddhist meditation instructions as a door to deep listening. *Buddhist-Christian Studies, 35,* 15–20.

Ortega, R. M., & Coulborn-Faller, K. (2011). Training child welfare workers from an intersectional cultural perspective: A paradigm shift. *Child Welfare, 90,* 27–49.

Overholser, J. C. (1993). Elements of the Socratic method: I. Systematic questioning. *Psychotherapy, 30,* 67–74.

Polcin, D. L. (2002). What if they aren't ready? Increasing motivation for treatment. *Counselor, 3,* 34–38.

Raines, J. C. (1990). Empathy in social work. *Clinical Social Work Journal, 18,* 57–72.

Reupert, A. (2007). Social worker's use of self. *Clinical Social Work Journal, 35,* 107–116.

Rogers, C. R. (1946). Significant aspects of client-centered therapy. *American Psychologist, 10,* 415–422.

Rogers, C. (1959). A theory of therapy, personality and interpersonal relationships as developed in the client-centered framework. In S. Koch (Ed.), *Psychology: A study of a* science (Vol. 3). New York, NY: McGraw Hill.

Rogers, C., & Farson, R. (1979). Active listening. In D. Kolb, I. Rubin and J. McIntyre (Eds.), *Organizational Psychology* (3rd ed.). Upper Saddle River, NJ: Prentice Hall.

Siporin, M. (2009). *Artistry in social work practice.* Bloomington, NY: iUniverse.

Tervalon, M., & Murray-Garcia, J. (1998). Cultural humility versus cultural competence: A critical distinction in defining physician training outcomes in multicultural education. *Journal of Health Care for the Poor and Undeserved, 9,* 117–125.

Waters, A.J. & Asbill. (2013, August 13). Reflections on cultural humility. *CYF News.* Washington, DC: American Psychological Association.

CREDITS

Fig 3.1: Source: http://thepeakperformancecenter.com/wp-content/uploads/2014/05/Maslows-Hierarchy-8-Levels.jpg.

Fig 3.2: Interprofessional Education Collaborative, Core Competencies for Interprofessional Collaborative Practice, pp. 13. Copyright © 2011 by American Association of Colleges of Nursing.

Highlight 3.2: Kathleen Cox and Sue Steiner, "What Are Your Signs of Stress?," Self-Care in Social Work: A Guide for Practitioners, Supervisors, and Administrators, pp. 46-47. Copyright © 2013 by National Association of Social Workers, Inc.

CHAPTER 4

Assessment

T HE VOLUME OF personal details that a client shares with their social worker can be regarded as a gift—one that offers a window into human nature, along with an assortment of keys to unlocking the hold that adversity takes on health and well-being. To understand and explain presenting problems, the practitioner must open a variety of doors and access information that relates to differing realms of human functioning: biological, psychological, social, cultural, spiritual, and environmental. As this occurs, social work assessment becomes multidimensional and holistic.

The holistic approach to assessment highlights the interaction between elements that comprise the whole person who is seeking services. It recognizes that this transaction produces an effect that is more significant than the contribution of individual elements. For example, while a mental illness may be a part of the problem plaguing an individual, their ability to cope with symptoms and with the attitudes of family members and friends toward their illness has a strong impact on the client's level of functioning. Likewise, an older adult with a terminal illness will make decisions about care that are impacted by the beliefs and customs of the cultural group with which they identify. Thus, the social worker who absorbs a wide range of relevant information is best prepared to avoid premature assumptions about the cause of a particular problem and/or its best remedy or resolution.

Another prominent feature of social work assessment is its focus on strengths. Practitioners seek to uncover the client's capacities, along with avenues for their expression, as a means of tackling problems and difficulties. This emphasis is consistent with the social work value placed on the dignity and worth of the person. It is also supported by research that reveals the power of resiliency and by the broad-based adoption of strengths-based models of practice. The following section provides in-depth discussion of the strengths perspective and how it can be utilized during assessment.

Strengths Assessment

The strengths-based approach to social work assessment has gained widespread recognition in recent decades. It represents a departure from conventional models that center on symptoms, pathology, and disorders. However, it must be emphasized that the strengths approach does not overlook problems, illnesses or adversity; it seeks to balance a focus on struggles with an appreciation for assets that may be tapped to support change, recovery, and goal attainment.

An underlying assumption of the strengths perspective is beautifully articulated by Dennis Saleebey (2009), the scholar who is credited with developing the strengths-based approach to social work. He wrote that all people have capacities and assets, including

> *the urge to be heroic, to transcend circumstances, to develop their powers, to overcome adversity, to stand up and be counted, to be a part of something that surpasses petty interests of self, to shape and realized their hopes and dreams.* (p. 7)

The aim of the strengths-based practitioner is to tune into these hopes, dreams, and desires, while helping clients perceive and embrace possibilities.

The strengths perspective also assumes that hardship, loss, or trauma may be damaging, but none inevitably lead to pathology or malfunction. A large body of research on resiliency substantiates this premise. For example, in his review of this literature, Bernard (2004) found that most youth and children from high risk backgrounds manage to do well in life and achieve good developmental outcomes. This includes youth who

- grew up in poverty,
- were sexually abused,
- participated in a gang,
- were placed in foster care, and/or
- had substance abusing or mentally ill families.

Overall, this research reveals that children are able to rebound from adversity and adopt "self-righting tendencies that move [them] toward normal adult development under all but the most persistent adverse circumstances" (Werner & Smith, 1992, p. 202).

A third assertion of the strengths approach is that social workers are most effective when they collaborate with clients. To do so, they must give up the role of "expert" and, instead, partner with their client as they solicit their perspective of the problem, its causes, and workable solutions. The strengths-based practitioner might reflect upon the following, as they conduct their assessment:

- To what extent has the client been consulted about matters that are pertinent to them?
- What do they want?
- What do they need?
- How do they think they can get it?
- How do they see their situation—problems as well as possibilities?
- What values do they want to maximize?
- How have they managed thus far? (Saleebey, 2009, p. 6)

A variety of tools have been developed to guide a collaborative approach to assessment, one of which is referred to as the ROPES model (Graybeal, 2001). The acronym ROPES can be used to guide interview questions falling into the domains of Resources, Options, Possibilities, Exceptions, and Solutions (see Highlight 4.1). The Narrative Application to follow illustrates the use of this tool.

HIGHLIGHT 4.1: The ROPES Model

Resources

Personal

Family

Social environment

Organizational

Community

Options

Present focus

Emphasis on choice

What can be accessed now?

What is available and hasn't been tried or utilized?

Possibilities

Future focus

Imagination

Creativity

Vision of the future

Play

What have you thought of trying but haven't tried yet?

Exceptions

When is the problem not happening?

When is the problem different?

When is part of the hypothetical future
   solution occurring?

How have you survived, endured, thrived?

Solutions

Focus on constructing solutions, not solving problems

What's working now?

What are your successes?

What are you doing that you would like to continue doing?

What if a miracle happened? (de Shazer, 1985)

What can you do now to create a piece of the miracle?
   (p. 237)

NARRATIVE APPLICATION: ROPES Interview

Laura is a 50-year-old woman who was referred to counseling by her physician. She has been in and out of abusive relationships since she was a teenager but is currently single and living alone. She is said to be suffering from anxiety, headaches, and thoughts of self-harm.

The social worker who is seeing Laura for counseling (Molly) has already read records about Laura's past, which include references to medical treatment for diabetes and depression. Molly spends the first few minutes of their first session setting the foundation for counseling before exploring issues in more depth. Her client responds as follows:

Laura: "I know the drill—seems like I've been in therapy my whole life."

Molly: "What brings you to counseling now, Laura?"

Laura: "I am stressed out, having headaches, starting to give up on life."

Molly: "Are you having thoughts of suicide?"

Laura: "No, not really. I just can't imagine life without pain and I am sick of it."

Molly: "Yes, pain is never easy."

Laura: "I am feeling really lonely too but don't want to get into another nasty and abusive relationship."

Molly: "Yes, I understand that you've had several. How have you managed to survive those experiences?"

Laura: "I think I just kept hoping things would get better, but they never did."

Molly: "So hope is important to you. What do you hope for in a relationship?"

Laura: "Kindness, respect, consideration."

Molly: "That sounds reasonable. Who in your life shows you the most kindness and respect right now?"

Laura: "My sons, I guess, but they get tired of me complaining about how miserable I am."

Molly: "Tell me about some times when you have enjoyed your sons' company and felt respected."

In the above narrative, Molly is feeling hopeless about her life. The social worker first rules out current suicidal thinking and then responds to her client's emotional pain. She asks her a question aimed at uncovering her ability to cope ("How have you managed to survive?"). Next, she keys in on hope as a strength, or potential *solution*, before focusing Laura on a future that holds more *possibilities*. Molly then explores *exceptions* to Laura's loneliness by asking about times when she has felt respected and cared for by her sons. The focus will then turn to building on her capacity and desire for caring relationships. This will entail more attention to *resources* and *options*.

Another strengths-based assessment tool, designed for use with children and adolescents, is referred to as the **Personal Strengths Grid** (Cox, 2008). This tool was developed as a means of identifying strengths in youth who have difficulty specifying them, when asked. It guides the practitioner as they inquire about the child or adolescent's capacities, interests, and resources across various realms of functioning: social, academic, athletic, artistic, mechanical, and cultural/spiritual. Examples are listed for strengths in each area. For instance, the youth may be asked about their skills and/or interests with regard to relationships with peers or adults; reading, writing, and use of computers; cooking, sewing, or other domestic arts; drama or other performing arts; drawing, painting, or ceramics; use of mechanical tools for building and fixing; or knowledge of their own heritage. They may also be encouraged to consider their resources: friends; mentors; trusted teachers; neighborhood art, recreational or vocational programs; and faith-based centers where they feel comfortable. Through the use of a grid of this kind, youth are better able to understand and articulate the assets they have and interests they would like to pursue (see Highlight 4.2).

The use of tools similar to the ones shared above can be extremely helpful; however, they don't ensure that the practitioner will adopt a strengths-based approach to practice. The application of a strengths perspective involves much more than listing strengths on a form or administering a questionnaire. This point is illustrated in a study conducted to examine the impact of strengths-based assessment used with youth seen in the public mental health system. Cox (2006) randomly assigned youth with severe emotional or behavioral disturbances to one of two conditions: one group received the usual diagnostic assessment, the other completed a strengths-based assessment protocol (Behavioral and Emotional Rating Scale; Epstein & Sharma, 1998) in addition to the usual format. The researcher also rated the assigned therapists' orientation toward strengths-based practice, gathered parent satisfaction and child functioning data, and reviewed case records. Results showed that the youth who received strengths-based assessment evidenced significantly better outcomes only when their therapist endorsed a highly strengths-based orientation to practice. Further, when the therapist utilized information from the Behavioral and Emotional Rating Scale, parent satisfaction was significantly greater, and rates of missed appointments were significantly lower. These findings suggest that social work services are enhanced when a focus on strengths is infused into all aspects of service delivery—engagement, assessment, intervention, goal setting, intervention, and evaluation.

HIGHLIGHT 4.2: Personal Strengths Grid*

Sources of Information Regarding Strengths:

Youth's Name: _____

Age: _____

- ❑ Youth Interview
- ❑ Teacher Interview
- ❑ Caregiver Interview
- ❑ Observation
- ❑ Other

Strength Domain	Social	Academic	Athletic
Capacities	❑ Initiates relationships with ease ❑ Sustains relationships over time ❑ Good interpersonal boundaries ❑ Relates well with peers ❑ Relates well with adults Comments: _____ _____ _____	❑ Good reading skills ❑ Good writing skills ❑ Good math skills ❑ Good verbal skills ❑ Good computer skills Comments: _____ _____ _____	❑ Good at team sports (e.g., basketball, football, baseball) ❑ Good at independent or non-competitive sports (e.g., swimming, gymnastics, jogging, rock-climbing, yoga) Comments: _____ _____ _____
Interests	❑ Wants to have friends ❑ Wants relationships with caring adults ❑ Wants to belong to peer groups, clubs ❑ Likes to help others ❑ Enjoys caring for animals Comments: _____ _____ _____	❑ Enjoys reading ❑ Enjoys writing ❑ Enjoys math or science ❑ Enjoys computers Comments: _____ _____ _____	❑ Wants to play team sports ❑ Wants to learn individual or non-competitive sports Comments: _____ _____ _____
Resources	❑ Has close (pro-social) friend(s) ❑ Has access to adult mentor ❑ Has access to naturally occurring groups, clubs, volunteer work, opportunities, etc. Comments: _____ _____ _____	❑ Has access to opportunities to display, share, or enhance academic abilities Comments: _____ _____ _____	❑ School offers athletics programs ❑ Neighborhood offers athletics programs Comments: _____ _____ _____

Strength Domain	Artistic/Creative	Mechanical	Cultural/Spiritual
Capacities	❑ Talent in visual arts (drawing, painting, etc.) ❑ Talent in performing arts (singing, dancing, drama, music, etc.) ❑ Skills in domestic arts (cooking, sewing, etc.) **Comments:** _____ _____ _____	❑ Able to assemble & disassemble bikes, appliances, computers, etc. ❑ Skills in using tools for carpentry, woodworking, etc. ❑ Skills in car maintenance/repair **Comments:** _____ _____ _____	❑ Knowledge of own heritage ❑ Knowledge of spiritual belief system ❑ Practices cultural/spiritual customs/rituals **Comments:** _____ _____ _____
Interests	❑ Desires to develop talent in visual arts ❑ Desires to develop talent in performing arts ❑ Desires to develop talent in domestic arts **Comments:** _____ _____ _____	❑ Enjoys fixing appliances, etc. ❑ Enjoys building, woodworking ❑ Enjoys working on cars or desires to learn mechanics **Comments:** _____ _____ _____	❑ Likes to attend church or other place of worship ❑ Desires to learn about own heritage ❑ Desires to participate in cultural or spiritually oriented activities **Comments:** _____ _____ _____
Resources	❑ School offers programs in type of art preferred ❑ Neighborhood offers programs in type of art preferred **Comments:** _____ _____ _____	❑ School offers vocational program in mechanical area of interest/skill ❑ Has opportunity to serve as apprentice in mechanical area of choice **Comments:** _____ _____ _____	❑ Connected to place of worship ❑ Has access to opportunities to participate in culturally oriented activities **Comments:** _____ _____ _____

Other strengths: _____

_____

Completed by: _____ **Date:** _____

Supervisory Review: _____ **Date:** _____

Content of Multidimensional Assessment

Social workers are often called upon to complete a comprehensive biopsychosocial assessment. This involves gathering information pertaining to a variety of domains of functioning in order to gain a clear and coherent view of the client's needs, strengths, and circumstances. Sources of information can include intake forms, assessment instruments, client interviews, direct observation of behavior, and collateral information from family members, friends, or other professionals involved with the client. The primary domains of this assessment will be covered below, along with associated theories and strategies for gathering pertinent information.

Biophysical Functioning

The assessment of biological functioning spans a wide territory that includes the client's physical appearance, general health, nutrition, brain activity, and use of alcohol and prescribed, or illicitly obtained, medications. This domain of assessment is rooted in biological theory and research that links behavior, cognitions, and emotions to medical issues. This section will provide an overview of this literature as well as strategies for gathering information that pertains to this realm of functioning.

Biological Theory and Research

A central premise of biological theory is that a person's genetic makeup impacts their risk for developing various medical conditions. Ample research reveals that family history is one of the strongest predictors of common illnesses, such as diabetes, cancer, and cardiovascular disease (Hernandez & Blazer, 2006). Of particular relevance to social workers is the large body of research demonstrating the role of heredity in increasing susceptibility to mental disorders.

It has been well established that mental illness runs in families. Family, twin, and adoption studies have shown that heredity contributes to the risk of developing schizophrenia, autism, bipolar disorder, major depressive disorder, ADHD, and panic disorder (Henry, 2012). Genetic risks appear to be strongest for those who have one or more first-degree relatives with a mental illness. According to the Centre for Genetics Education (2012), the lifetime chance of developing schizophrenia is 13 in 100 for the person who has a biological parent with this illness; 45 in 100 if both parents are afflicted. Similarly, the lifetime chance of developing bipolar disorder is 15 in 100 when one parent has the condition; 50 in 100 if both parents have the disorder. It is important to recognize, however, that most people who have a family member diagnosed with a mental illness do not develop one themselves.

The field of neurology has shed further light on the link between biology and the development of a behavioral or mental health disorder. Theories and research have suggested that imbalances of various neurotransmitters in the brain (e.g., dopamine, norepinephrine, serotonin) are associated with mental illness. For example, dopamine abnormalities have been seen in people with schizophrenia; recent research has indicated that the messenger chemicals glutamate, GABA, acetylcholine, and serotonin are also involved in the manifestation of this psychotic disorder (Brisch et al., 2014). Low levels of serotonin and norepinephrine have been found in depressed individuals; high levels have been associated with symptoms of anxiety. Researchers caution, however, that brain chemistry alone does not explain these conditions; multiple neurobiological and psychological mechanisms interact to produce mood, anxiety, and other mental health disorders (Willner, Scheel-Kruger, & Beizung, 2013).

Neuroimaging techniques have led to increased understanding of the structures in the brain that malfunction in people with mental health and substance abuse disorders. For instance, when shown unpleasant imagery, people with both depression and anxiety display elevated activity of the amygdala—the section of the brain that is responsible for signaling and processing fear and other emotions (Treadway & Zald, 2011). Individuals with schizophrenia appear to have a lowered level of grey matter in the brain that may be developmental or degenerative (Buckley, 2005). Drug addiction has been shown to hijack the brain's motivational (dopaminergic-mesolimbic) system, explaining why the addicted person is highly vulnerable to cravings and relapse when they stop using their drug of choice (Littrell, 2015). This field of study is expected to evolve in upcoming decades.

On the positive side, there is growing evidence of **neuroplasticity**—the ability of the brain to reorganize itself and form new connections between nerve cells. This is great news for those who have suffered from brain injury or exposure to psychological trauma. Imaging studies have shown that patients with traumatic brain injury (TBI) are able to recover functions over the course of their healing process. Moreover, rehabilitation programs have been successful in stimulating plasticity by reorganizing structures and prompting certain areas of the brain to compensate for those that have been damaged (Kou & Iraji, 2014). Treatments for post-traumatic stress disorder (PTSD) are aimed at reversing the hyperresponsivity of the amygdala, as well as the deregulation of the hippocampus and frontal lobe that occurs in response to psychological trauma (Bremner, 2006). Such treatments may combine the use of medications and therapies that include neurofeedback and/or reprocessing of traumatic events. Practitioners who work in trauma centers, rehabilitation programs, or mental health clinics are well advised to stay current on the evaluation of such methods.

Assessing Biophysical Functioning

Assessment of the biophysical dimension of functioning begins with a focus on the client's *physical characteristics*, *appearance*, and *mode of presentation*. More specifically, the social worker may attend to the following:

- Chronological age of client
- Body build (frail, medium build, overweight, or obese)
- Posture (upright or stooped)
- Dress and grooming (appropriate for occasion, disheveled, colorful)
- General behavior (mannerisms, gestures, tremors, twitching, tapping, calm demeanor)

Taken together, these observations may provide clues into the mood of the client, aspects of their personality, or the presence of physical or psychological conditions. On the other hand, they may reflect assets that support effective social functioning. When documenting biophysical assessment, it's important to avoid judgmental language (e.g., weird, ugly, provocative) and instead use words that describe concrete observations (e.g., long hair, facial tattoos, dressed in jeans and tennis shoes). As with all aspects of assessment, the practitioner must consider the sociocultural group with which a client identifies, as many aspects of dress, grooming, and behavior reflect the norms for that group.

The *health status* of the client is a second important area of biophysical assessment in that it has implications for the individual's psychological state and sense of well-being. Thus, social workers need to become knowledgeable about any chronic medical condition that the client is afflicted with, at present.

Many illnesses increase the likelihood of developing mental health challenges. For example, people with diabetes have been shown to have elevated rates of depressive symptoms which, in turn, can negatively impact their compliance with treatment for their medical illness (Adili, Larijani, & Haghighatpanah, 2006). Depression is also common in people with chronic illnesses, such as cancer, coronary heart disease, and HIV/AIDS (Kravitz & Ford, 2008).

The concept of **illness behavior** is useful to those who wish to understand the subjective response that a person has to being diagnosed with an illness. It refers to the meaning that the individual attributes to their illness, how it is defined, and the treatments they will consider. This subjective meaning is viewed as a "process that unfolds as over time as people struggle to achieve some accommodation or mastery over their health problems" (Institute of Medicine, 1987, p. 148). Awareness of this process is a valuable tool for helping the client cope with their medical challenges.

In some cases, what appears to be psychiatric in source is actually the symptom of a medical condition. For example, thyroid disease, autoimmune disorders, and various tumors can result in psychotic symptoms, such as hallucinations (Heinrich & Grahm, 2003; American College of Rheumatology, 1999; Bilgin, van der Wiel, Fischer, & De Herder, 2007), and Huntington's disease can cause severe mood and behavior changes. Therefore, it is important that the social worker refer their client to their physician to rule out a medical problem prior to assuming the presence of a mental health disorder.

If a client is taking **psychotropic medications** (as prescribed for a mental illness), it is useful to know the potential side effects for those medications. Antidepressant medications may cause nausea, weight gain, diarrhea, sleepiness, or sexual problems. The most common side effects for antianxiety medications are nausea, blurred vision, headaches, confusion, fatigue, or nightmares. Antipsychotic medications cause drowsiness, dizziness, restlessness, weight gain, dry mouth, nausea, or constipation. Medications used to stabilize mood may cause nausea, tremors, itching, excessive thirst, and frequent urination. See Table 4.1 for a more thorough listing of medications and potential side effects.

TABLE 4.1. Psychotropic Medications

Class of Medication	Examples	Conditions it Treats	Possible Side Effects
Anti-Depressant	Fluoxetine Citalopram Setraline Paroxetine Escitalopram	Depression Anxiety Pain Insomnia	Nausea/vomiting Weight gain Diarrhea Sleepiness Sexual problems
Anti-Anxiety	Clonazepam Alprazolam Lorazepam	Panic attacks Extreme fear Worry	Blurred vision Nausea Headaches Confusion Fatigue Nightmares

Stimulant	Methylphenidate Amphetamine Dextroamphetamine	Attention deficit disorder	Difficulty falling or staying asleep Loss of appetite Headaches Stomach pain
Antipsychotic	Chlorpromazine Haloperidol Perphenazine Fluphanazine	Schizophrenia Bipolar disorder Psychotic depression	Drowsiness Dizziness Weight gain Dry mouth Constipation Nausea/vomiting Blurred vision Tics/tremors
Mood Stabilizer	Carbamazepine Lamotrigine Oxcarbazepine	Mania Bipolar disorder Schizoaffective disorder	Itch, rash Excessive thirst Frequent urination Tremor Nausea/vomiting Slurred speech Hallucinations Loss of coordination

Note. The above information was obtained from the website for the National Institute of Mental Health (n.d.). Go to https://www.nimh.nih.gov/health/topics/mental-health-medications for more detail.

The biophysical portion of assessment should also include a focus on the client's *use or abuse of alcohol or other drugs.* The *Diagnostics and Statistics Manual (DSM-5)* (American Psychiatric Association, 2013), used to diagnose substance use disorders, identifies the primary criteria for determining a pathological pattern of substance use. These include the following:

1. Impaired control: The person has been taking greater amounts of the substance over increased periods of time; they may have made unsuccessful attempts to cut down or stop using. They are spending increased amounts of time focused on obtaining and using the substance. They may also have cravings for their drug of choice, or intense desires for it, when triggered.
2. Social and role impairment: Due to the abuse of substances, the client is unable to fulfill role responsibilities at work, home, or school. They continue to use the substance, despite on-going interpersonal problems related to the abuse. The person may even withdraw from others.
3. Risky use: The individual continues to use the substance even when it is hazardous to do so physically, psychologically, legally, and/or socially.
4. Pharmacological indicators: The client exhibits tolerance for the drug, as evidenced by the need to increase dosage in order to obtain the desired effect. They may also have symptoms of withdrawal when they abstain from using.

Numerous scales and instruments are available for use in a drug and alcohol assessment. A commonly used tool is the CAGE questionnaire (Mayfield, McLeod, & Hall, 1974). This brief scale includes four yes/no questions that ask about lifetime use of alcohol. The CAGE-AID adapts the original questionnaire to include screening for drugs other than alcohol. For detailed information on additional evidence-based substance abuse screening tools, visit the National Institute on Drug Abuse website (www.drugabuse.gov).

A common challenge encountered with the use of such standardized measures and/or informal questioning is that clients who abuse drugs are often unwilling or unprepared to acknowledge the extent of their problem. In response to this challenge, various interviewing techniques have been developed that are aimed at moving the client toward greater appreciation for the consequences of their abuse and to resources that support effective coping. Motivational interviewing strategies may need to be applied before the client will provide accurate information for a substance abuse assessment. These strategies will be discussed in depth in Chapter 7.

HIGHLIGHT 4.3: Aims of Biophysical Assessment

- Observe physical traits and characteristics that provide evidence of strengths and needs
- Understand general health-related strengths and challenges
- Rule out medical conditions that may explain behavior
- Gain knowledge of family history of mental health disorders
- Obtain information regarding the prescribed psychotropic medications being taken, along with the extent of alcohol and illicit drug use.
- Maintain appreciation for the role of brain functioning in the development and maintenance of mental health and substance abuse disorders.

Psychological Functioning

When delving into the domain of psychological functioning, client **emotions** often take center stage. Painful emotions such as anger, sadness, guilt, and shame are frequently shared by the client, as they relate to specific events or circumstances. Unlike emotions, **moods** are not linked to a particular event; they involve a more general feeling state and can exist without explanation (Baumeister, 2005). **Affect** is the term used to describe an immediate response to something viewed as positive or negative. "Affective reactions are extremely fast, arising within small fractions of a second" (p. 247) and expressed through tone of voice, facial expressions, and gestures, perhaps even laughter or tears. When conducting an assessment of psychological functioning, the social worker attends to all three. They ask about emotions (e.g., "How are you feeling about your upcoming retirement?") and more persistent moods (e.g., "What happens for you when you are depressed?"). They attend to the client's affect upon interview and note the extent to which it is congruent with the content of discussion. For example, if a client smiles or laughs while talking about a significant loss, this would be noted. The social worker also observes the range and intensity of feelings expressed.

Client behavior is also observed and explored. Presenting problems sometimes relate to behaviors over which the client exercises limited control (e.g., aggression, withdrawal, consumption of food, drugs or alcohol use). These behaviors may signal a need for enhanced social, communication, anger management, or other coping skills. It is equally important that attention be devoted to behavioral skills that are strong and may be leveraged to address difficulties. Behavioral assessment can utilize direct observation and/ or questions such as the following:

- How do you normally express your anger?
- What do you do in social situations? Avoid others? Interact? Observe?
- What do you do when you are feeling sad? Worried?
- How do you let people know when you are upset about something they have done?
- How do you manage your time so that you get things done?

Understanding how client mood, emotions, and behavior can be explained is complex and guided by a range of psychological theories. These conceptual frameworks encourage a focus on differing aspects of psychological functioning—attachments, stage of development, exposure to trauma, behavioral conditioning, and beliefs, thoughts, and perceptions. This section will review several theories that are commonly used to identify factors that help explain client concerns: attachment theory, developmental theory, trauma theory, behavioral theory, and cognitive theory.

Attachment Theory

John Bowlby is considered the father of attachment theory, developed in the mid-1950s. This theory argues that through natural selection, parents and infants have evolved in ways that preserve the bond between them. Because infants need the protection of the caregiver, they display various behaviors aimed at facilitating this bond and maintaining attachment. In the best of circumstances, the caregiver responds in kind.

Based on laboratory research, Mary Ainsworth proposed three styles of early attachment: secure, anxious, and avoidant. The *securely attached* infant is one who has experienced their primary caregiver as a secure base, one who is accessible and responsive. On the other hand, babies with an *anxious attachment* have no basis on which to believe that their caregiver will respond in a consistent and nurturing manner. Those with an *avoidant attachment* style have likely experienced their caregiver as rejecting, angry, and restrained in their expression of affect (Ainsworth, 1979). These styles are thought to impact emotional and relationship patterns that emerge later in life. Securely attached adults tend to have the highest levels of positive emotions, intimacy, and relational problem-solving ability, while anxiously attached individuals are prone to emotional lability. Those with an avoidant attachment style may structure their daily activities in a way that limits closeness with others (Tidwell, 1996).

Bowlby (1980) also recognized that the way an adult responds to grief and loss is influenced by their early life experiences with attachment. Individuals who are preoccupied with attachment anxiety and those who are avoidant of attachments are more likely to have difficulty navigating the phases of a normal grief reaction: they may suffer from chronic mourning and prolonged distress related to the loss of a loved one or some other treasured aspect of their life.

When conducting an assessment that is rooted in attachment theory, the practitioner is interested in learning about early life bonds with primary caregivers. This is particularly important when working with children who have experienced abuse, neglect, and/or disrupted home placements. In extreme cases, these children may suffer from reactive attachment disorder which is characterized by "a consistent pattern of inhibited, emotional withdrawn behavior toward adult caregivers" (American Psychiatric Association, 2013, p. 265). When working with adolescents and adults, it is important to gather information regarding significant losses, including the loss of a loved one, job, home, friend, or even hopes and dreams. It is also imperative that the practitioner conduct an assessment of the client's coping skills in response to loss.

Developmental Theory

A variety of theories focus on an individual's stage of development and associated tasks and conflicts. Sigmund Freud was interested in psychosexual development in early childhood and how it may determine one's personality. Eric Erikson departed from Freud's focus to include stages of psychosocial development across the life span. He identified eight stages of development that span from infancy to old age, each with differing psychosocial tasks that the person must master to achieve healthy adjustment (see Table 4.2). His model has been faulted for being obsolete and heterocentric, but it does provide a starting point for understanding the challenges faced by people at varying stages in life. For instance, adolescents often present with struggles related to identity formation, and older adults are often challenged by despair as they review their life and consider what might have been. When conducting an assessment, it can be useful to consider the psychosocial conflicts the client is facing based on their developmental stage.

TABLE 4.2. Erikson's Stages of Psychosocial Development

Stage	Crisis	Age
1	Basic trust versus basic mistrust	Birth to 18 months
2	Autonomy versus shame and doubt	18 months to 3 years
3	Initiative versus guilt	3 to 6 years
4	Industry versus inferiority	6 to 12 years
5	Identity versus role confusion	Adolescence
6	Intimacy versus isolation	Young adulthood
7	Generativity versus stagnation	Middle adulthood
8	Ego integrity versus despair	Older adulthood

Jean Piaget's theory of cognitive development helps guide social work engagement and assessment with children. This theory recognizes that cognitive structures, or schemata, develop in children as they organize information and adapt to their world. Piaget proposed that youth go through sequential stages as their mental structures evolve: sensory motor (from birth to age 2), preoperational (ages 2 to 7), concrete operations (ages 7 to 11), and formal operations (ages 11 and above). Table 4.3 provides an overview of the ways in which children think differently based on the period of their cognitive development. This framework makes clear the importance of tailoring communication to a child's cognitive abilities. For example, children age 11 and below may have difficulty comprehending abstract concepts, such as responsibility, morality, and generosity. They are likely to be more responsive to the use of concrete terms, as seen in the statement "when you share your toys with your sister, she smiles." Parents can also be encouraged to adopt developmentally appropriate expectations of their child based on their cognitive capabilities.

TABLE 4.3. Piaget's Model of Cognitive Development

Age	Stage	Cognitive Abilities
Birth–2 years	Sensorimotor	Uses senses and motor skill, object permanence learned
2–6 years	Preoperational	Language develops, imagination grows, egocentric thinking used
7–11 years	Concrete operational	Logic applied, has objective and rational interpretations, conservation learned
12 years to adulthood	Formal operational	Thinks abstractly, grasps hypothetical ideas and moral issues

Direct service practitioners who incorporate developmental theory into their assessment are attuned to the psychosocial tasks, conflicts, and challenges that typify the client's developmental stage. They use language and convey concepts in a way that is developmentally appropriate. They may also help the client's family members appreciate the struggles connected to differing stages of life.

Trauma Theory

A large body of research has documented the adverse effects of psychological trauma, including mental illness, conflicted relationships, behavioral difficulties, and continued instances of victimization (Stinson, Quinn, & Levenson, 2016). The literature has also focused on ways to conceptualize trauma. For example, the Substance Abuse and Mental Health Services Administration (SAMHSA) (Substance Abuse and Mental Health Services Administration, 2014) specified the **three "E's" of trauma**: events, experience of events, and effects. *Events* include circumstances that pose a threat of severe physical or psychological harm (e.g., violence, abuse, or natural disasters). *Experience* refers to the manner in which one interprets, assigns meaning to, and reacts to the event. *Effects* can be short lived or long lasting and may include poor coping, inability to trust others, heightened arousal, or avoidance of situations that trigger memory of the event. The three *E*'s are helpful in guiding assessment of trauma related issues. Information should be gathered about client exposure to traumatic events, their thoughts and emotions related to these incidents, and the presence or absence of troubling symptoms of traumatic stress, including heightened anxiety or arousal, emotional numbing, and avoidance of trauma-related triggers.

Trauma-informed care is guided by six key principles, as articulated by SAMHSA (2014), aimed at promoting recovery and resisting practices that may retraumatize a client.

- Safety: ensuring that the client feels physically and psychologically safe during service delivery
- Trustworthiness and Transparency: practice-based decisions are clearly stated and focused on maintaining trust between practitioner and client
- Peer Support: mutual self-help of trauma survivors is viewed as an important vehicle for advancing recovery
- Collaboration and Mutuality: emphasis is placed on partnering with clients and leveling power differentials

- <u>Empowerment, Voice, and Choice</u>: clients are empowered to share in decision-making and goal setting
- <u>Cultural, Historical, and Gender Issues</u>: services are responsive to gender identity, historical trauma, and the cultural needs of clients served

Behavioral Theory

As first proposed by John B. Watson in 1913, behaviorism assumes that all behavior is learned. Watson made use of laboratory experiments to demonstrate the process of **classical conditioning**, a form of learning that occurs when a previously neutral stimulus takes on the ability to evoke a response that was originally provoked by another stimulus. For example, if a woman was attacked by a man with a long, black beard, she might become frightened of all men with long, black beards. She now associates the previously neutral stimulus of the beard with a fear response. B. F. Skinner built on this type of learning and advanced the concept of **operant conditioning**. He observed that behavior increases in frequency when it is positively or negatively reinforced. Positive reinforcement is a reward that follows the behavior, while negative reinforcement involves the removal of an unpleasant stimulus.

A commonly used method of behavioral assessment applies the rules of operant conditioning—**functional behavior assessment**. This approach begins by gathering information about the *nature of a problematic behavior*, including when it started (onset), how often it occurs (frequency), and its intensity. Next, the circumstances that take place just before the behavior is exhibited are identified and referred to as *antecedents*. Finally, the events that occur immediately following the behavior are examined (*consequences*). This formula is intended to make clear the function of the problem behavior. For example, if a boy tantrums (behavior) when his parents fight (antecedent) and then the fighting stops (consequence), the child is being negatively reinforced to tantrum due to the removal of the aversive stimulus. The function of the boy's behavior is to exercise control over his parents' behavior and distract them from arguing. On the other hand, if the child tantrums when the parent ignores him and stops behaving badly when the desired attention is given, his use of tantrums is positively reinforced: its function is to obtain connection and belonging. The clues uncovered by functional behavior assessment are helpful in designing interventions aimed at changing behavior. Such interventions might focus on changing the antecedents and consequences or finding a replacement behavior that meets the underlying need.

Behavior assessment is also helpful in understanding the factors that surround substance abuse or addiction. Using this method, the practitioner seeks information pertaining to the onset, frequency, and amount of the client's substance use (behavior); places, people, and circumstances that trigger use (antecedents); and desired as well as undesired consequences of use. When the client is motivated to create a recovery plan, this information is critical to the development of strategies that account for triggers and the internal or external reinforcements that reward continued use.

Cognitive Theory

As advanced by Aaron Beck, cognitive theory asserts that thinking patterns have a strong influence on emotions and behavior. More specifically, Beck argued that low self-evaluation, negative expectations, and self-blame contribute to depression and other mood disorders (Beck, 1967). He introduced the concept of the **negative triad** that he observed in people suffering from depression. It includes irrational and negative views of self (I am a loser), the world (everyone hates me), and the future (I will never amount to anything). He also identified a variety of irrational thinking patterns, or **cognitive distortions**, that interfere with healthy functioning:

- Arbitrary influence: drawing a conclusion from a situation, event, or experience when there is no evidence to support this conclusion
- Selective abstraction: focusing on a detail taken out of context while ignoring other, more salient features of the situation
- Overgeneralization: drawing a general conclusion about one's ability, performance, or worth on the basis of a single incident
- Magnification: exaggerating the significance of an unpleasant event, inflating the magnitude of their problems (otherwise known as catastrophizing)
- Minimization: underestimating one's performance, achievement, or ability (pp. 204–205)

Social workers who adopt a cognitive approach to assessment attend to the thoughts and beliefs that may explain the client's psychosocial struggles. They ask questions intended to elicit client perceptions about the troubling events and circumstances they describe. These practitioners also remain attuned to the irrational thinking patterns that are apparent in the client's dialogue. Consider the following statements that might be made by a client who is distressed about receiving a C grade on a math test early on in the semester, never having taken a course by the instructor previously; the corresponding distortions are noted:

"The teacher hates me." (arbitrary influence)

"The teacher gave me a weird look when she returned the exam. I don't think she likes me now." (selective abstraction)

"I am not a very good student." (overgeneralization, minimization)

"I will never pass this class." (magnification)

Attribution bias is another type of cognitive error that may be made as individuals attempt to explain their own or others' behavior. The **hostile attribution bias**, in particular, is a social information processing problem that is often seen in individuals who display aggressive behavior (Nasby, Hayden, & De Paulo, 1980). It involves a tendency to erroneously infer hostility on the part of others in social situations when none is present. For example, when a person assumes a hostile motive on the part of someone who accidentally bumps into them in a crowded area, they may be operating on the basis of this bias. When assessing a client's triggers for aggressive behavior, this can be a fruitful area to explore.

In closing this section on psychological functioning, the author would like to offer a word of caution. A common temptation, particularly for beginning social workers, is to assume mental illness or pathology when symptoms are expressed. In some cases, this assumption may be warranted. Other times, it is not, but merely a case of over-diagnosing. See Highlight 4.4 for some reminders that are intended to help practitioners avoid this trap and maintain a balanced perspective.

HIGHLIGHT 4.4: Just Because: Avoiding a Tendency to Overpathologize

- Just because a client is sad, it doesn't mean they are depressed.
- Just because a client is worried, it doesn't mean they have a chronic problem with anxiety.
- Just because a client is having mood swings, it doesn't mean they have bipolar disorder.
- Just because a client is hearing voices, it doesn't mean they have schizophrenia.
- Just because a client drinks alcohol or uses marijuana, it doesn't mean they have a substance abuse disorder.
- Just because a client is mad, it doesn't mean they are aggressive.
- Just because a client negates alleged problem behavior, it doesn't mean they are in a state of denial.

Social and Environmental Systems

Based on the person-in-environment perspective, it is critical that the direct services practitioner has knowledge of their clients' social and environmental spheres of functioning. The ecological systems framework makes clear that problems and struggles don't occur in a vacuum—they exist in relation to a myriad of contextual variables. Therefore, an exploration of client strengths and needs with respect to their social and physical environment is a necessary component of social work assessment. It is a key element of the holistic approach, which accounts for forces outside of the person who is presenting for services. Suggested methods for approaching this area of assessment are provided below.

Physical Environment

The client's living situation can be assessed indirectly through client and family reports or directly through a home visit. Areas of focus are primarily related to health and safety features of the physical environment. Those include the following:

- Sanitation
- Access to clean water, heat, plumbing
- Provisions to ensure adequate nutrition
- Freedom from rodent or other pest infestations
- Adequate space and privacy

When assessing the physical environment of a frail, older adult, the social worker will determine if the living situation is safe and supportive of activities of daily living (ADLs) such as bathing, grooming, eating, toileting, and ambulation. If the client resides in a residential or convalescent facility, it is important that they have immediate access to personal items that offer pleasant memories and comfort.

When direct observation of a client's physical environment is possible, various items on display can serve as vehicles for establishing rapport. For example, a social worker might notice photographs of friends, family members, or vacations and ask about their importance to the client. A child's toys, games, or books might be the focus of conversation, as the practitioner seeks information about skills and interests. A robust assessment includes information about environmental assets as well as areas of deficiency.

Social Support

Client access to social support is another critical area of attention, as, under certain circumstances, it has been found to enhance health and well-being. According to Cohen and Wills (1985), research has shown that social support buffers the recipient from the negative impact of stress when the resources offered are responsive to the needs generated by the stressor. These authors also found that well-being is greater for those who are integrated into a large social network. Social networks can offer a variety of supports, including *emotional*, *informational*, and *concrete* (tangible) aid (Tracy & Whittaker, 1990). However, not all of the members of one's social network are supportive; in fact, some may be the source of criticism and conflict. A beneficial aspect of the social network is the ***reciprocity*** it affords, defined as the degree to which people both give and receive support from one another. In fact, reciprocity with family members reduces symptoms of stress to a greater extent than the amount of support given or received (Jung, 1990).

Comprehensive assessment should include exploration of the client's support system, including family, friends, neighbors, co-workers, and faith-based associates. To facilitate rich information on this topic, practitioners might use questions similar to the following:

- Who can you count on to listen when you share your worries and fears?
- If you were sick, who might help you with your daily chores?
- Who would you turn to for advice on how to handle a problem with your family?
- If you needed a loan or a ride to an appointment, who might be willing to help?
- Does the support between you and _____ go both ways?

Community Opportunities for Empowerment

In the late 1980s, Julian Rappaport presented the concept of empowerment and defined it as "a process, a mechanism by which people, organizations, and communities gain mastery over their affairs" (1987, p. 122). Empowerment theory recognizes that people are strengthened, to the extent that they are provided opportunities to (a) participate in decision-making processes that are meaningful to them and (b) access, as well as expand, resources capable of meeting their needs. Social workers may support the empowerment of their clients by identifying ways that the individual can not only access supportive services but contribute to their communities in significant ways. For example, a parent whose child was diagnosed with a mental illness might be encouraged to participate in the local chapter of the National Alliance on Mental Illness (NAMI). By connecting to this organization, the parent could access the support of other parents with similar challenges and, in turn, offer support to others in need. Likewise, an older adult might be aided in becoming a foster grandparent as a means of alleviating loneliness and helping at-risk children. The promotion of empowering activities of this kind requires knowledge of client assets as well as community involvement opportunities that provide a good match. The benefit of this work is increased self-efficacy on the part of clients as they discover that they, too, can make a difference.

TABLE 4.4. Psychological, Social, and Environmental Theories Guiding Assessment

Theory	Aim of Assessment
Attachment Theory	Gain knowledge of early life bonds with caregivers, major losses, coping skills for managing grief
Developmental Theory	Understand psychosocial tasks and conflicts based on stage; use of language consistent with cognitive development
Trauma Theory	Gather information about traumatic events endured, ways in which those events were experienced, and symptoms of traumatic stress
Behavioral Theory	Gain knowledge of onset, frequency, intensity of problem behavior, anteced-ents/triggers for behavior, positive and negative reinforcements
Cognitive Theory	Understand client core beliefs (regarding self, world, future), distorted thinking, attribution biases that impact behavior and emotions
Social Support Theory	Gather information concerning sources of emotional, informational, concrete resources, reciprocity between client and support givers or receivers
Empowerment Theory	Gain information regarding resources needed and available; assess client assets as they may lend themselves to community involvement opportunities

Cultural and Spiritual Assessment

As discussed in earlier chapters, it is imperative that the social worker explore and embrace the cultural identity of their clients. In conducting this assessment with diverse clients, it can be helpful to have general information pertaining to various cultural groups. However, practitioners should never assume certain beliefs, customs, traditions, or worldviews on the part of their clients based on demographic characteristics alone. There is a great deal of variation within groups due to the multiple dimensions that inform cultural identity. For example, a second-generation, 20-year-old Hmong American woman may have very different ideas about gender roles than her first-generation parents. Her cultural identity is rooted in not only ethnicity but her level of acculturation. The **intersectionality perspective** furthers understanding of this dynamic. It asserts that "people simultaneously occupy multiple positions (positionalities) within the socio-cultural-political and structural fabric of society" (Ortega & Coulborn-Faller, 2011). Thus, one's experiences within in a variety of groups and communities accumulate over time and shape identity. To access a client's multidimensional sense of themselves in relation to the world, the practitioner must embody a great deal of humility and willingness to learn from the client, thus giving up the role of expert. They must convey curiosity about the client's view of the benefits and challenges connected with various group affiliations. Table 4.5 provides a format for carrying out the discussion.

Another beneficial area to explore pertains to the client's customs and beliefs regarding appropriate healing practices. Many cultural groups prefer **indigenous healing methods** over westernized medicine and mental health practices. For instance, a Mexican American may turn to the curandero for medical assistance, while Hmong American families may utilize the shaman. The use of these practices should

TABLE 4.5. Areas of Intersecting Identity

Category	Group Examples
Race and Ethnicity	White, Black, Asian, Hispanic, Native American, Hmong, Pacific Islander
Gender	male, female, transgender, agender, genderqueer
Sexual Orientation	gay, lesbian, bisexual, heterosexual
Nationality	Mexican, Canadian, French, German, Iranian, Chinese, Vietnamese, United States American
Generation	baby boomer, Generation X (Y, Z), second- or first-generation immigrant
Socioeconomic Class	lower class, middle class, upper class
Education Level	student, high school graduate, college student or graduate
Religion	Jew, Buddhist, Muslim, Christian, Hindu, atheist
Politics	conservative, liberal, Republican, Democrat, independent
Geography of Residence	rural, semirural, urban
Occupation	military, law enforcement, law, education, hospitality, social work, psychology, mechanics, agriculture

Note. Table 4.5 is intended to guide discussion of intersecting aspects of a person's culture. Examples are not exhaustive, and it's best to use the client's language in identifying groups within one or more categories that are central to their identity. Next, explore their views with regard to the benefits and challenges associated with group membership(s).

never be denigrated or dismissed; rather, they should be acknowledged, celebrated, and, if indicated, incorporated into a treatment plan.

Spiritual assessment should move beyond asking if the client attends church, temple, or synagogue. In fact, spirituality is distinct from religion in that it encompasses a broad understanding of the way in which the person makes meaning of life, and relates to their interpretation of God, or spirit. Hodge (2001) provides a framework for conducting a spiritual assessment that includes questions about early life experiences with religious practices as well as the person's current orientation. The model also entails inquiry into the role of spirituality in helping the client cope with pain, maintain hope, deal with challenges, and determine right from wrong. When the social worker conducts a less direct, or implicit spiritual assessment, they listen for clues as to the client's spiritual views (Hodge, 2013). The value in the latter approach is apparent when one considers a Muslim woman who confesses to her social worker that she has suicidal thoughts and then follows up with assurances that she would never take her own life, as it is forbidden by the Koran. Such comments open the door for discussion related to the ways in which faith supports recovery and well-being.

The Process of Assessment

Assessment is not only a product or document submitted to a social work agency, it is a process through which the social worker establishes a level of safety that allows clients to disclose their personal concerns and challenges. The process needs to be flexible and adaptable to agency mandates as well as the circumstances at hand. For example, a child protective services social worker performing an investigation of alleged neglect must attend to safety issues in the home and assess the extent to which basic needs of a child are met (food, shelter, clothing, hygiene, etc.). In other cases, the preliminary focus of the practitioner may need to be on stabilizing crisis—an activity that will be covered in depth in Chapter 7. Once safety is ensured, the practitioner can begin assessing the realms of functioning described above with the aim of forming a working hypothesis about key factors that contribute to presenting problems. It should be understood, however, that the assessment process is on-going and ideally doesn't end with an initial interview. In fact, the written assessment should be considered a "live" document that is modified and updated as additional information comes to light.

The process of gathering information often involves interviewing collateral or significant others to gain their perspective with regard to presenting problems and client concerns. The NASW Code of Ethics makes clear that a consent for release of information must be signed by the client in order for the practitioner to speak to collateral individuals about their care. Those might include family members, teachers, physicians, or public service workers (e.g., probation officers, child welfare workers, law enforcement). With proper consent, this endeavor can be very informative and, in some cases, vital to efforts aimed at increasing client access to needed resources. An example is provided in the following narrative application.

NARRATIVE APPLICATION: Mezzo Level Approach to Assessment

Marcie was conducting an assessment for her 15-year-old client, Juan, who was on probation for stealing and on-going problems with truancy. Upon interview, she asked him why he skipped school, but he was not very forthcoming and merely stated, "It's boring." His probation officer had informed Marcie that Juan was at risk of being cited for violation of probation if his school attendance didn't improve. Marcie made a home visit to speak with his mother, Alejandra, who was monolingual Spanish speaking. Thankfully, Marcie had Spanish speaking ability and was able to understand Alejandra's point of view.

During the home visit, Alejandra stated that she was worried about her son getting into trouble but was at a loss as to what to do. Juan's father was a farm laborer who worked long hours and expected her to manage things at home. Every morning, Juan told her he was going to school, and she wanted to believe him. Alejandra didn't understand the voicemail messages left on their phone from the high school. When Alejandra tried to call the school, the staff in the office were unable to understand her, as none of them spoke Spanish. Marcie obtained consent to speak with school personnel about the situation.

Upon contacting the school counselor, Marcie learned that Juan did fairly well in class when he attended, but he had missed most classes every day last week. He did attend art classes, however, as he seemed to have a special talent and connection with the art teacher. When Marcie explained Alejandra's challenge in communicating with the office, the counselor admitted that there was only one employee who spoke Spanish, but she would work out a way for the staff to reach out to Juan's mother and keep her in the loop. Marcie relayed the information back to Alejandra, who was very pleased with the idea of having improved communication with Juan's school.

In the above narrative, Marcie is carrying out mezzo-level work by accessing information about the nature of the relationship between two systems—home and school. This sets in motion efforts to empower Alejandra by providing her with access to needed information and support. Marcie is exhibiting cultural humility as she attempts to shift the power imbalance between Alejandra and the school system. In addition, she is learning important information about two of Juan's strengths—his artistic talent and relationship with his art teacher.

Self-Care: Safety in Social Work

The process of assessment may, at times, involve venturing into territory that is experienced as threatening, either by the social worker, the client, or both. The practitioner may routinely visit homes or neighborhoods that present with safety risks. When this is the case, self-care involves being proactive, anticipating challenges, and minimizing risk. Ideally, the worker will have access to a supervisor who will assist in the process of planning and preparing.

The National Association of Social Workers (2013) has established guidelines for social worker safety that includes the following suggestions for those who conduct home visits:

- Vehicle should be in good repair
- Cell phone should be charged and in good working order
- Visit should be planned at a time of day that presents with low risk
- Information should be made available to your supervisor about the time and location of the visit
- One needs to be informed of any violent incident that has occurred within the last 48 hours in the neighborhood where the visit will take place

Go to http://naswpress.org/publications/standards/index.html for a complete set of guidelines.

The need for self-care may also arise when a practitioner interviews an involuntary client who is not happy about having to meet. The person may escalate if the conversation touches on their insecurities and fears related to the referral for mandated services. The client may become angry or agitated, which can be alarming for the unprepared social worker. The best way to handle situations of this kind is to remain calm, while ensuring that there is a clear path to exit the room, if needed. Various techniques can be used to help de-escalate the client, such as speaking slowly in a soft, gentle but confident tone of voice and allowing the client to talk about what is upsetting to them. The social worker should avoid arguing with the client and, as an alternative, should validate their emotions. This doesn't mean that the practitioner must agree with the client's beliefs, behaviors, or attitudes. **Validation** involves communicating understanding of the client's emotions, given their current circumstances. "I understand that it is hard to talk with someone you don't know about personal issues." "It must be stressful having child welfare at your front door."

Self-care during this process can include taking slow, deep, breaths to help sustain a calm and well-reasoned approach. It also entails avoiding a tendency to personalize the client's upset. Instead, the professional should understand that the reaction is not about them (unless they have said something rude or disrespectful) but about the client's loss of control, self-blame, and/or frustration due to legal mandates. Once the encounter has ended, it is advised that that practitioner take some time to decompress and share their experience with a trusted colleague or supervisor.

SUMMARY

This chapter begins with a focus on strengths discovery, which can be viewed as the cornerstone of social work assessment. It continues with the application of theory and methods for conducting a comprehensive assessment that includes information about client functioning across multiple domains: biophysical, psychological, social, environmental, cultural, and spiritual. The process of assessment is also discussed, including a mezzo-level approach to gathering information. The section on self-care is devoted to safety as well as strategies for managing risk and coping with difficult encounters with clients who are angry, agitated, or upset. As in previous chapters, sample dialogues and narrative illustrations are provided to exemplify the use of suggested methods.

KEY TERMS

Classical conditioning
Cognitive distortions
Emotions/mood/affect
Functional behavior assessment
Hostile attribution bias
Illness behavior

Indigenous healing methods
Intersectionality perspective
Negative triad
Neuroplasticity
Operant conditioning
Personal Strengths Grid

Psychotropic medications
Reciprocity
ROPES model
Three *E*'s of trauma
Trauma-informed care
Validation

DISCUSSION QUESTIONS

1. What challenges do you anticipate in conducting a strengths assessment with clients? How will you resolve them? Why is this important?

2. In what ways is reciprocity important as it relates to social support? What is the impact of limited reciprocity on the part of support givers? Receivers?

3. What categories of intersectional identity are most important to you in defining your culture?

SKILL DEVELOPMENT ACTIVITIES

1. Review the ROPES model and narrative application that follows. Utilize this approach to strengths-based assessment with a client or another consenting individual. What did you learn about your interviewee that you might not have discovered had you conducted a more deficit-based format for assessment?

2. Research opportunities in your community for client empowerment, similar to those discussed in this chapter.

3. Watch the presentation on Cultural Health Beliefs and Practices by Caroline Fee, as sponsored by San Jose University and Stanford Geriatric Education Center. Go to http://www.sjsu.edu/at/atn/webcasting/events/gerontology/index.html and scroll down from the first slide to find the link to this video. Which aspect of the film did you find most informative or interesting?

REFERENCES

Adili, F., Larijani, B., & Haghighatpanah, M. (2006). Diabetic patients: Psychological aspects. *Annals of the New York Academy of Sciences, 1084*, 329–349.

Ainsworth, M. D. (1979). Infant-mother attachment. *American Psychologist, 34*, 932–937.

American Psychiatric Association. (2013). *Diagnostic and statistical manual of mental disorders* (5th ed.). Washington, DC: American Psychiatric Publishing.

American College of Rheumatology. (1999). The American College of Rheumatology nomenclature and case definitions for neuropsychiatric lupus syndromes. *Arthritis Rheumatology, 42*, 599–608.

Baumeister, R. F. (2005). *The cultural animal: Human nature, meaning, and social life*. Don Mills, Ontario: Oxford University Press.

Beck, A. T. (1967). *Depression: Causes and treatment*. Philadelphia: University of Pennsylvania Press.

Bernard, B. (2004). *Resiliency: What we have learned*. San Francisco, CA: WestEd.

Bilgin Y. M., van der Wiel, H. E., Fischer, H. R., & De Herder, W. W. (2007). Treatment of severe psychosis due to ectopic Cushing's syndrome. *Journal of Endocrinological Investigation, 30*, 776–779.

Bowlby, J. (1980). *Attachment and loss: Sadness and depression* (Vol. 3). New York, NY: Basic Books.

Bremner, J. D. (2006). The relationship between cognitive and brain changes in posttraumatic stress disorder. *Academy of Sciences, 1071*, 80–86.

Brisch, R., Saniotis, A., Wolf, R., Bielau, H., Bernstein, H., Steiner, J., … Gos, T. (2014). The role of dopamine in schizophrenia from a neurobiological and evolutionary perspective: Old fashioned, but still in vogue. *Frontiers in Psychiatry, 5*, 1–11.

Buckley, P. F. (2005). Neuroimaging of schizophrenia: Structural abnormalities and pathophysiological implications. *Neuropsychiatric Diseases and Treatment, 1*, 193–204.

Centre for Genetics Education. (2012). Mental illness and inherited predisposition-schizophrenia and bipolar disorder. Retrieved from www.genetics.edu.au

Cohen, S., & Wills, T. A. (1985). Stress, social support, and the buffering hypothesis. *Psychological Bulletin, 98*, 310–357.

Cox, K. (2006). Investigating the impact of strength-based assessment on youth with emotional and behavioral disorders. *Journal of Child and Family Studies, 15*, 287–301.

Cox, K. (2008). Tools for building on youth strengths. *Reclaiming Children and Youth, 16*, 19–24.

De Shazer, S. (1985). *Keys to solution in brief therapy*. New York, NY: W. W. Norton.

Epstein, M. H., & Sharma, J. M. (1998). *Behavioral and emotional rating scale*. Austin, TX: Pro-Ed.

Graybeal, C. (2001). Strength-based social work assessment: Transforming the dominant paradigm. *Families in Society: The Journal of Contemporary Human Services, 82*(3), 233–242.

Heinrich, T. W., & Grahm, G. (2003). Hypothyroidism presenting as psychosis: Myxedema madness revisited. *Journal of Clinical Psychiatry, 5*, 260–266.

Henry, S. G. (2012). The genetics of mental illness: Implications for practice. *Bulletin of World Health Organization, 78*, 460–485.

Hernandez, L. M., & Blazer, D. G. (Eds.). (2006). *Genes, behavior, and the social environment: Moving beyond the nature/nurture debate*. Washington, DC: National Academies Press.

Hodge, D. R. (2001). Spiritual assessment: A review of major qualitative methods and a new framework for assessing spirituality. *Social Work, 46*, 203–214.

Hodge, D. R. (2013). Implicit spiritual assessment: An alternative approach for assessing client spirituality. *Social Work, 58*, 223–230.

Institute of Medicine. (1987). *Pain and disability: Clinical, behavioral, and public policy perspectives*. Washington, DC: National Academies Press.

Jung, J. (1990). The role of reciprocity in social support. *Basic and Applied Social Psychology, 11*, 243–253.

Kou, Z., & Iraji, A. (2014). Imaging brain plasticity after trauma. *Neural Regeneration Research, 9*, 693–700.

Kravitz, R. L., & Ford, D. E. (2008. Introduction: Medical conditions and depression—the view from primary care. *American Journal of Medicine, 121*, S1–S7.

Littrell, J. (2015). *Neuroscience for psychologists and other mental health professionals: Promoting well-being and treating mental illness*. New York, NY: Springer.

Mayfield, D., McLeod, G., & Hall, P. (1974). The CAGE questionnaire: Validation of a new alcoholism screening instrument. *American Journal of Psychiatry, 131*, 1121–1123.

Nasby, W., Hayden, B., & DePaulo, B. M. (1980). Attributional bias among aggressive boys to interpret unambiguous social stimuli as displays of hostility. *Journal of Abnormal Psychology, 89*, 459–468.

National Association of Social Workers. (2013). Guidelines for social work safety in the workplace. Retrieved from https://www.socialworkers.org/

National institute of Mental Health. (n.d.). Mental health medications. Retrieved from https://www.nimh.nih.gov/health/topics/mental-health-medications/index.shtml

Ortega, R. M., & Coulborn-Faller, K. (2011). Training child welfare workers from an intersectional cultural humility perspective: A paradigm shift. *Child Welfare, 90*, 27–49.

Rappaport, J. (1987). Terms of empowerment/exemplars: Toward a theory for community psychology. *American Journal of Community Psychology, 15*, 121–148.

Saleebey, D. (2009). *The strengths perspective in social work practice*. Boston, MA: Pearson.

Stinson, J. D., Quinn, M. A., & Levenson, J. S. (2016). The impact of trauma on the onset of mental health symptoms, aggression, and criminal behavior in an outpatient psychiatric sample. *Child Abuse & Neglect, 61*, 13–22.

Substance Abuse and Mental Health Services Administration. (2014). *SAMHSA's Concept of Trauma and Guidance for a Trauma-Informed Approach*. HHS Publication No. (SMA) 14-4884. Rockville, MD: Substance Abuse and Mental Health Services Administration.

Tidwell, M-C. O., Reis, H. T., & Shaver, P. R. (1996). Attachment, attractiveness, and social interaction: A diary study. *Journal of Personality and Social Psychology, 71*, 729–745.

Tracy, E. M., & Whittaker, J. (1990). The social network map: Assessing social support in clinical practice. *Families in Society: The Journal of Contemporary Human Services, 71*, 461–470.

Treadway, M. T., & Zald, D. H. (2011). Reconsidering anhedonia in depression: Lessons learned from translational neuroscience. *Neuroscience and Biobehavioral Reviews, 35*, 537–555.

Werner, E., & Smith, R. (1992). *Overcoming the odds: High risk children from birth to adulthood*. New York, NY: Cornell University Press.

Willner, P., Scheel-Kruger, J., & Belzung, C. (2013). The neurobiology of depression and antidepressant action. *Neuroscience and Biobehavioral Reviews, 37*, 2331–2371.

FIGURE CREDIT

Highlight 4.1: Selections from Clay Graybeal, "Strengths-Based Social Work Assessment: Transforming the Dominant Paradigm," Families in Society, vol. 82, no. 3, pp. 237. Copyright © 2001 by SAGE Publications.

Table 4.1: Source: https://www.nimh.nih.gov/health/topics/mental-health-medications.

CHAPTER 5

Goal Setting

*The tragedy of life doesn't lie in not reaching your goal. The tragedy lies in having
no goals to reach.*—BENJAMIN MAYS

W HEN A PERSON feels stuck, unmotivated, or uninspired, goal setting provides a way out of the quagmire. It can free one from the tug of apathy and indifference by providing focus and direction. Yet, not all goal formation is helpful or transformative. In fact, studies have shown that when it is indiscriminate, narrowly focused, or adopts inappropriate timelines, it can reduce motivation (Ordonez, Schweitzer, Galinsky, & Bazerman, 2009). Conversely, when goal setting is carefully executed, it supports problem resolution, growth, and well-being. However, effective goal setting requires skill and nuance. It resists the "one size fits all" label and takes on a tailored approach that provides a good fit with the person's assets, needs, and desires. Likewise, goal setting with clients is most successful when aims and objectives are individualized to their unique strengths, preferences, and circumstances. Further guidelines for effective goal setting in direct social work practice will be discussed in this chapter; but first, key terms and concepts will be reviewed.

Goal Setting Basics

Client goals specify the purpose of service delivery and anticipated outcomes. They provide a road map for what is to be accomplished that includes "mileage markers" that guide movement forward (Hepworth, Rooney, Rooney, Strom-Gottfried, & Larsen, 2010, p. 303). **Long-term goals** represent the ultimate destination that the client intends to reach, such as the completion of court-ordered probation, management of mental illness, or graduation from college. **Short-term goals** are those that need to be accomplished before long-term goal attainment is likely or possible. For someone who has the long-term goal of completing probation, a short-term goal might be to pay off restitution or secure employment. **Objectives** are the task-related goals or action steps that the client intends to take that will bring him or her closer to short-term goal attainment. For the individual who is seeking employment, objectives might be to turn in three applications per week and/or practice job interviewing skills. In addition to setting goals and objectives, effective goal setting entails the anticipation of potential **barriers** to goal attainment and planning how the client will manage and resolve these impediments.

Goal Setting That is S.M.A.R.T.

S.M.A.R.T. goal setting was first introduced by management consultant George Doran in 1981. He asserted that organizational goals and objectives should be as follows:

> **Specific:** target a particular area for change or development
> **Measurable:** quantify aims, with clear indications of progress

Assignable: clarify who will do what
Realistic: possible to attain, given resources available
Time-bound: indicate when outcomes should be accomplished

Doran (1981) suggested that not all objectives will necessarily meet all five of the criteria, but "the closer we get to the smart criteria as guidelines, the smarter are objectives will be" (p. 36).

The S.M.A.R.T. acronym has since been adapted and popularized by leadership trainer and consultant Jose Luis Romero (2009), who provides a slightly different interpretation of smart goal setting. He suggests that goals should be as follows:

Specific: clear regarding outcomes to be attained
Measurable: include performance targets with quantitative or qualitative measures
Attainable: challenging yet realistic, given resources needed and available
Relevant: address issues of importance
Time-bound: provide timeline with regular dates for performance review

The revised format for smart goal setting is often used as a guideline in direct social work practice. *Goal specificity* is encouraged in order to avoid ambiguity as it relates to desired outcomes. As an illustration, consider the client goal to "work toward recovery." This aim is very vague and could be interpreted in a variety of different ways. A further specified goal would be to "reduce marijuana use from two times daily to once a week." Tasks and objectives should be very specific, even when long- or short-term goals are broader: "Client will attend substance abuse recovery counseling sessions two times per week."

Client goals should also be *measurable* so that progress toward attainment can be monitored and recognized. If the client sets a goal to "increase self-esteem," it would be very difficult to ascertain if they were making headway. A more measurable objective would be to participate in self-esteem-building activities at least once a week or maintain a daily log of personal successes.

It is always advisable to set goals that are *attainable*, given the client's attributes and access to resources, otherwise they are being set up for failure. Imagine the behaviorally challenged child who is expected to follow instructions 100% of the time. This goal is not realistic for any child, much less one who exhibits oppositional behavior. A more realistic aim would be to increase the child's compliance with instructions from zero times daily to three times a day.

It goes without saying that goals should be *relevant* and devoted to areas of importance. Yet, relevance is value laden and may be viewed differently across practitioner and client. A social worker might like to see a client comply with court mandates to obtain employment and abide by local laws. The client might value a focus on resolving symptoms of depression that limit their motivation to actively pursue employment. Acting on the principle of relevance can present with a number of challenges that will be addressed below in the upcoming section devoted to self-determination theory.

Timelines are important in promoting accountability for outcomes established. They provide a trajectory for goal attainment and an anticipated end point for service delivery. Ideally, they prompt social workers and their clients to evaluate what's working and what might be improved at various points between the onset and ending of services. This feedback reinforces momentum and motivation on the part of both practitioner and client.

HIGHLIGHT 5.1: Sample SMART Service Plan for Depressed Teen

Problems/Needs: Depressed and anxious moods, self-harm behavior, fatigue, loss of interest in pleasurable activities

Strengths & Resources: Support from mother, interest in volunteer work, artistic ability, reading and writing skills

Cultural Considerations, Needs & Resources: Stigma related to bisexual orientation, interest in connecting with LGBTQ resource center

Long-Term Goals: Improved ability to regulate depressed and anxious moods, elimination of self-harm behaviors (cutting) by (date)

Short-Term Goals: Improved cognitive coping skills as practiced in session and observed by mother, increased activity level per self-report

Objectives:
- I will develop a safety plan for use when I have the urge to cut by (date)
- I will keep a daily log of my negative thoughts, replacement thoughts, and emotions for one month
- I will use painting to self-soothe at least two times a week
- I will take daily walks for exercise
- I will visit the LGBT community center by (date) and inquire about volunteer opportunities

Barriers: Rude or mean comments by peers is a trigger. If this happens, I will cope by deep breathing and watching my thoughts.

Periodic Review Dates: May 15, June 15, July 15

Peeling Layers Off the Onion

The development of relevant client goals requires flexibility on the part of the social worker along with a willingness to adapt to newly acquired information. Certain objectives that seemed appropriate early on in the goal setting process may miss the mark with respect to addressing core issues that contribute to the presenting problem. Fine-tuning client goals is akin to the process of peeling layers off an onion. As one strips the layers of an onion that are dried and unproductive, they eventually reach the savory bulb. Likewise, after pruning away unrealistic client goals, the practitioner may reach material that is vital to the change process.

As an example, consider a pre-teen client who is leaving home without permission and staying out late at night. An initial goal might be to increase the youth's compliance with curfew. Upon working with the family, it may become increasingly apparent that the parent provides little discipline or enforcement of rules; based on this information, a new goal is established to increase structure in the home. After coaching the parent on ways to set and enforce house rules, it may become clear that they are unable to make use of behavior management tools due to severe depression. Thus, the immediate goal will change so as to address the parent's mental health problems. It is vitally important that direct service practitioners remain alert to barriers that interfere with goal attainment, and change course accordingly.

Applying Theory to Goal Setting

One of the most challenging aspects of goal setting is carrying out a process that supports and invigorates client commitment. A rote method of cutting from one client plan and pasting onto others is much less likely to foster motivation than an approach that is collaborative and customized to the individual. A meaningful process of goal setting is one that is inspiring and empowering for the client. Self-determination theory sheds light on how such a process may be conducted.

Self-Determination Theory

Self-determination, a central value in social work, is sometimes difficult to apply during the goal-setting process. The challenge is exacerbated when clients are mandated to receive services and prompted by external forces and court-imposed sanctions to make change. **Self-determination theory** provides a foundation for steps that can be taken to maximize the control clients experience during this goal-setting process, thereby increasing their motivation to pursue court-enforced objectives. This conceptual model begins with the premise that, to be effective, goals must be internalized and integrated. Essential to the processes of internalization are a sense of autonomy, competence, and relatedness to others who are recommending change (Ryan, Patrick, Deci, & Williams, 2008). *Autonomy* is experienced when the individual endorses the importance of a goal as it relates to their own personal values. Social workers can support autonomy and integration of goals by helping clients link externally imposed goals to their own core values, such as family, freedom, independence, or self-worth. *Competence* is attained when one has the skills and resources needed to make change, along with self-efficacy, or task-related confidence. Research has shown that self-efficacy is positively associated with goal-directed performance (Hirsh, Nitzl, & Reemts, 2018). Practitioners can support competence by providing the tools needed for success as well as on-going recognition that the client has what it takes to be successful. *Relatedness* develops when a person feels respected and understood by significant others. Social workers who practice effective engagement foster a sense of relatedness with their clients. They can further support relatedness by helping clients focus on the family members and friends who will celebrate their goal-related accomplishments.

Advances in Goal Theory

Goal setting theorists Locke and Latham have reviewed hundreds of studies that pertain to task performance in organizations. In a recent article (2006), they discuss advances in this research, one of which highlights the importance of **framing** as a means of supporting goal attainment. Framing can be helpful when an individual views a goal as threatening due to its potential for personal failure. The application of this technique involves helping the person reappraise the goal as a challenge and opportunity for success versus a threat to their self-worth. Framing is widely used in social work practice to help clients broaden their perspective. When utilized in goal setting, it promotes a focus on potential victory as opposed to failure, as illustrated in the narrative application below.

NARRATIVE APPLICATION: Supporting Self-Determination

Bob is a 35-year-old man who was recently released from jail under the condition that he participate in a local day treatment program. He had been arrested during a manic episode in which he had sliced the tires of his girlfriend's truck after she broke up with him. This was the third episode over the course of 2 months in which law enforcement had been called due to his loud and belligerent behavior in public. Bob started attending the program and seemed to appreciate the structure it provided, but he refused prescribed medications for bipolar disorder. He expressed his concerns about medication to his social worker.

> Bob: I don't like how it slows me down. I really like being manic!
>
> Social Worker: Ok, Bob. No one can force you to take it. What do you want for yourself?
>
> Bob: I want to stay out of jail and for my girlfriend, Sandy, to take me back.
>
> Social Worker: So freedom and your relationship with Sandy are important to you?
>
> Bob: Yep.
>
> Social Worker: What do you think would need to happen for Sandy to take you back?
>
> Bob: I'd have to start acting like somebody, not like a fool.
>
> Social Worker: So, when you are acting like somebody, what are you doing?
>
> Bob: I am more chill, but it's hard with all the thoughts racing around in my head.
>
> Social Worker: Tell me about a time when your thoughts didn't race so much.
>
> Bob: I was in the hospital.
>
> Social Worker: Were you taking meds then?
>
> Bob: Yes, they said I should if I wanted to leave by my birthday.
>
> Social Worker: Did you leave by your birthday?
>
> Bob: Yep. [He smiles slyly.] OK, the meds did help, but here's the thing. If I start taking them again and I screw up anyway, I might as well give up.
>
> Social Worker: Well, there is that possibility, but I think that you have a real shot at acting like somebody if you try the meds for 3 months at the dose the psychiatrist recommends and keep working on the coping skills we practice in group.
>
> Bob: OK, I'll try, but no mood charting—it's totally pointless. I do like having things to do during the day and being with people that understand what it's like to have bipolar.
>
> Social Worker: OK, we'll work that into your plan and set an appointment for you to see the doctor. Are you in agreement?
>
> Bob: Yes, that works. Can my girlfriend come for family counseling?
>
> Social Worker: That's up to her, but if she agrees, we can definitely include her.
>
> Bob: Will you call my probation officer and tell her that I'm working the program?
>
> Social Worker: Absolutely. We don't want you going back to jail, that's for sure.

In the above narrative, we see the social worker reassure Bob that his choices are respected. His autonomy and relatedness are supported as she recognizes his desire for freedom and reunification with his girlfriend. Lastly, she encourages a focus on success that is likely as he pursues his interest in "acting like somebody." By doing so, she is able to negotiate a medication trial and link this goal with his stated interests.

Strategies for Goal Setting

A variety of strategies have been developed to guide goal setting in social work, and several will be discussed below. One is a model for individual or group-based work that is rooted in Native American principles. The second is a method for specifying goals that has been used effectively with frail, older adults and youth who have physical and developmental disabilities. Finally, an approach consistent with ecological systems theory will be examined.

Goal Wheel

A unique approach to goal setting founded in Navaho philosophy is offered by Garner, Bruce, and Stellern (2011). They adapted the Native American medicine wheel for use in group counseling with adolescents, but stressed that their method can be utilized with all age groups. The process begins by establishing an atmosphere of trust and respect between group members as the sacred wheel is introduced. It is described as a "universal symbol of wholeness and courage to embrace life" (p. 63), with its four quadrants representing the seasons of the year. Each season is said to have associated themes, colors, and cardinal directions (see Table 5.1).

TABLE 5.1. Navajo Medicine Wheel

Quadrant	Season	Themes	Color
1 – East	Spring	Hope, Anticipation, Imagine, Visualization (Ni'tsa'hake'e's)	White
2 – South	Summer	Compassion, Planning (Nahat'a')	Turquoise
3 – West	Autumn	Satisfaction, Self-Worth, Action (Aadi'i'li'il)	Yellow
4 – North	Winter	Accomplishment, Fulfillment, Refection (Bee niise'e'ldoo)	Black

Following this introduction, group members are invited to share their hopes and dreams for the future along with realistic steps they might take to move toward fulfillment. They then draw a large circle on a piece of paper, fold it into fourths, and number each quadrant in a clockwise direction. Each quadrant (Q) is labelled: Q1—Imagine and Visualize; Q2—Planning; Q3—Action; Q4—Enjoy and Reflect. Next, they enter the four cardinal points of the compass and decorate each section with the associated color. The goal wheel is then ready for the insertion of personal information related to the assigned topics.

In quadrant #1, participants are asked to write about the future they envision for themselves, with emphasis placed on how they will feel and the benefits that will come their way when they accomplish the goal. For example, if they imagine a future having friends, they might note that when this is achieved, they will feel a sense of belonging and acceptance. Within quadrant #2, group members identify what will be needed to help them accomplish their goal. Brainstorming with fellow group participants is used to aid in this exploration. The youth who wants to make friends might decide to write about managing social anxiety and joining a teen club in their community. Quadrant #3 is devoted to the creation of a detailed plan that includes action steps that will be taken and associated timelines. Here they also note the barriers that might occur and how they will feel in response to these obstacles. In completing quadrant #4, members are asked to meditate or otherwise reflect upon their goal and the activity as a whole. They represent this reflection with a poem, drawing, or plan for sharing with others.

Goal Menu

Another approach to goal setting makes use of the goal menu, a list of options that clients may select from in establishing their own goals and objectives. These menus have been created in response to difficulties encountered in specifying goals for select populations. One example is discussed by Yip and colleagues (1998), who studied a menu created for goal setting with frail elders in an inpatient rehabilitation center. The tool was developed by identifying *functional areas for clients served* (e.g., self-care, mobility, nutrition, cognitive functioning, depression, behavior management) and a *concrete hierarchy of possible outcomes* for each goal area. The authors then studied the impact of the tool utilizing a retrospective chart review; results supported the menu's validity and yielded descriptive information about its benefits and limitations. Noted benefits included time saved by interdisciplinary team members who "avoided reinventing the wheel each time a new patient was admitted" (p. 741). The template also allowed for flexibility and individualization during the goal setting process, as each patient ended up with a different combination of goal areas and anticipated outcomes. However, the researchers caution that the tool should not be rigidly applied, as the specified outcomes may not apply in every case.

Gerhardt and colleagues (2015) discuss the development of a goal menu for use with children who have disabilities and struggle to make friends. These researchers conducted a focus group with youth at a children's rehabilitation hospital, and semistructured interviews with expert clinicians. Qualitative data analysis produced five themes related to the friend-making process:

- Person factors influencing friend making (e.g., social skills, age appropriate interests)
- Making friend making a priority (by youth, family, and school)
- Opportunity for friend making (e.g., extracurricular activities, walking home from school)
- Motivation to make friends (as facilitated by family, peers, healthcare workers)
- A little bit of luck (it just happens!) (p. 1024)

The authors illustrate the creation of a goal menu as it relates to the opportunity for friend-making theme. They identify three goal target areas: joining an extracurricular activity, attending get-togethers with friends, and taking public transit with peers. For each target area, they provide specific and measurable outcomes. The authors encourage practitioners to utilize such menus as a means of delineating functional steps toward friend making that move beyond person factors (social skill) and are aimed at improving motivation, opportunity, and the priority placed on this area of social development.

Risk/Resiliency Ecological Framework

Consistent with the ecological systems orientation of social work, Corcoran and Nichols-Casebolt (2004) propose a risk and resilience model for guiding assessment and goal setting with at-risk youth and families. Based on an extensive review of empirical research, they specify risk and protective factors at the micro, mezzo, and macro system levels. Those include the following:

- <u>Micro</u>: child temperament, self-efficacy, intelligence, parental monitoring, family violence versus home safety and stability

- Mezzo: economic advantages or disadvantages of neighborhood, social supports, access to illegal substances, community safety
- Macro: poverty, unemployment, discrimination, segregation

Next, the authors identify potential points of intervention aimed at reducing risks and bolstering youth and family strengths across all levels of practice. For example, a micro-level risk of family violence might be addressed at a micro level by improving anger management skills, at the mezzo level by furthering access to domestic violence shelters in the community, and at the macro level by advocating for policies that increase funding for domestic violence programs. Similarly, the mezzo-level risk of violence in the neighborhood could be managed through the micro-level goal of family relocation to a new neighborhood, through the mezzo-level goal of increasing neighborhood policing, or the macro-level aim of increased funding to enhance the safety of violence-plagued neighborhoods. Corcoran and Nichols-Casebolt acknowledge that social workers may not have the resources needed to intervene across all system levels, but argue that they all "must be knowledgeable about the potential range of micro, mezzo, and macro factors that affect the functioning of individuals and families" (p. 229).

Team-Based Approaches to Goal Setting

A significant development over the last few decades has been the widespread adoption of team-based approaches to goal setting and service planning. They each exemplify the integration of micro practice with mezzo- and/or macro-level work.

Wraparound/Family Conferencing

The **wraparound process**, otherwise known as family team conferencing, was developed in the 1980s as an approach to service delivery with multi-need families who were being served by the public child welfare, mental health, and/or juvenile probation system. It involves the creation of a team of individuals who meet on a regular basis with the aim of ensuring the safety, permanency, and well-being of a child who is at risk of removal from their home and community. The child-family team includes family members, their natural supports, and agency-based professionals, all of whom are guided by 10 principles as they develop a plan for services and supports (Bruns et al., 2004). Those include the following:

1. Family voice and choice are prioritized.
2. Service planning and delivery is team based.
3. Natural supports of the family are involved and recognized.
4. Collaboration between team members is required.
5. Services are community based and provided in the least restrictive setting possible.
6. The team respects and builds on the family culture.
7. Strategies are individualized and tailored to family strengths and needs.
8. The team recognizes and validates family strengths.
9. Providers persist in working toward goals until wraparound process is no longer needed.
10. The team determines and tracks outcomes on an on-going basis.

Team-based goal setting begins with the translation of presenting problems into needs that are basic to all human beings. When left unmet, such needs result in problematic circumstances and conditions. The process of identifying critical, unmet needs often involves digging deeper than what presents as an immediate concern. For example, a family may express a need for housing after being evicted from their apartment due to loud arguments and calls for law enforcement. An affordable housing arrangement might be provided to the family, but this would not address the underlying need for safe and sound conflict resolution within the home.

As a guide for need identification, team members are presented with visual prompts (a worksheet, chart, or labelled cards) that facilitate consideration of family needs spanning a wide range of **life domains**. The *emotional/psychological* domain includes needs for emotion regulation, and mood and symptom management. The *social* domain covers needs for friendship, social support, and community connection. The *behavioral* domain encompasses skills and supports needed to enhance anger or stress management and/or recovery from substance abuse or dependence. Needs falling into the *safety* domain may relate to concerns about community or domestic violence, or campus-based or cyberspace bullying. *Medical needs* may be met through medications, medical appointments, and/or insurance coverage for medical care. However, in some cases, *transportation issues* need to be addressed so that family members are able to attend scheduled appointments. *Legal needs* may relate to child custody, or court mandates as overseen by child protective services and/or juvenile or adult probation. The *residential* domain includes needs for stable housing along with adequate plumbing, heating, clean water, and electricity, and freedom from household pests. *Educational needs* might include help with homework or getting up on time for school, while *vocational needs* might be met through job training or childcare so a parent can attend a vocational training program. Finally, *spiritual needs* may be fulfilled through access to faith-based affiliations, supports, or materials.

Following the exploration of family needs across the applicable life domains, the team prioritizes them. For those deemed most important, the **members establish goals** by answering the following question:

"If this need is met, what behavior or outcome would we see?"

For instance, if a family need for conflict resolution skill is met, we would expect to see arguments settled without violent outbursts. Similarly, if a boy's need for connection and belonging are met, we might expect to see fewer disruptive behaviors in the home that escalate into verbal violence. If the boy's sibling's need for privacy are met, we might see her spending more quality time with her brother. Thus, needs are linked to pathways aimed at achieving family goals.

Collaboration is another important feature of team-based goal setting. The philosophy behind family-team conferencing stresses the importance of positive relationships among group members: "Relationships based on power, fear, anger, and control" must be changed (Burford & Hudson, 2000, p. 2). Nonnegotiable or safety-related issues are clarified by professionals on the team, but the family is provided choices as to how these obligations will be met. Key in facilitating collaboration are ground rules that include the expectation that *members speak directly to each another, rather than about one another* (Child Welfare Policy and Practice Group, 2001).

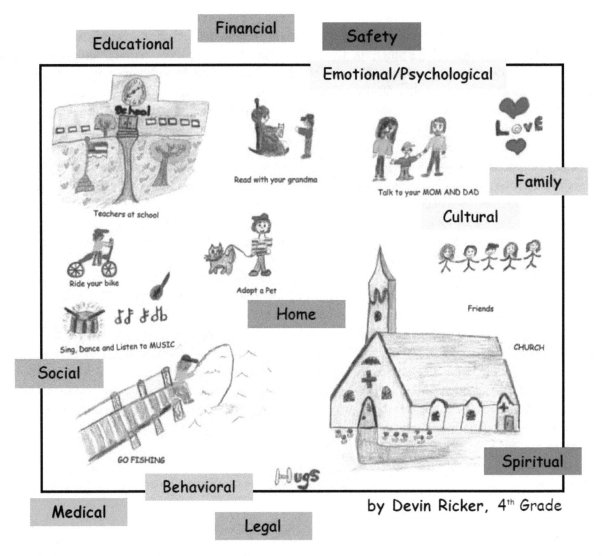

FIGURE 5.1. Youth Drawing of Family Needs.

Children can be engaged in drawing their family needs, as seen in this illustration by Devin Richter, 4th grade, a participant of The Nashville Connection Wraparound Program. He has emphasized needs across the educational, emotional, family, social, behavioral (recreational), and spiritual domains.

NARRATIVE APPLICATION: Wraparound

Child protective services (CPS) worker Rose Stevens was concerned about the Mills family and referred them for wraparound services. The family consisted of 33-year-old Kristin and her 9-year-old daughter, Becky. Three years prior, Becky had been removed from Kristen's care due to Kristen's drug abuse and domestic violence in the home that was perpetrated by Kristen's then boyfriend. The young girl was placed with her maternal grandmother. After getting sober and cutting off her boyfriend, Kristen regained custody of Becky. She now has a job working at a convenience store and makes just a little more than minimum wage. She also receives social security benefits on behalf of her deceased husband, who died of an overdose 8 years ago. Becky is a bright girl and has done well in school for the most part, but her grades have fallen during the last few months, and her teacher states that she often appears distracted.

Recently, Kristen resumed drinking, sometimes to excess. CPS was called out to investigate after Becky told her teacher that her clothes were dirty because her mom was passed out on the couch for most of the weekend and didn't take them to the laundromat. When CPS went out to the house, they noticed that trash, dirty dishes, and liquor bottles were piled up in the kitchen. Kristen admitted to drinking and stated that she was planning to quit. She said that she was stressed out and exhausted between her job and parenting responsibilities. Another stressor was that PG&E had been threatening to shut off power if she didn't pay her electricity bill. Short on cash, Kristen called her mother and asked for help. Her mother agreed to pay the bill but lectured Kristen about her irresponsibility, asking why she can't be more like her sister who kicked drugs and now owns a beauty supply store. This intensified Kristen's negative feelings about herself.

The wraparound team included Kristen, her mother, her sister, Becky, Becky's teacher, and the CPS worker, along with the team facilitator. They identified Kristen's need for support in her recovery and for skills in stress management as well as childcare once a week so that she could attend AA meetings with her sister, who was active in the 12-step community. These needs all related to her goal of sustaining sobriety. Following a process that involved brainstorming solutions, Kristen's mother agreed to babysit Becky, thus supporting Kristen's progress toward sobriety. The team also noted Becky's need for improved concentration in order to complete her school assignments. She and her mother decided to attend mindfulness meditation classes each Wednesday night at the neighborhood church. Becky's teacher agreed to send a note home each week reporting on her academic improvements. Kristen agreed to reward completed assignments with praise and an occasional movie. The team monitored the family's progress, stuck with them during setbacks, and celebrated their successes.

Team and Data-Based Decision-Making

Another recent development is the proliferation of team and data-based decision-making models in primary and secondary schools. These system-wide approaches are exemplified by **positive behavioral interventions and supports** (PBIS), a widely-used framework aimed at enhancing academic, social, and behavioral outcomes for students. Data is utilized by the school-based team to clarify needs and evaluate progress based on a 3-tiered continuum of supports. The first tier is focused on primary prevention practices for use with all students; tier 2 is devoted to group support for some higher-risk students; tier 3 is dedicated to individual intervention with a few students who have evidenced behavioral challenges.

Goal setting occurs at the school-wide and individual student level. Common campus-wide goals are to improve the school climate and create a culture that embodies the values of respect for self, others, and school property. Also promoted are safety on campus, the bus, and in the community; responsibility for attending school on time and completing assigned work; and the development of positive relationships with teachers, staff, and other students (Office of Special Education Programs, 2017). Progress toward school-wide goals are often measured by rates of attendance and disciplinary referrals.

At the individual student level, goal setting is guided by *functional behavior assessment* (FBA) with select youth who have not responded adequately to tier 1 and 2 strategies (see the behavior theory section of Chapter 4 for an overview of FBA). Based on the antecedents and consequences of the target behavior, its function is determined (e.g., avoidance of difficult tasks, connection and belonging with peers). Goals are set to promote replacement behaviors for the student that meet the underlying need in a more functional way; or, they may focus on altering the triggers and consequences in the school environment (e.g., punishment might be replaced with offering choices, assistance in understanding assignments, or support in engaging with peers). Progress toward improved impulse control, acceptance of instruction, and decreased disruptive behavior on campus is tracked on a daily basis. Ample positive reinforcement is provided in response to gains made. PBIS is a novel approach that blends prevention and intervention in school-based social work.

NARRATIVE APPLICATION: Britney's Story

Britney was in first grade when she started with the PBIS program that had been implemented at her school. She had been diagnosed with Down's syndrome. Her strengths included being smart and easily redirected, having a good memory and a supportive and loving family. She enjoyed reading and playing outdoors. Behaviors that had been targeted for tier 3 intervention were: hitting, frustration, and saying "no" when asked to complete a task. A variety of goals were set with Britney and her family.

1. Develop a behavior support team that would include immediate and extended family members, her teacher and speech therapist, and the school administrator.
2. Solidify a person-centered plan focused on her dream to have friends, stay included, be independent, join Girl Scouts, and stay on grade level and involved with church.
3. Specific, shorter-term goals were to express frustration appropriately, have a friend at school, resolve her hearing problems, increase her level of independence during classroom activities, and move on to second grade in an inclusive setting.

A functional behavior assessment was conducted that tracked her behavior over time, along with triggers and consequences. Based on this assessment, it was determined that the function of her disruptive behaviors (e.g., laying on floor, saying "no") was to gain adult interaction and delay or gain assistance with a task. Proactive strategies were used to support her success:

1. More time given to complete work
2. Expanded social interaction with teacher's assistant
3. Use of peer buddy
4. More choices offered
5. Increased use of positive reinforcement (praise, star system, library time)
6. Coaching in appropriate ways to request a break or help, as needed

Updates revealed that the PBIS team worked well together, and new members were added. Britney's mother and father were supportive and used behavioral support strategies at home.

She was able to enroll in second grade with typical peers.

This account was adapted from a case study posted on the website for the Positive Behavioral Supports and Interventions (https://www.pbis.org/).

Assertive Community Treatment

In response to concerns regarding reoccurring inpatient admissions for adults with severe and persistent mental illness, **assertive community treatment** (ACT) was born in the 1970s. ACT involves the use of a multidisciplinary team that typically includes a psychiatrist, nurse, social worker, psychologist, substance abuse/rehabilitation specialist, and peer support worker. The team oversees a small caseload and the provision of crisis management, assessment, supportive therapy, medication, intervention with support networks, and assistance for consumers in meeting basic needs for housing, transportation, supported employment, and medical care (Assertive Community Treatment, 2009).

The goal-setting process in ACT is client directed, with the consumer assuming a primary role in decision-making (Appelbaum & LeMelle, 2008). While the team provides clinical guidance in goal setting, ultimately the client is in the driver's seat. Long-term goals focus on improved quality of life and stable community living. Short-term goals are measurable and specific, often devoted to relapse prevention, housing stability, employment, and the development of illness management skills. Research has found that the inclusion of *illness management skill building* in assertive community treatment further reduces psychiatric hospital use over time (Salyers et al., 2010). Goals pertaining to illness management may be dedicated to understanding facts about mental illness and medications, building social supports, or learning coping skills and strategies for responding to stigma (Substance Abuse and Mental Health Services Administration, 2009). As with wraparound and PBIS, collaboration between disciplines is of paramount importance in achieving maximum results with ACT.

NARRATIVE APPLICATION: Paolo's Story

When Paolo was in graduate school studying chemistry, he began fearing for his life. He was consumed with paranoia, including beliefs that others were following him, wanted to kill him, and were inserting evil thoughts into his mind. He also started hearing voices of condemnation. Paolo refused to take public transportation and withdrew from everyone. Before long, he was hospitalized (twice in 3 months) due to his psychotic symptoms and spent a year in day treatment. When his psychiatrist finally explained his diagnosis of schizophrenia, Paolo felt a great deal of relief, as he had always believed that he was to blame for his symptoms and misfortunes. The physician also put him on the right dose of medication. Feeling better, he tried to enter the workforce, but when his attempts failed, he became very depressed.

Paolo was in his early 40s when his psychiatrist recommended that he shadow a peer support worker on an Assertive Community Team. Paolo took advantage of this opportunity and was quite impressed with the dedication and caring approach used by the team—his newly acquired goal was to be a part of this program. He enrolled in a Psychosocial Rehabilitation Certificate Program, where he learned illness management skills that he was able to use in his own life. Based on his lived experience, he understood well the incremental steps that individuals need to take to work toward their ultimate goal of recovery from a mental illness. After completing his field placements with an ACT team, he was hired as a peer support worker for a program nearby. In his first-person account of his own recovery (Scotti, 2009), Paolo wrote:

After living in darkness for many years and having died to my old self thinking that my life was over and futile, a new birth emerged from within me that has made my life more meaningful and purposeful than ever before. (p. 13)

Self-Care and Goal Setting

Social workers often shoot for the moon in their approach to direct services, taking on highly ambitious goals for themselves and their clients. While this tendency is understandable, and benefits some, it may also have unintended, negative consequences. In fact, this tendency can be a "formula for frustration," resulting in distress for the social worker, not to mention the client who is unable to meet unrealistic expectations (Briar, 1974). Recognizing this potential pitfall, Cox and Steiner (2013) stress the importance of **adaptive goal processes** as an essential element of self-care in social work.

As discussed by Folkman (2008), adaptive goal processes prompt the individual to evaluate the odds of success with their goals and to relinquish those that are more likely than not to result in failure. As adopted by social workers for purposes of self-care, these adaptations involve "redirecting focus away from things over which they have not control to things they can reasonably accomplish" (Cox & Steiner, 2013, p. 66). For example, the practitioner who aims to eliminate mood swings in a client that has been diagnosed with borderline personality disorder would be well-served to adjust this goal and instead strive to arm the client with coping skills that support emotion regulation. Or the social worker who intends to eliminate arguments in a conflicted family might instead focus on helping them learn how to negotiate when disputes occur. Realistic goal setting is as important for the practitioner as it is for the client—it supports **self-efficacy**, or the belief that one has what it takes to be effective.

Realistic goal setting can be achieved by **partializing goals**, breaking them down into manageable pieces (Hepworth et al., 2010). This process is important because many practice aims are complex and can easily lead to feelings of overwhelm in the client and practitioner. When goals are partialized, success can be acknowledged each step of the way, thereby buttressing long-term goal attainment. The following narrative illustration serves as an example.

NARRATIVE APPLICATION: Adaptive Goal Processes

Rhonda was promoted to a new position that was aimed at "bridging the gap" between her agency and several others. There had been perpetual conflict between this group of human service organizations, and she was charged with resolution. Rhonda shared in an interview how she coped with the overwhelming responsibility that she had acquired.

I was very frustrated and worried, but in order to stay optimistic, I had to overcome feelings of inadequacy and a tendency to blame other workers for the troubles we were having. I stayed positive by focusing on clear and specific tasks that I could take on, such as having respectful conversations with cross-agency partners, facilitating productive interagency meetings, and educating our clients on resources provided by the other organizations. Probably most important, I took the time to cherish these small victories each and every time they occurred.

Another means of supporting self-care in social work involves the creation of agency-wide goals toward improving workplace wellness. These goals can focus on establishing a routine for self-care in which, at a certain time of day, all workers stop their activities and stretch, sing, pray, meditate, tell jokes, or express gratitude. This practice can do wonders toward promoting a positive agency climate. Another approach is to place visual reminders of success around the office. These items can take the form of drawings, cartoons, thank you letters, or photographs that bring to mind the benefits of the work being done. Finally, employees might collaborate in creating a silent space designed for relaxation and refocusing. The location might be decorated with calming pictures, comfortable chairs, and a small water fountain. Earphones might be made available for listening to music. Rooms of this kind have been assigned a variety of different names (*serenity space, rejuvenation room, zen den*) and have become quite popular in recent years. When workers take a break in a serene room or space, they are endowed with the strength to shake off the stress involved with their difficult assignments.

SUMMARY

This chapter is devoted to goal setting with clients, an important vehicle for promoting change. Basic terms are reviewed, as well as the characteristics of S.M.A.R.T. goals and objectives. Self-determination theory is tapped for guidance in goal setting, specifically as it is carried out with clients who are mandated to receive services. Several approaches are shared including the use of a goal wheel, goal menu, or ecologically oriented framework. Various models for team-based goal setting are also discussed, including wraparound, positive behavioral interventions and supports, and assertive community treatment. The chapter ends with a discussion of methods that support self-care in practitioners and organizations.

KEY TERMS

Adaptive goal processes	Long-term goals	Self-efficacy
Assertive community treatment	Objectives	Short-term goals
Barriers	Partializing goals	Wraparound process
Collaboration	Positive behavioral intervention	
Framing	and supports	
Life domains	Self-determination theory	

DISCUSSION QUESTIONS

1. Review the basics of goal setting. What is a long-term goal that you have? What short-term goals and objectives might be adopted to support movement toward your long-term goal? What barriers might interfere with your goal attainment, and how will you handle them when/if they occur?

2. How would you go about furthering the autonomy of a client who is ambivalent about setting goals?

3. What underlying needs might be unmet for a client who presents with homelessness as a primary problem?

SKILL DEVELOPMENT ACTIVITIES

1. Create your own goal wheel by following the instructions provided above in the section entitled Approaches to Goal Setting. What did you learn about yourself as a result of completing this activity?

2. Explore one of the following resources and share what you learned about the team-based model for goal setting:

    https://nwi.pdx.edu/ (Wraparound)

https://www.pbis.org/ (Positive Behavioral Interventions and Supports)

http://dhhs.ne.gov/medicaid/Documents/ACT.pdf (Assertive Community Treatment)

3. Design your own safe and silent space for rejuvenation in the workplace. What would you use to enhance serenity?

REFERENCES

Appelbaum, P. S., & LeMelle, S. (2008). Techniques used by assertive community treatment (ACT) teams to encourage adherence: Patient and staff perceptions. *Community Mental Health Journal, 44*, 459–464.

Assertive Community Treatment. (2009). Retrieved from http://dhhs.ne.gov/medicaid/Documents/ACT.pdf

Briar, S. (1974). The future of social work: An introduction. *Social Work, 19*, 514–518.

Bruns, E. J., Walker, J. S., Adams, J., Miles, P., Osher, T. W., Rast, J., VanDenBerg, J. D., & National Wraparound Initiative Advisory Group. (2004). Ten principles of the wraparound process. Portland, OR: Portland State University, National Wraparound Initiative, Research and Training Center on Family Support and Children's Mental Health.

Burford, G., & Hudson, J. (Eds.). (2000). *Family group conferencing: New directions in community-centered child and family practice*. New Brunswick, NJ: Aldine Transaction.

Child Welfare Policy and Practice Group (2001). *Handbook for family team conferencing: Promoting safe and stable families*. Montgomery, AL: Author.

Corcoran, J., & Nichols-Casebolt, A. (2004). Risk and resilience ecological framework for assessment and goal formulation. *Child and Adolescent Social Work Journal, 21*, 211–235.

Cox, K., & Steiner, S. (2013). *Self-care in social work: A guide for practitioners, supervisors, and administrators*. Washington, DC: NASW Press.

Doran, G. T. (1981). There's a S.M.A.R.T. way to write management's goals and objectives. *Management Review, 70*, 35–36.

Folkman, S. (2008). The case for positive emotions in the stress process. *Anxiety, Stress, & Coping, 21*, 3–14.

Garner, H., Bruce, M. A., & Stellern, J. (2011). The goal wheel: Adapting Navajo philosophy and the medicine wheel to work with adolescents. *Journal for Specialists in Group Work, 36*, 62–77.

Gerhardt, S., McCallum, A., McDougall, C., Kennan, S., & Rigby, P. (2015). The goal of making friends for youth with disabilities: Creating a goal menu. *Child: Care, Health, and Development, 41*(6), 1018–1029.

Hepworth, D. H., Rooney, R. H., Rooney, G. D., Strom-Gottfried, K., & Larsen, J. (2010). *Direct social work practice: Theory and skills*. Belmont, CA: Brooks/Cole, Cengage Learning.

Hirsh, B., Nitzl, C., & Reemts, S. (2018). The neglected mediating role of self-efficacy in the goal setting process in local public administration. *Journal of Business Economics, 88*, 41–63.

Locke, E. A., & Latham, G. P. (2006). New directions in goal setting theory. *Current Directions in Psychological Science, 15*, 265–268.

Office of Special Education Programs. (2017). Technical Assistance Center on Positive Behavioral Interventions and Supports. Positive Behavioral Interventions & Supports [Website]. Retrieved from www.pbis.org

Ordonez, L. D., Schweitzer, M. E., Galinsky, A. D., & Bazerman, M. H. (2009). Goals gone wild: The systematic effects of overprescribing goal setting. *Academy of Management Perspectives, 23*, 6–16.

Romero, J. L. (2009, August 4). *Effective goal setting*. Retrieved from www.Skills2lead.com

Ryan, R. M., Patrick, H., Deci, E. L., & Williams, G. C. (2008). Facilitating health behavior change and its maintenance: Interventions based on self-determination theory. *European Health Psychologist, 10*, 2–5.

Salyers, M. P., McGuire, A. B., Rollins, A. L., Bond, G. R., Mueser, K. T., & Macy, V. R. (2010). Integrating assertive community treatment and illness management and recovery for consumers with severe mental illness. *Community Mental Health Journal, 46*, 319–329.

Scotti, P. (2009). Recovery as discovery. *Schizophrenia Bulletin, 35*, 844–846.

Substance Abuse and Mental Health Services Administration. (2009). Illness management and recovery: Practitioner guides and handouts. HHS Pub. No. SMA-09-4462, Rockville, MD: U.S. Department of Health and Human Services, Substance Abuse and Mental Health Services Administration, Center for Mental Health Services.

Yip. A. M., Gorman, M. C., Stadnyk, K., Mills, W. G. M., McPherson, K. M., & Rockwood, K. (1998). A standardized menu for goal attainment scaling in the care of frail elders. *Gerontologist, 38*, 735–742.

CREDITS

CHAPTER 6

Intervention with Individuals

The expectations of life depend upon diligence; the mechanic that would perfect his work must first sharpen his tools.—CONFUCIUS

C ARRYING OUT INTERVENTION requires skill in the use of an assortment of tools and techniques that have proven success in promoting change. Knowing when to use what tool is a particularly important aspect of intervention planning. Just as one wouldn't use a screwdriver to hammer a nail, a social worker would not problem solve with a client whose primary need is to process grief and loss. Thus, having access to a range of techniques allows the practitioner to respond skillfully to a variety of client needs. However, mastery of change-oriented strategies takes time and sustained effort. It is not uncommon for a social worker to feel awkward and clumsy the first time or two that they utilize a particular tool. With practice, they will exhibit greater ease and a more natural flow in applying the technique. This chapter will assist social work students with practicing basic skills and strategies that are commonly used with individuals. Subsequent chapters focus on basic skills for application with groups and families.

Social Work Practice with Individuals

Some social workers have a preference for individual work with clients in that it allows for an in-depth focus on the person's strengths and needs. When utilizing this modality, the social worker need not divide their time and attention across multiple clients. They can zero in on issues that underlie the client's presenting problems. Their efforts toward building client insight and self-awareness are more concentrated than they might be in group or family practice. This section presents a range of techniques that are aimed at helping individuals manage crisis, transition from institutional environments, problem solve, build skills, regulate emotions, and process grief.

Crisis Intervention

Social workers are often called upon to perform crisis intervention with individuals who have encountered a time-limited, distressing event—one perceived as an "intolerable difficulty that exceeds [their] resources or coping mechanisms" (James, 2008, p. 3). The precipitating event might be a traumatic loss, stressful transition, or a situation posing a significant threat to the person's physical or emotional safety. For example, the client may have been the victim of a verbal, physical, or sexual assault; they may have witnessed community or domestic violence, or encountered circumstances that triggered severe anger, anxiety, or depression. The practitioner intervenes to help the client cope effectively and to prepare them for tackling future crises on their own.

Clear steps have been defined for the process of crisis intervention that are applied in a client interview. Author and human services professor Kristi Kanel (2015) advocates for the use of a three-stage approach to crisis management. Its foundation is the *development and maintenance of rapport*, defined as a "state of understanding and comfort" between the client and practitioner (p. 50). The crisis worker uses a variety of skills during this stage, including several discussed in Chapter 3. Attending skills are used to defuse intense emotions and establish a sense of calm and composure. They are evident in relaxed posture, eye contact, and a warm and soothing vocal style of the social worker. Questions asked are mostly open ended and followed by clarifying prompts, reflections of the feelings expressed by the client, and paraphrasing of their main concerns. During the second stage, the practitioner seeks to *understand the nature of the precipitating event* from the client's perspective, as well as their beliefs and perceptions about both the circumstances and their ability to cope. Next, the social worker begins *exploring coping methods* that the client has used, along with additional strategies that might work for them. Various alternative thoughts and behaviors might be introduced, encouraged, and practiced; referrals may be made for on-going assistance. The latter might include a referral for legal aid, shelter services, medical care, a support group, or long-term therapy.

When collaborating with a client to access their coping abilities, the social worker is leveraging the benefits of crisis in triggering needed change. It has been well established that negative events can promote skill development and growth (McMillen, 1999). Thus, crisis holds potential—it can prompt the client to enhance material, personal, and social resources. It also provides an opportunity to practice coping skills, transform irrational beliefs, and improve functioning in the face of challenge.

Suicide Prevention

When carrying out crisis intervention with a person who is severely depressed or feels overwhelmed with life, it is important to consider their risk for suicide. Warning signs include giving away possessions, withdrawing from activities, the recent death of a loved one, and feelings of hopelessness and worthlessness (Aguilera, 1990). **Risk factors for suicide**, as delineated by the American Foundation for Suicide Prevention (2018), span health, environmental, and historical domains. *Health factors* include having a mental health condition, a physical health condition, or a traumatic brain injury. *Environmental factors* are rooted in prolonged stress (e.g., from harassment or bullying) and exposure to another person's suicide. *Historical risk* occurs in individuals who have made a previous suicide attempt, have a family history of suicide, or have experienced child maltreatment or trauma.

The assessment of suicide risk involves first asking the person if they have thoughts of ending their life. If they respond in the affirmative, the practitioner needs to inquire about the *frequency and intensity of their thoughts concerning suicide*. A client with a lower level of risk may have occasional, fleeting thoughts of suicide or a passive wish to die; one with a much higher level of risk will have persistent and consuming thoughts of ending their life. If they have current thoughts of suicide, it is particularly important to ask the individual if they have a *plan for suicide and the means to carry it out*. If they do have a detailed plan and access to the materials needed to act on the plan, intensive intervention is required.

The form intervention takes will depend on the seriousness of the risk and the supports available to the client. In severe cases, the client may need to be psychiatrically hospitalized either voluntarily or involuntarily; this would be initiated by contacting the local police or psychiatric emergency team. Hospitalization may be avoided if the client is willing to participate in a partial hospitalization or intensive outpatient program. In this case, family members will be enlisted to monitor the client and confiscate any materials (drugs, knives, guns, ropes) that could be used to inflict self-harm. In some cases, a no-suicide contract may be signed by the client who is willing to abstain from suicidal behavior for a period of time while other interventions are put into place (e.g., medication, therapy, increased structure and support). *No-suicide contracts* are most successful with clients who are low or medium risk for suicide (Kanel, 2015).

Safety planning should always be performed with a suicidal client, whether their risk is high, medium, or relatively low. Ideally, a written plan will be created collaboratively between the client and social worker. This plan will indicate what the client will do when/if they have thoughts of suicide. It might note who they will talk to when feeling distressed and what efforts they will take to manage their emotions and minimize risk. The plan should also include phone numbers of supportive people and of an emergency psychiatric clinic or crisis line.

Any time a new social worker interviews a suicidal client, it is advisable that they access supervisory support when determining risk and appropriate intervention. Even when the worker is confident in their assessment and plan for managing risk, it is wise for them to consult with a supervisor. Consultation brings a new set of eyes to the situation and allows the practitioner to process their own stress related to life-threatening circumstances. It is a strategy for enhancing both risk management and self-care in the social worker.

NARRATIVE APPLICATION: Suicide Risk Assessment

Jed was a husky, 17-year-old who lived with his mother. He was sensitive and had a great sense of humor but was prone to episodes of severe depression. Jed had been hospitalized briefly due to a mild suicide attempt prior to entering the intensive outpatient program where he was currently a participant. The program included group therapy, three times a week, with other teens who had a mental health diagnosis. Jed participated actively for 2 months. On his last day of group, Jed displayed a wide grin as he shared a chocolate cake that his mother had baked for the occasion. Yet, something sorrowful seemed to be brewing underneath the surface of his smiles. He asked to see the therapist alone after the group meeting ended. During his individual session with the clinical social worker, he shared that he had been considering suicide.

> Therapist: "I sensed that something was troubling you, Jed. How long have you been thinking about ending your life?"
>
> Jed: "For about a week. It comes up when I am alone, at night mostly."
>
> Therapist: "Every night?"
>
> Jed: "Pretty much."
>
> Therapist: "Which of your coping skills have you been using when these thoughts come up?"
>
> Jed: "I have been trying to distract myself with my favorite movies, but it hasn't helped."
>
> Therapist: "Are you concerned about leaving the program?"
>
> Jed: "No ... yes ... I don't know."
>
> Therapist: "OK. It's common for people to have mixed feelings about this. Tell me, Jed, do you have a plan for ending your life?"
>
> Jed: "Yes."

Therapist: "Would you be willing to share it with me?"

Jed sighed, "I think about hanging myself with a rope off the bridge near my house. I have the rope hidden in my backyard."

Therapist: "What has stopped you from doing it?"

Jed: "I don't want to hurt my mom."

Therapist: "Yes, that would hurt her a great deal. I am so glad you told me, Jed. That tells me that a big part of you wants help in managing these thoughts. Let's talk about options."

Based on this conversation, it was clear to the therapist that Jed was at high risk for suicide because he had a plan, access to the means to carry out his plan, and a previous suicide attempt. Upon further discussion, Jed agreed that he should return to the hospital to ensure his safety. He called his mother and asked her to take him to the crisis unit for evaluation. He stayed at the inpatient facility for a week before returning to the outpatient program. As a result of this experience, he learned that he needed to stop masking his feelings with humor and share them more openly with people whom he trusted.

Community Transitional Support/Rehabilitation

Over the last decade, there has been an expansion of services provided to vulnerable populations, with the primary purpose of supporting their transition from institutional settings such as nursing homes, inpatient hospitals, and correctional facilities. These services typically include case management for individuals who are reintegrating into their community. The central aim of these services is to prevent recidivism and/or readmissions to institutional care, while promoting public safety, rehabilitation, and self-management of problematic behaviors or illnesses.

Transition from Jail

According to the National Institute of Corrections (NIC), over nine million adults pass through jails in the United States every year (National Institute of Corrections, 2008). These individuals have, traditionally, received little in the way of support upon reentering their community. To address this need, NIC launched the Transition from Jail to Community Initiative (TJC) in 2007. The aim of this initiative was to develop, implement, and evaluate a model for improving reentry outcomes. In 2012, TJC published a practice brief that outlines their recommended case management strategies (Warwick, Dodd, & Neusteter, 2012). They include the following:

- Use of a *triage approach* for assessing risk and matching offenders to appropriate interventions.
- *Jail-in-reach* by the case manager who meets with the client prior to their release from jail; the focus is on building trust and providing education regarding post-release services.
- Maintaining an *inventory of available community-based programs* and services; development of a resource packet that is provided to all inmates upon release.
- Close coordination between case managers, jail personnel, and probation/parole officers.

Discharge from Acute Care Hospital

The Centers for Medicare and Medicaid Services estimates that "nearly one in five Medicare patients discharged from a hospital—approximately 2.6 million seniors—are readmitted within 30 days, at a cost of over $26 billion every year" (Centers for Medicare and Medicaid Services, 2018). Although hospitals provide discharge planning services, they do not adequately address the multiple factors that contribute to read-missions. The Community-Based Transitions Program (CCTP) was created by the Affordable Care Act to address these deficiencies. Funding is provided to community-based organizations for transition services, including medication review/management and *patient-centered self-management support*. Practitioners use an empowerment-based approach when helping patients set realistic goals and self-management plans. They also provide *disease-specific information*, while promoting competencies in medication adherence and the use of community healthcare options.

Transitions for Homeless Adults with Co-Existing Disorders

Another population served by community transitional support comprises homeless individuals with severe and persistent mental illness and a co-existing substance abuse disorder (COD). Upon release from a psychiatric hospital, residential treatment program, or prison, they are provided assistance in obtaining housing, employment, and treatment for COD. Practitioners serving this population are guided by a framework developed on the basis of an extensive literature review (Sun, 2012). Recommendations of the author include the following:

- Critical time intervention that occurs during the first few months after discharge. The social worker will visit the client's residence, accompany them to appointments, and provide crisis intervention, as needed.
- Emphasis on housing-first versus treatment-first practice in which the outreach team provides linkage to "low demand" housing that offers supportive counseling.
- Assistance in creating a detailed vocational profile that includes the client's status with regard to substance use. Case managers assist the client in finding a job that supports recovery. Ideally, a money management plan is developed that ensures wages earned are not used to purchase alcohol or drugs.
- Counseling on illness self-management aimed at enhancing client motivation to comply with their antipsychotic treatment regime.
- Focus on reduced use and harm reduction as an alternative to total abstinence from substances.
- Contingency management approach that systematically reinforces desirable behavior. Incentives may be established to support reduced substance use, paid for with donations from community and corporate organizations.
- Referral to a 12-step program or specialized group that addresses issues related to mental illness and addiction.

NARRATIVE APPLICATION: Transitional Services

Nik, 30 years of age, was recently released from prison where he had served time for the sale and distribution of methamphetamine. He had been diagnosed with schizoaffective disorder in his mid-20s due to alternating periods of psychosis and depression, but his symptoms were managed successfully with medication. He had been abusing a variety of substances, including alcohol, prior to his commitment to the state correctional facility. While in prison, he participated actively in a 12-step program and was motivated to maintain his sobriety upon release.

Nik was now living with his maternal grandmother, who had raised him since he was a toddler. His social worker, Jim, had been visiting him weekly at her home to support Nik's goals to find employment and further his recovery.

Nik's grandmother was unable to drive, so Jim transported him to his appointments with his psychiatrist. Nik had been walking to a local Narcotics Anonymous meeting 1–2 times a week.

Within a month post-release, he began hearing voices and started drinking to drown them out. When he met with Jim, he admitted that he had stopped taking his medication; he also shared his despair about relapsing.

Nik (sadly): "My recovery is done."

Jim: "You fell off the wagon, but you can jump right on again. Recovery is a process ... but what do you want to do about those voices?"

Nik: "I thought I could handle things without the meds, but I guess not. I'll start them up again."

Jim: "That's great to hear because I have some good news. There is a landscaper in town who needs an assistant and might be willing to hire you. You would have to be on your meds and off drugs and alcohol for it to work, though."

Nik: "Huh. That's something to work for. I am good with plants."

Jim: "Well then, let's build that into your self-management plan."

Problem-Solving Intervention

Problem solving with clients incorporates a task-centered approach that is commonly used in a wide range of social work settings. It places an emphasis on addressing the problems and concerns identified by the client and on collaborating with them to develop tasks aimed at problem resolution. Incremental movement toward task completion is recognized so as to empower the client and enhance their self-efficacy.

The method begins by *eliciting the client's target problems* and then *prioritizing them*. It is recommended that priority concerns be limited to three that will be addressed within a circumscribed time period (Hepworth, Rooney, Rooney, Strom-Gottfried, & Larsen, 2010). Next, goals are agreed upon for each problem and partialized by *delineating general and more specific tasks* (action steps) that will be undertaken. Brainstorming is useful in facilitating creative thinking and consideration of a wide range of task options.

Preparing clients for task implementation often involves helping them acquire various skills and abilities. For example, a woman who intends to talk with her mother about their difficult living situation may need to practice assertive communication skills prior to having this conversation. Otherwise, the plan may backfire and result in failure to resolve the problem successfully. In other cases, the social worker may need to strengthen the client's motivation to complete an unpleasant task. This may be particularly important when a client is planning to participate in an activity (e.g., group meeting or interview) that is likely to result in a great deal of stress and anxiety. Preliminary efforts may be needed to process the client's worries and facilitate the development of relaxation skills. Some clients are also aided by thinking through all the benefits of task completion. Others respond well to planned incentives and to rewards that they will self-administer upon carrying out their plan.

A crucial and often overlooked component of the problem-solving approach is the *close monitoring of client progress*. When barriers interfere with task completion, it is important that they be addressed and resolved; alternative tasks may need to be established that have a greater likelihood of success. Most importantly, incremental progress toward problem resolution should be acknowledged and celebrated so as to build client confidence in their ability to master the problem.

Liz is 27-year-old who complained to her social worker that she is feeling overwhelmed and having occasional panic attacks. She works full time at a retail store and has just been promoted. She has a new boss and a new set of responsibilities. Liz is the single parent of 5-year-old Trevor; the boy's father is out of the country and has never been a part of his life. Trevor just received the diagnosis of autism spectrum disorder; he has a great deal of social and communication difficulties. Liz and her son live in a small apartment, and she would like to move once she saves up enough money to afford a new home.

Upon meeting her social worker (Jean), Liz was asked to identify the problem or challenge that bothers her the most. She responded, "My son's diagnosis. I just don't know what to expect, and it's stressing me out." Jean validated Liz's concerns, describing them as common for parents who have a child with special needs. The social worker then assured Liz that, while she can't change her son's diagnosis, she can learn how to cope with the disorder so that it is less likely to trigger severe anxiety. She can also learn ways to further Trevor's emotional and social development. They established a goal for Liz to build understanding of autism and make connections with others who have experience in parenting a child with this condition. They then developed some general and specific tasks that she would carry out toward achieving these goals:

Goal 1: Build Understanding of Autism Spectrum Disorder
    General Task: Read about autistic spectrum disorder
    Specific Tasks: Obtain and read two books about this disorder (e.g., *Thinking Person's Guide to Autism; Ten Things Every Child with Autism Wishes You Knew*); explore two websites devoted to autism.

Goal 2: Build Connections with Knowledgeable Others
    General Tasks: Learn about community resources for parents of a child with autism
    Specific Tasks: Consult with a medical practitioner who specializes in treating autism; attend a local support group for parents of children with autism.

In preparing to carry out these tasks, Liz decided to explore websites, read one book, then develop some questions to ask the medical practitioner. She asked for help from Jean in managing her worries about entering uncharted waters and making new social connections. Jean also supported her in carrying out parenting strategies that she was learning from the reading and other parents.

Skill Building

The acquisition of new skills is frequently needed to support an individual's success in resolving problems, enhancing functioning, and increasing well-being. Interpersonal skills, such as ways of talking, listening, and communicating nonverbally, are often the focus of intervention with individuals. Independent living skills programs guide individuals in all aspects living independently. Coping skill development is another common aim of service delivery that includes efforts to enhance stress management, emotional self-regulation, and self-compassion. The skill development process that is recommended can be applied across many more skill categories—it essentially entails presenting concepts, building self-awareness, providing tools, and promoting practice.

Assertive Communication Skill

Clients often present to their social worker with concerns about conflicted relationships at home, work, or with family members and friends. Assessment may reveal that the individual has a tendency to respond to disagreement by either withdrawing or lashing out at the significant other. Or, the person may vacillate between passive and aggressive reactions to interpersonal disputes. These are indications that skill development in assertive communication may be beneficial.

Skill building begins with education about the differences between passive, aggressive, and assertive communication. Characteristics of these communication styles, including verbal and nonverbal behaviors and the associated thinking pattern, are reviewed in Table 6.1. **Passive communication** is briefly explained as a style in which the person avoids expressing their true thoughts and feelings or conveys them in a submissive and self-effacing manner. **Aggressive communication** violates the rights of others through blaming, boasting, and putting others down; it is typically experienced by the listener as degrading or demeaning. **Assertive communication** involves expressing one's thoughts and feelings honestly, openly, and respectfully. It is characterized by the use of "I" statements that express likes, wants, and needs without blaming or suggesting that others shouldn't feel or behave in certain ways that the person finds objectionable.

Clients may be asked to identify the style that they exhibit most often, with the caveat that no judgement will be attached to their selection. The social worker might help the individual explore the costs associated with this pattern of communication and the benefits of learning to communicate more assertively. Concurrently, the practitioner will demonstrate appreciation for the challenges that arise when learning a new style of communication. These typically include self-doubts, discomfort, and concerns about how others will react to their behavior change.

TABLE 6.1. Styles of Communication

Style	Verbal Behavior	Nonverbal Behavior	Associated Thinking
Passive	Soft, unsteady, hesitant speech; apologetic; self-dismissing; self-critical	Avoids eye contact; slouched posture; wringing hands; jaw trembling	"My needs are less important than yours."; "I don't want to upset anyone or cause them to dislike me."
Aggressive	Firm voice; sarcastic, cold, or harsh tone; use of threats, put-downs; boastfulness	Intrusive; staring or glaring; pointing or fist clenching; scowling or sneering; jaw set firm	"My needs are more important than yours."; "I am out for #1."; "I must win every argument."
Assertive	Firm but relaxed voice; steady pace; use of "I" statements; seeks out others' opinions; provides constructive criticism without blaming	Receptive listening; direct eye contact without staring; erect, open posture, open hand movements, facial expressions congruent with emotions	"I will stand up for myself but I won't attack you."; "The needs of both of us are important."

Note. This chart is informed by information provided by Fiona Michel and Dr. Anthea Fursland in their training module entitled: How to Recognise Assertive Behavior. This module is part of a larger training package: Michel, F. (2008). *Assert yourself.* Perth, Western Australia: Centre for Clinical Intervention.

While practice may not result in perfection, it will further success in the adoption of a new behavior. assertive behavior. Role play is an ideal method for helping a client learn how to communicate assertively. They benefit by the modeling of the practitioner, when the latter plays the role of the communicator. They also learn through opportunities to think through how they will communicate assertively in an upcoming situation where this skill will be needed. Better yet, some will engage in a simulated role play in which they play the communicator and receive constructive feedback from the social worker.

In preparing to use assertive communication in real-life circumstances, it is important that the client understand that there is no guarantee that their listener will respond kindly or appropriately. While they don't have control over their significant other's reaction, the individual can always take pride in their own efforts to communicate effectively and respectfully. Whenever possible, the practitioner will follow up with the client and process their experiences adopting this new skill.

Independent Living Skills

Individuals with disabilities or other functional limitations are often aided by intervention aimed at enhancing their independent living skills (ILS). The aim of this work is to provide the client with the tools needed to live as independently as possible. Skills taught may include the following:

- Personal hygiene
- Telephone skills
- Use of public transportation
- Money management (counting, budgeting, banking)
- Shopping skills
- Nutrition/cooking
- Leisure time skills
- Home safety
- Accessing healthcare, law enforcement, and other public services
- Survival reading (signs, labels, recipes, schedules)

The process for teaching ILS begins with an assessment of the client's functional abilities, needs, and priorities. Next, short- and long-term goals are established; skills are taught individually or in a group format (see Chapter 7 for an illustration of group ILS work with transition-aged youth in the foster care system). Some may be introduced in a classroom setting using films, worksheets, role plays, or hands-on activities. However, key to the effectiveness of ILS intervention requires practice generalizing skills to real-life community settings. For example, clients may be accompanied to banks, stores, or bus stations and coached in the application of the newly acquired skills. Correction should be offered supportively and followed by liberal use of praise when a task is completed successfully.

HIGHLIGHT 6.1: Independent Living Support for Older Adults

Two skill sets that are particularly important in supporting independent living in older adults are *medication manage-ment* and *money management*. The management of medication is vital given that 40% of adults age 65 and older take at least five medications per week; 12% take at least 10 (Zhan et al., 2001). The consequences of mismanagement can be life threatening. Skill building in this area may focus on learning how to read a prescription bottle, order refills, and utilize a pill box (Mc Dougal, Becker, Vaughan, Acee, & Delville, 2010).

Money management is crucial, as many seniors are at risk of economic insecurity and/or financial fraud and abuse. The National Council on Aging (NCOA) (n.d.) provides a wide range of online resources to support seniors in attaining financial security:

- *You Gave, Now Save*: a guide to benefits for older adults related to healthcare, food, housing, income, and transportation
- *Savvy Saving Seniors:* toolkits for budgeting, avoiding scams, and applying for benefits
- *Senior Debt Reduction*: tips for managing debt; debt hotline toolkit
- *Scams and Security*: information concerning financial scams and how seniors can protect themselves
- *Ready, Set, Bank:* video instruction pertaining to online banking

Go to https://www.ncoa.org/economic-security/money-management/ for further information on these resources.

Stress Management Skill

When a soup is simmering in a pot over a low flame, it is in its comfort zone; if the flame is turned up high for a lengthy period of time, the pot will boil over. Likewise, when a person experiences low levels of stress, they are likely to sustain interest and cope effectively with responsibilities and challenges. Higher levels of chronic stress may excite or exacerbate negative emotions that then spill over into the individual's relationships and day-to-day activities.

Stress management is a skill that assists individuals in regulating the impact of difficult situations on their physical, emotional, mental, and behavioral functioning. Developing this skill requires that the person first recognize the early signs of stress before they accumulate and cause significant harm. As noted in Chapter 3, *physical signs of stress* can include headaches, neck stiffness, fatigue, heart palpitations, excessive thirst, insomnia, and intestinal problems. *Emotional signs* are feelings of helplessness, despair, anxiety, or anger. *Behavioral indictors* of stress include irritability, impatience, and increased use of alcohol and other substances. *Mental signs* are poor concentration, memory loss, or confusion.

After recognizing their signs of stress, the client can be helped to *identify its sources*. If they involve circumstances over which they have some control, problem solving may be useful. For example, a student who has a problem with procrastinating might be helped to structure their time and break assignments down into smaller tasks. Conversely, if the client is stressed about things over which they have no control, they can be coached in the use of a variety of coping strategies, including *controlled breathing*, *self-soothing*, or *mindfulness activities* (see Table 6.2 and Highlight 6.2). It is also helpful to explore the thoughts and perceptions the client has about their stressor, as these impact the amount of distress they will carry. Reappraising the meaning of the event often helps the person see it in a new and more positive light. Reappraisal is used in cognitive behavioral intervention, a model that will be discussed in depth in Chapter 7.

TABLE 6.2. Stress Management Activities

Activity	Description	Benefits
Controlled Breathing	Slow, deep inhale; slow, deep exhale; repeat at least 3 times	Reduces physiological arousal
Self-Soothing	Activities that bring comfort without negative side effects (e.g., warm bath, candles, music, being in nature)	Reduces negative emotions; calms mind and body
Mindfulness	Awareness without judgment; attending to touch, smell, sights, sounds, taste	Increases concentration; reduces pain, depression, anxiety; improves sleep
Cognitive Reappraisal	Changing perceptions about stressors	Decreases pessimism; increases optimism and hope

HIGHLIGHT 6.2: Mindfulness

The concept of **mindfulness** has its origins in ancient Buddhist teachings but is now integrated into many contemporary mental health practices. It refers to present moment awareness and appreciation, without judgement. According to Siegel (2010), the cultivation of mindfulness changes brain structure and function in ways that help individuals let go of worries, make peace with change, and tune into the beauty and richness of day-to-day experiences. He suggests a variety of formal and informal strategies for enhancing mindfulness:

Body Scan: Attend to breath, as well as pleasant and unpleasant sensations from the bottom of the body to the top.

Stepping into Sadness Anger or Fear: Concentrate on the breath and sensations in the body that are associated with these emotions; ramp up their intensity and stay with them for several moments to increase your distress tolerance. Let them go as you bring your attention back to your breath and body.

Thinking Mindfully: Focus on your breath and let thoughts arise. Utilize imagery to consider your distressing thoughts as clouds passing through the sky or bubbles bursting. Recognize that you are not your thoughts; they come and go.

Eating Meditation: Sit quietly and attend to the process of eating. First, look at your food and notice its color, shape, and texture; visualize where it came from (plant, tree, animal). Slowly lift a bite of food to your mouth and take in its scent; place it in your mouth, chew slowly, and concentrate on its flavor. Stop eating when you are full.

Nature Meditation: Go outdoors or look out a window. Bring attention to the sights, sounds, and scents of your world. If outdoors, feel the sensation of the breeze on your skin or the warmth of the sun.

The strategies noted above are brief adaptations of a select few of Siegel's mindfulness practices that can be found in his book *The Mindfulness Solution: Everyday Practices for Everyday Problems* (2010).

Emotional Self-Regulation Skill

A client who has episodes in which they are consumed with excessive amounts of anger, sadness, fear, frustration, or jealousy may benefit by skill development in emotional self-regulation. This skill allows one to respond thoughtfully to emotionally charged situations versus reacting in a knee-jerk manner. The coaching process begins with a focus on identifying a variety of emotions. Clients can usually name the basic ones (anger, fear, sadness, joy) and may be prompted to consider many more. The use of an emotions list or chart can be helpful here; handouts for children attach named emotions to associated facial expressions (happy face, sad face, angry face, etc.). These strategies are all aimed at *building an emotions vocabulary*.

Emotions are normalized through discussion of their benefits and the fact that all have played a role in human survival. Negative emotions, such as sadness, frustration, and fear, provide important clues that certain circumstances require our attention. Even anger, while unpleasant, isn't bad—its various forms of expression can be helpful or unhelpful in a difficult situation. By offering this perspective, direct service practitioners enhance client awareness of their emotions and how they might be communicated in a congruent and constructive manner.

Social workers might also notice when their clients confuse thoughts with emotions. For example, when asked how they feel about losing their job, the person might say "It's unfair. I didn't deserve to be laid off. I don't think I can find a new job." Such comments provide an opportunity for the practitioner to point out that the individual has shared beliefs they have in relation to the situation. They might then prompt the client to consider the emotions that are connected to those thoughts. Next, the social worker might explore alternative ways of thinking that could help the person manage their emotions of anger, frustration, and hopelessness. This is another example of reappraisal, a cognitive behavioral strategy that was discussed in the section above.

The use of **coping cards** has been found to be effective in helping clients deal with strong emotions (Henriques, Beck, & Brown, 2003). This tool consists of a small, hand-written index card or an app on a mobile device that is easily accessed. It contains coping statements that the client has selected as reminders about how to think about stressful or emotionally laden circumstances. For example, the client who experiences social anxiety might note statements such as: *What others think is not important; I am safe; Just Breathe* (see Highlight 6.3).

As with all the skills discussed above, social workers strengthen the learning process by reviewing occasions in which the client made an attempt at using the new skill. This review may be enhanced through the use of a weekly or daily diary in which the client notes the situations that triggered strong emotions and the actual emotion that occurred, along with the thoughts that accompanied the emotion and how they coped. The record is completed, then examined and discussed in counseling with their social worker.

HIGHLIGHT 6.3: Sample Coping Card

My Coping Card

When my heart races, I will remember that it is just anxiety taking hold.

I will know that I am safe, unless something really dangerous is happening.

I will practice slow, deep breathing. If my panic is serious, I will breathe into a paper bag until I am calm.

If I am worried that I will look foolish by speaking up or talking in a social situation, I will remember that it doesn't matter what others think. I am just as good as everyone else. I don't have to prove anything.

I am a good person, just the way I am.

Self-Compassion

Over the last several years, growing attention has been devoted to the concept of **self-compassion** as a tool for furthering recovery, mental health, and well-being. Although it is similar to self-esteem, there are important differences between these two concepts as they relate to attitudes toward oneself. Self-compassion does not involve evaluation of one's self-worth or a social comparison with others. Instead, it focuses on the adoption of a warm, caring, and accepting attitude toward self, as an alternative to over-identification with feelings of inadequacy. According to leading experts on self-compassion Neff and Vonk (2009), it comprises three main components: "self-kindness, a sense of common humanity, and mindfulness when considering personal weaknesses or hardships" (p. 25). Self-compassion has been linked to numerous aspects of psychological health, including life satisfaction, emotional intelligence, and reduced depression and anxiety (p. 26).

When a client is highly self-critical and overly concerned about rejection or disapproval from others, skill building in self-compassion is indicated. This process begins by helping the person recognize that flaws and failure are part of the human experience. Clients are then taught methods for establishing mindful awareness of painful feelings in response to criticism, defeat, or potential humiliation. On her website, Neff offers a variety of exercises that may be used by clients for this purpose (Neff, 2019), including those noted below:

- Think about what you would say to a friend who is struggling with self-criticism or insecurity.
- Get in touch with your inner critic, the criticized, and the compassionate observer; sit in different chairs as you explore the perspectives of each.
- Write a letter to yourself from a place of self-compassion.
- Notice when you are becoming self-critical; soften the critical voice by reframing its observations so that they are more supportive and encouraging.
- Keep a journal for processing difficult events through a lens of self-compassion.

Go to https://self-compassion.org/ for further details on these and other exercises.

Self-Compassion as Self-Care

Many social workers hold very high performance expectations and low tolerance for their real or perceived mistakes. When they fail to meet these high expectations, they may experience anxiety or anger toward clients, colleagues, and themselves. The practice of self-compassion is an important tool for professional helpers, one that is aimed at countering negative self-evaluation and performance anxiety. In fact, research has shown that it is an effective approach to self-care—it has been found to buffer social work students from stress and burnout, while increasing the effectiveness of their practice (Iacono, 2017). Bohlinger, Wahlig, and Trudeau-Hern (2014) offer a self-guided meditation for enhancing self-compassion in clinicians. It includes the following elements:

- Sit comfortably in a quiet place.
- Let your eyes close and look inward.
- Focus on your breath—if your mind wanders, simply notice this without judgement and bring your attention back to your breath.
- Imagine a small, white light in your chest where you experience caring and empathy.
- Grow the light bigger and radiate it to others toward whom you feel warmth—imagine it touching their fears or self-criticism and dissolving it.

- Grow the light even bigger to encompass all of humanity and see your compassion fill the universe.
- Send messages of hope, peace, and forgiveness.
- Bring your light of compassion back to yourself. Imagine placing your troubles in a box and sending your white light inside. See it glowing with warmth.
- Return the light to your chest, where it will remain available, whenever you need it next.

A full transcript of the meditation can be found in Chapter 10 of Bean, R. D., Davis, S. D., & Davey, M. (Eds.). (2014). *Clinical supervision activities for increasing competence and self-awareness.* **Hoboken, NJ: John Wiley and Sons.**

Processing Grief

Supportive counseling is often needed by individuals who are grieving the loss of a person, role, relationship, living situation, or aspects of their own functioning, such as hearing, vision, and mobility. Social workers provide the space, comfort, and acceptance that grieving clients may need to navigate the complex thoughts and emotions that accompany a significant loss, particularly the death of a loved one. In approaching grief work, it is crucial that one appreciate the vast number of ways in which people grieve; there is no one, right way to handle loss. Some people express their sadness overtly; others experience emotional numbness or anger and confusion. The social worker must honor the process of their client and tailor their interventions accordingly.

Research conducted by Bonanno and Kaltman (2001) provides useful insight into the bereavement process. Their review of the empirical evidence showed that most grieving individuals (between 50% and 85%), display a normal grief pattern with moderate disruptions in functioning during the first few months following their loss. The most common forms of disruption that occur in the first year following the death of a loved one are as follows:

- <u>Cognitive Disorganization</u>: difficulty making sense of the loss, confusion, preoccupation, difficulties concentrating or making decisions, uncertainty about the future
- <u>Dysphoria</u>: distressing emotions, such as sadness, anger, and loneliness
- <u>Health Deficits</u>: somatic symptoms of shortness of breath, heart palpitations, loss of appetite, restlessness, insomnia
- <u>Disrupted Social and Vocational Functioning</u>: difficulty fulfilling social and/or occupational roles
- Positive experiences associated with bereavement were also noted, including appreciation for newfound independence, pride in the deceased, and humor.

A theoretical model for explaining bereavement sheds additional light on the process. The dual process model developed by Margaret Stroebe and Hank Schut (1999, 2001) delineates two main endeavors associated with the process of grieving the death of a close friend or family member. First, **loss-oriented coping** involves activities that are related to the loss itself, such as crying, reminiscing, and yearning for the loved one. In some cases, the grieving person may ruminate about events and circumstances surrounding the death, or about life with the loved one as it had been. The second main endeavor is **restoration-oriented coping**, which includes adjustments to the changes that are secondary to the actual loss and to an environment in which the deceased person is missing. These adjustments may involve taking on new responsibilities, roles, and identities that were previously assumed by the loved one. It is common for grieving individuals to vacillate between these two main tasks in a dynamic way.

Gillies and Neimeyer (2006) made a significant contribution to the dual process model when they researched the topic of meaning reconstruction as it occurs during the bereavement process. These authors suggest that restoration-oriented coping includes efforts to *make sense of the loss* and a reason for the death. After months or years of grieving, the person may even *find benefits* to the loss, such as enhanced wisdom, spiritual growth, or the strengthening of relationships with other family members and friends. The individual may also *broaden their sense of self and identity* by establishing a new purpose in life.

Social workers can support both loss-oriented and restoration-focused coping with clients who are grieving the loss of a loved one (due to death, separation, or divorce). They can provide a listening ear as the person shares their pain, anger, and confusion about the loss, and memories of the missing person (both positive and negative) can be explored and processed. When the client is ready, the practitioner may assist them in adjusting to life without the deceased. This adjustment can take many forms, but for many, it means thinking about themselves in a new and expanded way, learning how to take on new roles, meeting new people, or becoming involved in activities aimed at helping others who are struggling with similar challenges. Powerful examples of the latter are seen in the recent activities of high school students who were suffering due to the death of their classmates and friends through gun violence. By becoming politically active, they, to the extent possible, transformed a tragedy into an opportunity to make a difference.

NARRATIVE APPLICATION: Coping with Grief

Kathryn and Don had been married for over 60 years. They were a very hard working and self-sufficient couple but had few friends and rarely reached out to others for help. When Don turned 90 years old, his functioning deteriorated; he was almost completely blind due to macular degeneration, had poor hearing, and was in chronic pain resulting from a back injury. When his kidneys began to fail, Kathryn's two adult children encouraged her to contact the local hospice. The hospice nurse responded immediately; he initiated a care plan for Don, arranged for in-home assistance, and requested social work services for Kathryn to help her cope with her role as caregiver. Not long after hospice began serving them, Don passed away. For the first few weeks following his death, Kathryn engaged in loss-oriented coping by crying, reminiscing, and yearning for her husband. She had difficulty sleeping in the empty bed they had once shared, and struggled with loneliness and uncertainty about her future. At the same time, she felt relief that Don was no longer suffering and that she was free of the monumental stress involved in caring for him. Her hospice social worker continued to see her for a brief time following Don's death. She normalized Kathryn's mixed feelings about his passing and helped her consider ways to ease her loneliness. For the first time, Kathryn experienced the benefits of supportive counseling. She also maintained frequent phone contact with her children in processing her loss, and her emotional connection with them flourished. Over time, she came to the realization that she needed to accept assistance from them in sorting through all of Don's belongings, putting her home up for sale, and moving into her son's home. While her bereavement process had been extremely painful, it helped her recognize the importance of accepting help from others.

SUMMARY

This chapter focuses on intervention strategies for use with individuals. First, it covered crisis intervention, including suicide risk assessment. Next, it delved into key elements of transitional support provided to clients reintegrating into their communities from institutional settings. A problem-solving approach was presented that is task centered; skill building was covered, as applied to assertive communication, independent living, stress management, emotional self-regulation, and self-compassion. Finally, concepts related to bereavement were discussed, along with strategies for processing grief with bereaved clients. Skill in the use of these varied techniques provides an important foundation for the adoption of specialized methods that will be covered in upcoming chapters.

KEY TERMS

Coping cards

Loss-oriented coping

Mindfulness

Passive, aggressive, assertive

communication

Restoration-oriented coping

Risk factors for suicide

Safety planning

Self-compassion

DISCUSSION QUESTIONS

1. How would you approach suicide risk assessment with individuals?

2. To what extent do you practice self-compassion? When is it the hardest to utilize this skill?

3. Consider someone you know who has recently lost a loved one. How did they make sense of their loss?

SKILL DEVELOPMENT ACTIVITIES

1. Explore the money management resources provided on the NCOA website. How might you introduce them to an older adult in need of financial assistance?

2. Practice one or more of the mindfulness activities suggested in Highlight 6.2. Describe your experience.

3. Design a coping card for yourself. Include reminders and affirmations that will help you manage the stress associated with school and internship.

REFERENCES

Aguilera, D. C. (1990). *Crisis intervention: Theory and methodology* (6th ed.). St. Louis, MO: Mosby.

American Foundation for Suicide Prevention. (2018*). Risk factors and warning signs*. Retrieved from https://afsp.org/about-suicide/risk-factors-and-warning-signs/

Bohlinger, A. I., Wahlig, J. L., & Trudeau-Hern, S. (2014). Teaching self-compassion to decrease performance anxiety in clinicians. In R. A. Bean, S. D. Davis, & M. P. Davey (Eds.), *Clinical supervision activities for increasing competence and self-awareness* (pp. 61–65). Hoboken, NJ: John Wiley & Sons.

Bonanno, G. A., & Kaltman, S. (2001). The varieties of grief experience. *Clinical Psychology Review, 26*, 705–734.

Centers for Medicare and Medicaid Services (2018). Community-based Care Transitions Program. Retrieved from https://innovation.cms.gov/initiatives/CCTP/

Gillies, J., & Neimeyer, R. A. (2006). Loss, grief, and the search for significance: Toward a model of meaning reconstruction in bereavement. *Journal of Constructivist Psychology, 19*, 31–65.

Henriques, G., Beck, A., & Brown, G. (2003). Cognitive therapy for adolescent and young adult suicide attempters. *American Behavioral*

Hepworth, D. H., Rooney, R. H., Rooney, G. D., Strom-Gottfried, K., & Larsen, J. (2010). *Direct social work practice: Theory and skills*. Belmont, CA: Brooks/Cole, Cengage Learning.

Iacono, G. (2017). A call for self-care in social work education. *Journal of Teaching in Social Work, 37*, 454–476.

James, R. K. (2008). *Crisis intervention strategies* (6th ed.). Belmont, CA: Thomson-Brooks/Cole.

Kanel, K. (2015). *A guide to crisis intervention* (5th ed.). Stamford, CT: Cengage Learning.

McDougal, G. J., Becker, H., Vaughan, P. W., Acee, T. W., & Delville, C. L. (2010). The revised assessment of functional status for independent older adults. *The Gerontologist, 50*, 363–370.

McMillen, J. C. (1999). Better for it: How people benefit from adversity. *Social Work, 44*, 455–468.

Michel, F. (2008). *Assert yourself*. Perth, Western Australia: Centre for Clinical Intervention.

National Council on Aging. (n.d.). *Money management*. Retrieved from https://www.ncoa.org/economic-security/money-management/

National Institute of Corrections. (2008). *Transition from Jail to Community Initiative*. Retrieved from https://nicic.gov/transition-from-jail-to-community

Neff, K. (2019). Exercises. Retrieved from https://self-compassion.org/category/exercises/#exercises

Neff, K., & Vonk, R. (2009). Self-compassion versus self-esteem: Two different ways of relating to oneself. *Journal of Personality, 77*, 23–50.

Siegel, R. D. (2010). *The mindfulness solution: Everyday practices for everyday problems*. New York, NY: Guilford Press.

Stroebe, M., & Schut, H. (1999). The dual process model of coping with bereavement: Rationale and description. *Death Studies, 23*, 197–224.

Stroebe, M., & Schut, H. (2001). Meaning making in the dual process model of coping with bereavement. In R. A. Neimeyer (Ed.), *Meaning reconstruction and the experience of loss*. Washington, DC: American Psychological Association.

Sun, A. P. (2012). Helping homeless individuals with co-existing disorders: The four components. *Social Work, 57*, 23–37.

Warwick, K., Dodd, H., & Neusteter, S. R. (2012). Case management strategies for successful jail reentry. National Institute of Corrections. Retrieved from https://nicic.gov/case-management-strategies-successful-jail-reentry

Zhan, C., Sangl, J., Bierman, A. S., Miller, M. R., Friedman, B., Wickizer, S. W., & Meyer, G. S. (2001). Potentially inappropriate medication use in the community-dwelling elderly: Findings from the 1996 Medical Expenditure Panel Survey. *Journal of the American Medical Association, 286*, 2823–2829.

CREDITS

CHAPTER 7

Social Work Practice with Groups

Alone we can do so little, together we can do so much. —HELEN KELLER

ENTERING THE FIELD of social work almost inevitably means working with groups of individuals to provide education, support, problem solving, skill building, service planning, outreach, or program development. There are many advantages to group work, including its value in establishing mutual support and aid between individuals who share a common challenge or concern. Most importantly, groups hold potential for promoting **synergy** in relation to goal attainment. According to the Merriam-Webster dictionary (Synergy, n.d.), the word *synergy* comes from the Greek word *synergos*, meaning combined action. This term also conveys meaning about the benefits accrued through group participation. When one or more persons come together and create synergy, they are able to achieve combined effects that are greater than the sum of their individual contributions. When synergy is established through group process, members are motivated and inspired to build on the contributions of others. The result can be enhanced insight, understanding, and creativity, and shared enthusiasm to reach personal or organizational objectives.

This chapter will cover two main types of groups in which social workers participate: therapeutic groups and task groups. **Therapeutic groups** are formed in order to provide support, psychoeducation, skill building, self-actualization, self-help, or therapy. Group members are expected to self-disclose in these groups and work toward meeting their socioemotional needs. **Task groups**, commonly used in social work organizations, are more structured than therapeutic groups; they are focused on service or program planning, strengthening professional partnerships, enhancing community resources, and advancing an agency's vision for service delivery or a social justice agenda. This section will discuss skills needed to effectively facilitate both therapeutic and task groups, but first some common terms will be discussed.

Group Formation

When a group is formed, there are a variety of practical questions that should be considered. One is whether the group will be open or closed. **Open groups** have changing membership—as participants leave, others enter. A challenge with open groups is that as new members join, it can be difficult to reestablish trust that had been built prior to the new member's entrance. An advantage to this type of group is that veterans can be called upon to show leadership by orienting new members and explaining the ground rules, which, in a therapeutic group, include guidelines related to confidentiality. **Closed groups** do not incorporate new members once sessions have begun. These groups usually have a predetermined number of meetings that will occur before the group ends. A challenge with closed groups is that potential members often need to wait until a new group cycle begins before they will be included. An advantage is that the work need not stop midstream in order to orient new members to the group purpose and process.

Another important consideration is the degree to which the group composition will be homogenous or heterogeneous. **Homogenous groups** are those in which members have a great deal in common with respect to age, gender identification, education, ethnicity, socioeconomic status, type of problem, and/or level of motivation to make change. An example of a relatively homogenous group is one that includes female survivors of intimate partner violence. A group that is even more homogenous might be composed of female residents of a domestic violence shelter who are preparing to reenter the community. **Heterogeneous** groups are composed of clients who differ with respect to age, gender identification, life experience, primary presenting problem, and motivation level. There are advantages to both types of group composition: homogenous groups allow for a great deal of connection and understanding between members; heterogeneous groups promote appreciation for diversity and alternative ways of approaching various challenges. In most cases, social workers facilitate groups that are somewhere in between these two extremes. For instance, they may be working with a group of males with substance abuse problems who are of differing ages, primary presenting problems, and levels of motivation to make change. Here, the younger or less motivated members may learn from the older or more motivated participants. On the other hand, the group members who are serious about recovery may become frustrated with those who are unmotivated to make change. Such challenges can be managed, however, as seen in the narrative application below.

NARRATIVE APPLICATION: Group Composition

Emma worked at a juvenile corrections facility and was asked to start a therapeutic group with eight of the youth in the program. These young men had been assigned to her caseload without consideration of their similarities or differences. Her first few groups with them were very stiff and uncomfortable: it was like pulling teeth to get any interaction going. She tried hard to initiate conversation by mentioning some of the things that they had in common, but it didn't seem to make a difference. After a period of struggle, Emma finally realized what the barrier had been: the teens in the group came from rival gangs. After consulting with her supervisor, she decided to process this issue with the participants in group. When she brought it up, the youth were quick to acknowledge the problem. One of the group members said that he actually liked two of the other youth who were from a different gang, and they responded in kind. After some discussion, the group members made a pact; they would be friendly with their rivals while in the program, but after they were released to the community, they would have to consider them as enemies, once again. Emma thought over their agreement following the group session. It wasn't ideal, but it seemed like a compromise that might work. Her hope, of course, was that after forming a bond with their opponents, the young men might think differently about who could be trusted in the world and who couldn't. She concluded that it was worth a try. The group continued without incident and with increased interaction.

Group Norms

As a group is established, **norms** emerge—these are the shared assumptions about how members should conduct themselves over the duration of the group's life cycle. Sometime these norms are *overt*, or explicitly stated in the form of ground rules concerning attendance, self-disclosure, mutual respect, acceptable language, and confidentiality. Such clearly stated norms help reduce anxiety by making clear how members are expected to behave in order to further trust and inclusion. Facilitators often begin a newly formed group with a request that members identify rules for their own conduct that will allow all to feel safe and respected; such norms might be listed in a location that may be revisited, as needed. Groups also have *covert* norms that are fully understood but not explicitly stated. They develop over time in response to modeling by the facilitator and other members of the group. Covert norms are reflected in the shared use of certain terms or phrases, the content of material open for discussion, and the extent to which emotional expression is expected and/or tolerated. Group facilitators should be aware of the norms that have been created and the extent to which they further or detract from group goals and satisfaction with the group experience.

Group Roles

Group roles can be thought of as the parts members play in carrying out the group's purpose. They differ to the extent that they involve task-oriented behavior or a focus on the maintenance of group relationships and fulfillment of socioemotional needs. Based on their research, Benne and Sheats (1948) argued that both types of roles are needed for a group to survive. They developed a taxonomy of group roles that is composed of task roles, maintenance roles, and individual roles. The latter are described as those intended to satisfy individual needs that are not relevant to group functioning. **Task-oriented roles** include the *initiator-contributor,* who proposes new ideas or a shift in perspective about the group goals. The *information seeker* requests information and facts that concern the problem under discussion; the *information giver* offers facts or relays their own experience pertaining to the problem. **Group building and maintenance roles** (otherwise referred to as *socioemotional roles*) include the *encourager,* who offers warmth and praise, and the *harmonizer,* who mediates differences of opinion. **Individual roles** are exemplified by the *aggressor,* who expresses criticism and disapproval toward other members, and the *dominator,* who tries to assert superiority and control over the group. The *playboy* is said to display cynicism and a lack of interest in the group process. A complete list of roles in this taxonomy are provided in Highlight 7.1

HIGHLIGHT 7.1: Benne and Sheats's Taxonomy of Group Roles

Task Roles

- Initiator-contributor: offers new ideas or a changed way of considering the group problem or goal
- Information seeker: asks for clarification regarding suggestions or for information pertaining to the problem under discussion
- Opinion seeker: asks for clarification of the values connected to suggestions made
- Information giver: offers facts or relays their own experience pertaining to the group problem
- Opinion giver: shares their own beliefs or opinions concerning suggestions made and values that should be considered
- Elaborator: offers a rationale for suggestions made and tries to deduce how a proposed solution would work out, if adopted

- Coordinator: clarifies the relationships among various ideas and suggestions; coordinates activities of subgroups
- Orienter: summarizes what has occurred or raises questions about the direction that the group is taking
- Evaluator-critic: evaluates or questions the quality of the group's performance
- Energizer: stimulates the group to continue moving toward goals
- Procedural technician: performs routine tasks for the group, such as rearranging seating or handing out material
- Recorder: serves as the "group memory" by taking notes and recording decisions

Group Development and Maintenance Roles

- Encourager: agrees with the contribution of others; offers praise, understanding, and acceptance
- Harmonizer: mediates differences of opinion between members; attempts to relieve tension in conflict situations
- Compromiser: offers compromise when in conflict with others so as to maintain group harmony
- Gate-keeper and expediter: encourages and facilitates the participation of others or proposes regulation of the flow of communication
- Standard setter or ego ideal: applies standards in evaluating the quality of group functioning
- Group observer and commentator: maintains records of group processes and provides data for the group's evaluation of its own procedures
- Follower: passively accepts the ideas of others; serves as an audience in group discussion

Individual Roles

- Aggressor: expresses disapproval of the values, acts, or feelings of others; attacks the group or the problem it is working on; shows envy toward the contributions of others
- Blocker: tends to be negative and resistant; disagrees and opposes without reason
- Recognition seeker: calls attention to themselves by boasting or acting in unusual ways
- Self-confessor: expresses personal, non-group oriented feelings and insights
- Playboy: displays cynicism, nonchalance, horseplay; communicates a lack of interest in the group's processes
- Dominator: tries to assert authority or superiority in manipulating the group process; may interrupt the contributions of others
- Help-seeker: attempts to generate sympathy from other group members; expresses insecurity, personal confusion, or self-depreciation
- Special interest pleader: attempts to speak for others or communities in need, usually masking their own biases

Source: Benne, K. D., & Sheats, P. (1948). Functional roles of group members. *Journal of Social Issues, 4,* 41–49.

Group Cohesion

A key determinant of a group's effectiveness is the extent to which **group cohesion** has been created. The term *cohesion* is defined as "the act of sticking together tightly" (Cohesion, n.d.). In a group setting, it refers to the sense of solidarity, "we-ness," and unity that has been fostered. When groups have a high level of cohesion, members are committed to the group process; they participate actively toward creating a safe climate and cooperative working relationships with other participants. On the other hand, when group cohesion is low, conflict is left unresolved, trust is elusive, and members become alienated from the group process.

Several strategies for furthering group cohesion have been advanced by Engleberg and Wynn (2010). One method involves the creation of *group identity and traditions*. This can be done through the use of plural terms, such as *we* and *our* versus *I* and *my*; some groups adopt a name or slogan and various routines and rituals. Secondly, the facilitator should *strengthen teamwork* by emphasizing the importance of combined contributions and achievements. They must also create a supportive climate in which *success is praised* and *otherwise rewarded*. Most importantly, *respect should be shown to all group members*, along with sensitivity to their needs. "Treating members with respect, showing concern for their personal needs, and appreciating diversity promotes a feeling of acceptance" (p. 226).

Group Interaction

In understanding a group's dynamics and interaction, the group facilitator must attend to both the content of what is being said and the process of communicating used by group members. All communications, both verbal and nonverbal, are aimed at relaying a message. If a group participant rolls their eyes as another one speaks, this facial expression conveys meaning. Other messages are communicated nonverbally through gestures, seating choice, gaze or eye contact, smiling and head nodding, or nervous mannerisms such as foot or finger tapping. Once these nonverbal behaviors are observed, the group leader must decide how to respond constructively. In some cases, the facilitator will avoid putting a group member on the spot by mentioning their behavior, particularly if it seems to reflect uneasiness or discomfort. Other times, they may respectfully invite the nonverbal communicator to express what they are thinking or feeling. "I saw that you nodded your head when ... was speaking. Are you feeling the same way?" Another option for the group leader is to share a more general observation, such as "I notice that everyone seems a bit quiet and uneasy today. Am I right?" A key competency in group facilitation is maintaining awareness of the group process and utilizing it effectively.

The group facilitator must also guide and support the patterns of group interaction that members will use in contributing to discussion. Toseland and Rivas (2009) distinguish between leader-centered and group-centered patterns. When interaction is **leader centered**, the group facilitator structures the process of communication. One example is the *maypole* in which the leader is the central figure and interacts with individual members who then respond. The *hot seat* involves "extended back-and-forth between the facilitator and one member, as the other members watch." (p. 70). In the *round robin* pattern, members are prompted to take turns speaking as the sharing proceeds around the circle. This last pattern is frequently used as an "ice-breaker" aimed at helping members learn more about each other. One advantage of the round robin technique is that it ensures that each member has an opportunity to speak. However, the downside to all leader-centered patterns is that they limit the member-to-member interaction that is needed in order for mutual aid and support is to evolve.

Group-centered communication is the preferred pattern in therapeutic groups, as it strengthens trust and cohesion. This style promotes *free-floating* interaction in which members speak directly to one another. Group-centered interaction allows members to assume ownership over the group process and responsibility for the work to be done. Group facilitators can promote free-floating interaction by resisting the temptation to fill every silence with their own observations or comments. This allows group members some time to process internally what they are hearing and work up the courage to verbalize their own thoughts and emotions.

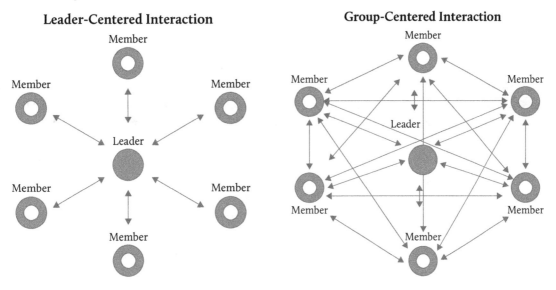

FIGURE 7.1. Leader- and Group-Centered Interaction Patterns.

Group Leadership

Leadership involves the ability to mobilize, coordinate, and motivate individuals toward the achievement of a common goal. More specifically, group leadership requires skill in providing structure and focus for group members while also promoting trust, cohesion, and collaboration. However, leaders tend to lean toward either task motivation or relationship motivation in their approach to group work (Fiedler, 1981). Based on this premise, Blake and Mouton (as cited in Forsyth, 1999) developed a **leadership grid** that distinguishes between five primary leadership styles; each is based on the extent to which the leader displays concern for people and/or productivity:

1. Apathetic or impoverished leader: is disinterested in people and production results
2. Taskmaster or authoritarian leader: has a high degree of concern for productivity, little concern for people
3. Country club or laissez-faire leader: is very concerned with people and relationships; minimally focused on productivity
4. Middle-of-the-road leader: displays moderate concern for people and productivity, may sacrifice both
5. Authoritative leader: has a high degree of concern for both productivity and people; Blake and Mouton assert that this is the most effective leadership style

Other theorists have focused on the traits of good leaders, such as intelligence, personality, and expertise. Others study the behaviors of effective leaders. For example, the demonstration of confidence, competence, trustworthiness, and optimism have been associated with model leadership (Chemers & Ayman, 1993). Some argue that leadership should be situational and adapted to group needs and circumstances (Hersey & Blanchard, 1982). All of these conceptual models provide useful guidance in understanding group leadership, but they are limited by their focus on the style, traits, or behaviors of the formally assigned leader.

While many social work groups have designated leaders, additional group members often emerge as informal leaders based on respect earned and contributions made toward group goals. Thus, recognizing the process through which **shared leadership** evolves is relevant to effective group practice. Shared leadership has been found to benefit groups in several important ways. It furthers the development of trust (Bergman, Rentsch, Small, Davenport, & Bergman, 2012), increases opportunities for group members to interact (Aime, Humphrey, DeRue, & Paul, 2013) and enhances group performance (Wang, Waldman, & Zhang, 2014).

To promote shared leadership in a task group, the facilitator might encourage members to rotate responsibility for various functions, such as preparing the meeting agenda, bringing refreshments, timekeeping, or taking minutes. In a therapeutic group, the assigned leader might stress that each member plays an important role in furthering group growth by offering support, providing feedback, reviewing group norms and rules, and recognizing healthy risk taking. Such efforts at distributing leadership functions "may lead to empowerment as group members employ positive influence techniques" (Drescher, Korsgaard, Welpe, Picot, & Wigand, 2014, p. 773).

Therapeutic Groups

As noted above, therapeutic groups are aimed at promoting the personal growth and well-being of participants. By sharing personal struggles with others in an accepting and trusting environment, groups members learn about themselves, explore changes they wish to make, and consider various strategies for making them. They are also given an opportunity to receive feedback, as well as encouragement to steady the course as they implement new skills. There are a variety of different types of therapeutic groups. In this section, discussion will focus on the nature of psychoeducational, support, self-help, growth, and therapy groups.

Psychoeducation Groups

The goal of the psychoeducational group is to provide knowledge and skill building as it relates to a specific topic, such as anger management, parenting, communication, leadership, or methods for attaining academic success. This approach is commonly used in programs aimed at the prevention of substance abuse, intimate partner violence, or school-based bullying. In comparison with the other therapeutic groups to be covered, psychoeducational formats are relatively structured, with information imparted, then discussed, and skills introduced and applied. The focus is on learning about and increasing awareness of problem areas, common challenges, and strategies for furthering success.

HIGHLIGHT 7.2: Group Work with Transition-Aged Youth

Youth who are aging out of foster care and out-of-home placement face monumental challenges on their path to young adulthood. Many lack the skills and competencies needed to live independently (Dworsky, 2008); most have limited familial support in navigating the healthcare, mental health, and social service systems (Allen & Williams, 2012). To address the psychoeducational needs of these youth, independent living programs have sprung up across the nation.

Group work is the modality of choice in preparing transition-aged youth (TAY) for independent living, because it offers a "base of support and a culture of social learning" (Allen & Williams, 2012). A framework for group practice offered by Allen and Williams includes skill-building activities across the following domains:

- Job seeking skills (completing applications, interviewing, sustaining employment)
- Personal development (sense of pride, confidence, respect for self and others)
- Home management (food preparation, cooking, cleaning)
- Open expression of feelings related to problems that arise
- Career exploration (knowledge of various vocations and occupations)
- Money management (banking, budgeting)
- Personal hygiene (grooming, health habits)
- Sex education (STD prevention)
- Community resources (accessing social services)

The recommended group format exposes members to videos, didactic presentations, experiential activities, positive role models, and carefully crafted projects aimed at strengthening mastery of skills needed for self-sufficiency. Group facilitators are encouraged to support the creation of group norms that permit the open expression of uncertainties, anxiety, and other emotions that arise with the movement toward independence. The authors stress that how the above content is presented can make a fundamental difference in how it is received.

Support Groups

The primary goal of a support group is to help participants cope with challenging life circumstances, such as receiving a medical diagnosis, taking on caregiving responsibilities for an aging parent, adjusting to civilian life after military service, or parenting a child with disabilities. Members are encouraged to share their experiences with the stressful event and give, as well as receive, empathic understanding and mutual aid. Support groups help individuals overcome alienation through the recognition that they are not alone in their struggle. Often, a psychoeducational component is incorporated into the group process to normalize stress, stigma, and isolation associated with the life event.

HIGHLIGHT 7.3: Connecting with Group Support

Local face-to-face or online support groups are sponsored by many organizations, including the following:

- Alzheimer's Association (https://www.alz.org/): support for patients living with Alzheimer's and their caregivers
- American Association of Suicidality (www.suicidology.org): support for families and friends who have lost a loved one to suicide

- Anxiety and Depression Association of America (https://adaa.org/supportgroups): support for individuals with a variety of anxiety and depressive disorders
- CHADD (https://chadd.org/): support for individuals and families affected by ADHD
- Caregiver Action Network (https://caregiveraction.org/): support for family caregivers
- Compassionate Friends Grief Support (https://www.compassionatefriends.org/): for families that have suffered the death of a child
- Autism Spectrum Connection (www.aspergersyndrome.org): support for families dealing with the challenges of autism spectrum disorder
- National Alliance on Mental Illness (https://www.nami.org/): support for individuals and families coping with mental illness
- ARC (https://www.thearc.org/): support for people with intellectual or developmental disabilities

Self-Help Groups

When a support group is facilitated by an individual who shares the problem or challenge of other group members, it is considered a self-help group. A guiding principle of self-help groups is that the lived experience of participants is key to problem resolution and healing. Examples include 12-step groups such as Alcoholics Anonymous that offer group members a community connection, a safe harbor, and an opportunity to learn from the stories of others who have embraced recovery (Davis & Jansen, 1998). In addition to addressing substance abuse, 12-step groups are used to support recovery from co-dependency, emotional difficulties, eating disorders, self-harm, and gambling or sex addictions.

HIGHLIGHT 7.4: Twelve-Step Model

Twelve-step self-help groups support participants in their recovery from substance abuse or other addictive behaviors. The 12-step philosophy emphasizes the importance of accepting addiction as a disease that can managed through the completion of the following activities:

1. Admitting powerlessness over the addiction
2. Believing that a higher power (in whatever form) can help
3. Deciding to turn control over to the higher power
4. Taking a personal inventory
5. Admitting to the higher power, oneself, and another person the wrongs done
6. Being ready to have the higher power correct any shortcomings in one's character
7. Asking the higher power to remove those shortcomings
8. Making a list of wrongs done to others and being willing to make amends for those wrongs
9. Contacting those who have been hurt, unless doing so would harm the person
10. Continuing to take personal inventory and admitting when one is wrong
11. Seeking enlightenment and connection with the higher power via prayer and meditation
12. Carrying the message of the 12-steps to others in need

Source: 12-Step Drug Rehabilitation and Addiction Treatment Programs (2018). American Addiction Centers. Retrieved from https://americanaddictioncenters.org/rehab-guide/12-step

Growth Groups

The growth group is used as a vehicle for self-improvement or self-actualization, as opposed to problem resolution. Members are provided support as they learn new strategies for enhancing self-awareness, relationships, and emotional or spiritual development. They bond with one other as they explore their thoughts, feelings, and behavior or apply new skills. Mindfulness-based, prayer-focused, or intimacy-oriented encounter sessions are examples of the growth group.

HIGHLIGHT 7.5: Mindfulness-Based Growth Group

Betsy Nelson (2011), program director at the Sarasota Mindfulness Institute, shares her format devoted to the furthering of mindfulness in group participants:

- Group begins with 5 minutes of quiet centering
- Introductions are made
- Facilitator offers a brief reading and stimulates discussion
- Meditation period of 20–25 minutes or more focused on:
  - ✓ Noting what is; resisting the impulse to fix or change it
  - ✓ Taking a few breaths to steady the body and move into a relaxed posture
  - ✓ Conducting a general body scan
  - ✓ Attending to the breath, as the mind wanders from the present moment and is gently returned

Go to https://www.mindful.org/setting-up-a-mindfulness-meditation-group/ for further detail on mindfulness group work.

Therapy Groups

Therapy groups help clients manage the symptoms associated with a mental, emotional, or behavior disorder. They may promote coping with depression, anxiety, substance abuse, or trauma. Their aim is to improve the functioning level of members, enhance their insight, and assist them in acquiring new skills. Depending on the theoretical orientation of the facilitator, the group process may include exploration of early life experiences, work on interpersonal relationships, or restructuring of thinking patterns associated with problematic moods or behavior.

Irvin Yalom, professor of psychiatry and author of the widely acclaimed textbook *The Theory and Practice of Group Psychotherapy* (2005), extols the virtues of group therapy in promoting hope and universality in clients with mental health disorders. He states that

> *many patients enter therapy with the disquieting thought that they are unique in their wretchedness, that they alone have certain frightening or unacceptable problems, thoughts, impulses and fantasies. … After hearing other members disclose concerns similar to their own, patients report feeling more in touch with the world and describe the process as a "welcome to the human race experience."* (p. 6)

Consistent with this perspective, Yalom (2005) promotes the use of interpersonal group therapy. He views the group as a social microcosm within which members reveal their interpersonal style. Maladaptive interpersonal behaviors become evident and are recognized and addressed within the group. The therapist maintains a focus on process, on the immediate relationships between group members—a focus that is considered the "power cell of the group." (p. 150). Yalom has produced video demonstrations of his approach to group therapy; several can be found on YouTube.

Basic Skills for Facilitating Therapeutic Groups

Many clients begin their first group meeting with a great deal of apprehension. They may wonder why they are there, if other group members can be trusted, or if the group leader has what it takes to facilitate a safe and productive process. To counteract these concerns, it is important that the facilitator establish a tone that is conducive to therapeutic work. They should create safety by *clarifying the purpose of the group*, helping members establish group norms, and normalizing the stress related to entering a group for the first time. These efforts require contracting skills that are aimed at establishing structure during the beginning phase of a group. Shulman (2016) asserts that contracting should involve the use of a "simple, non-jargonized statement" that describes the group purpose in terms that group members can understand and embrace (p. 423). He also recommends that the facilitator clarify their role in the group and review issues concerning confidentiality. Group members should agree to upholding privacy as it relates to personal contributions by others; they must also understand the limits of confidentiality resulting from the facilitator's ethical responsibility as a mandated reporter.

Secondly, effective group leaders have in skill in *helping members help each other*. As with other forms of mezzo-level practice, therapeutic group work entails strengthening the connection between individuals. This is accomplished by prompting member-to-member interaction when it appears appropriate and likely to strengthen trust and rapport. For example, if group member Rosie shares sadness that she feels at the loss of a friend, the facilitator might respond with one of the following:

> "Who understands how Rosie feels and can share with her a similar experience?"

> "Who else knows what it's like to lose a friend and is willing to share that with Rosie?"

Another example is seen when group member Tim discusses a problem he is having at home and the facilitator asks:

> "Who can share with Tim some ideas about how to handle this problem?"

> "Who has had a similar challenge and is willing to share with Tim and the others how it worked out."

> "How might we use our knowledge of coping skills to help Tim out?"

The key here is to encourage members to speak directly with one another rather than through the leader, which they may be inclined to do. Group-centered communication can feel awkward at first but, in time, the group will become more accustomed to free-floating interaction.

Another strategy for promoting mutual aid and support is to highlight common ground, similar challenges, and shared strengths that are apparent in group members. This can be done by noting prevailing themes that emerge out of group discussion and making them explicit. For instance, after a period of dialogue concerning school-related challenges, the group facilitator might follow up with one or more of the following:

"It's clear that you all really want to do well."

"I am hearing a common struggle with motivation."

"You all seem to know what it's like to be treated badly by other kids at school."

"How have you all managed to cope with bullying by peers?"

Efforts to identify commonalities enhance group cohesion and commitment to the group process. They allow members to develop a sense of belonging and acceptance by others who genuinely understand what they are going through.

A third basic skill for group facilitators entails *building bridges* from the group experience to the outside world. This is important because the insights, new behaviors, and skills acquired during group sessions are beneficial to the extent that they generalize to other arenas of the client's life, such a work, home, and social support networks. Group workers can build bridges by encouraging members to apply what they are learning in one or more of these outside arenas and then report back to the group what occurred. This allows members to address barriers that arise as they apply new concepts and practice new areas of competency. When group membership comes to a close, it is important that participants be guided in anticipating challenges that may come up when they no longer have group support. They should be aided in considering alternative sources of support and ways that they will maintain and utilize what they have learned on an on-going basis.

Multicultural Group Work

Therapeutic group work is an ideal modality for furthering appreciation for various aspects of culture, as they influence the attitudes and experience of self and others. As discussed in Chapter 2, culture embodies the values, beliefs, and traditions of a group based on ethnicity, national origin, gender identification and expression, age, sexual orientation, religion, political beliefs, and/or rural versus urban place of residence. Thus, every individual approaches their involvement in group from their own unique cultural vantage point.

A multicultural approach to group work acknowledges the **etic** and **emic** approach to observing and understanding culture. Linguist and anthropologist Kenneth Pike (1954) introduced these terms in the mid-20th century. The etic model views a cultural group from the perspective of an outsider who compares and contrasts it with other culturally defined groups. Conversely, the emic approach examines the internal dynamics of a culture from the perspective of persons within that group. In applying these concepts to multicultural group work, Anderson (2007) offers an additional view—the **dialectic perspective**. This lens is focused on understanding the differential power dynamics as they emerge within groups. Anderson argues that multicultural group counselors must apply skill in the use of dialectic interactions through which members share their differing experiences with power, privilege, and oppression. He states

the ultimate goal of multicultural group interventions is to reconcile the dialectic of human and cultural diversity through directing forces of group conflict, contradictions, and tensions to promote higher levels of unity in experience, self, and self in relationship to others. (p. 230)

Consistent with the dialectic perspective, Corey, Corey, and Corey (2018) encourage group practitioners to develop "diversity and multicultural and social justice competence" (p. 15). This begins with an understanding of their own stereotypes and biased notions about other cultural groups. It continues with the unfolding of comfort and skill in inviting dialogue about culture between group members. When built on a foundation of safety and respect, such conversations help group members recognize their differences and also the common ground they share. Sue (2016, pp. 45–46) suggests the following guidelines for counselors as they initiate group discussion of culture and racial/ethnic differences:

- Understand your own racial and cultural identity
- Recognize and be open about your racial biases
- Encourage discussion about feelings
- Pay more attention to the process than to the content of race talk
- Encourage and support people who are willing to take the risk of expressing themselves

Task Groups

Well-run task groups provide problem-solving support and direction for organizations, family decision-making teams, neighborhood coalitions, and communities. Participation in such groups can be challenging and time consuming, yet well worth the effort. In fact, "there are few experiences in the workplace to equal the sense of cohesion, commitment, and satisfaction that members feel when their ideas have been heard, appreciated, and used in resolving a difficult issue and arriving at a solution" (Toseland & Rivas, 2009, p. 314). Social workers are often called upon to facilitate these teams and coordinate their activities.

Leadership of task groups requires a unique skill set that allows the social worker to provide the structure needed for effective teamwork. The group facilitator must, first, carry out adequate *preparation for team meetings*. This begins with the development of a written agenda that is, ideally, distributed to team members for review and suggestions regarding additional items to include. Members should be prepared to approve the agenda at the upcoming meeting. Another task for the facilitator is to ensure that the data needed for decision-making is available to group members either prior to or during each team meeting.

During the task group meeting, the facilitator must help the team *maintain focus* as they discuss the issues listed on the agenda. The leader will check in with group members to ensure that they understand each issue and its relevance to their stated purpose. They prompt discussion of each agenda item in a sequential fashion and redirect the group members if they sway off topic. Brainstorming may be initiated to generate ideas and options for problem solving. When specific decisions must be made, the leader ensures that the agreed-upon process for decision-making is followed. For example, if decision-making is to be made by majority rule, the facilitator prompts a voting process. If consensus decision-making is the preferred mode, they will check for agreement from all members before a final decision is recorded. As the team meeting comes to a close, the leader should summarize what was decided as well as the work to be done before the next meeting.

It is essential that task group facilitators establish an overall atmosphere at team meetings that is safe for open sharing of information. Moreover, varying perspectives should be recognized and embraced. Effective task group leaders invite participation from all members and support norms that welcome creative and innovative ideas. They also *promote the acceptance of diverse viewpoints* and respect for varying approaches to problem solving. Group facilitators support collaboration by recognizing that varying modes of thinking are important in effective collaboration. See Highlight 7.6 for an activity aimed at illustrating this point.

NARRATIVE APPLICATION: Facilitating a Team Meeting

Marcy had been assigned by her supervisor to facilitate a committee charged with improving employee morale at their community-based social service organization. The first meeting was tense, with committee members challenging her about the purpose of the group. They questioned the assumption that agency morale was broken and asked why it had become the focus of administration. Marcy had no answers, as she was confused herself about what prompted this effort. Discussion went around in circles, and members were clearly frustrated. One committee member came to Marcy's rescue and suggested that morale might be improved if salaries were increased. Everyone appeared to support this suggestion, but several members voiced doubt that a pay raise would come to pass. The meeting ended with little support for setting follow-up committee meetings.

Marcy sought help from her supervisor, Julia, in processing what had occurred. Julia acknowledged that, in her haste to comply with the request for committee action, she failed to adequately prepare Marcy for this assignment. She arranged a meeting for them with the unit manager to obtain clarification. At this meeting, Marcy was provided data showing a steady increase in turnover at the agency, despite step salary increases. She was also given a research article that tied turnover to various morale concerns in similar agencies. Based on this information, she and Julia discussed an improved approach to committee facilitation. At the next department staff meeting, the data was presented and volunteers were requested for committee participation. The aim of the committee was clarified—it would explore morale issues and the extent to which they were contributing to turnover. Solutions would be developed to help resolve issues that were identified. Eight employees volunteered to sit on the committee. Marcy and Julia created and disseminated a survey to elicit staff perspectives on morale and turnover.

At the first meeting of this newly focused committee, Marcy thanked members for their willingness to devote time to this endeavor. She reviewed the purpose of the committee and presented data from the staff survey. This jump-started a robust discussion aimed at identifying and addressing issues that were, in fact, impacting morale. Based on this experience, Marcy learned the importance of clarity in team purpose and of adequate preparation for committee meetings.

Specialized Strategies and Techniques

Among the techniques used to facilitate the work of a task group is **brainstorming**. Introduced by Alex Osborn (1957), this strategy is commonly adopted by teams and organizations as a means of generating a full range of ideas over a short period of time. Brainstorming is based on the idea that the quality of ideas increases with quantity. Put simply, it assumes that as members build on each other's ideas, creativity is enhanced. An important guideline for the facilitation of brainstorming is that ideas should not be analyzed, opposed, or critiqued until the process is over. Some group members may have difficulty complying with this guideline, as they are compelled to offer their opinion immediately after a solution is proposed (e.g., "That won't work."). When this occurs, the facilitator should redirect the group process with a gentle reminder that "all ideas are good" at this stage of discussion.

Once the group has finished brainstorming, the ideas must be refined and narrowed. One method for doing so is the **nominal group technique** (NGT). This strategy was developed by Delbecq, Van de Ven, and Gustafson (1975) with the aim of maximizing involvement in group decision-making. The facilitator begins by presenting a clear problem to be solved. Group members are asked to write down their ideas, then a round robin pattern is used for sharing (each member presents one idea at a time from their private list until all are exhausted). Every idea is posted in full view of all group members (on a flip chart or projected computer screen). Next, all recorded ideas are discussed, and members are free to state their opinions. Discussion is followed by voting; each member ranks the ideas in their order of preference, and a pooled outcome of votes is tallied.

A simplified version of the nominal group technique is the decreasing options technique (DOT) (Engleberg & Wynn, 2010). Members write their ideas on separate pieces of paper and post them all on a wall in the meeting room. Similar ideas are grouped together, and a title is given to each grouping. Next, members are given a set number of colored sticker dots and instructed to place one next to each of their preferred ideas. When this process is complete, the overall ranking of ideas is usually quite apparent. Those with the most votes are then discussed. The DOT method is helpful in narrowing ideas to a manageable number and in ensuring equal input from all members in the decision-making process.

HIGHLIGHT 7.6: Six Thinking Hats

The six thinking hats technique can be used to promote effective decision-making within teams. It was created by psychologist Edward de Bono (1999) as a means of furthering parallel thinking and productive collaboration within organizations. The strategy assumes that a variety of different modes of thinking should be used in communal problem solving and decision-making. Six varying colored hats are used to represent each mode, as follows:

- White Hat: focuses on information that is available to the team as well as additional data needed to make a well-informed decision
- Black Hat: identifies the flaws, weaknesses, and risk associated with a particular decision
- Yellow Hat: adopts an optimistic perspective by examining the strengths and benefits that can be attained by employing a particular solution
- Red Hat: tunes into the feelings and emotions associated with the decision
- Green Hat: emphasizes creativity, innovation, and "out of the box" thinking
- Blue Hat: assumes the role of mediator, ensuring the inclusion of all other hats

This technique can be applied in differing ways. One approach is to divide a large group up into five smaller ones and assign a hat (white, black, yellow, red, or green) to each small group. The moderator wears the blue hat in order to facilitate the process effectively. For teaching purposes, the groups are all presented with the same agency-based decision to be made or mock scenario. Each small group approaches the proposed solution from the perspective of the hat that they were assigned to wear. When the whole group reconvenes, each small group reports their ideas for general discussion. The moderator then points out the importance of considering information from all modes of thinking when approaching a decision.

A second approach is to introduce the six thinking hats to an already-formed group or team that is grappling with a decision. Again, the facilitator wears the blue hat and facilitates the discussion. The team as a whole puts on one hat at a time as they consider each proposed solution. The facilitator then highlights the importance of taking each perspective into account when making a final, fully informed decision.

The benefits of this strategy have been discussed in the academic literature. Patre (2016) examined its potential for use by a human resource team contending with a hypothetical challenge. She concluded that six thinking hats is a "powerful tool for organizations in optimizing their workforce decisions" (p. 198). Nursing scholar Cioffi (2017) applied the technique to a clinical case discussion used by a family and healthcare team. She asserted that it is a valuable method for moving groups beyond repetitive thinking styles and for promoting partnership in decision-making.

Self-Care: Group Supervision

Group supervision is a valuable tool that supports the self-care of social workers. It offers opportunities for practitioners to process stressful circumstances on the job and gain the support of others who share these challenges. Further, it provides a rich source of learning, as group members contribute a variety of viewpoints about practice-related issues, including ethical dilemmas and challenges related to engagement, assessment, or intervention. Cases are often presented by group participants with the aim of sharing successes and receiving feedback from others about steps that might be taken to enhance positive outcomes. Modeling by more seasoned workers can also be very helpful for entry-level social workers. Taken together, these functions contribute to the self-efficacy of social workers, as reflected in beliefs about their own capabilities with respect to practice.

According to Kadushin & Harkness (2002), some social workers are more comfortable with group supervision than they are with individual supervisory sessions. They may find it easier to accept "criticism, suggestions, and advice from peers than from parental surrogates, such as the supervisor" (p. 394). In addition, they may be energized by the mutual sharing of relevant experiences that takes place during the group process. When membership is diverse, the group conference provides an ideal opportunity for multicultural education and the development of cultural awareness. As group cohesion develops, relationships with colleagues are fostered, both inside and outside of supervisory sessions. Peer and supervisory support contribute to the self-care of employees and the maintenance of a positive organizational climate (Cox & Steiner, 2013).

SUMMARY

This chapter provides an overview of concepts, skills, and strategies pertinent to group work, a commonly used modality in social work. The differences in purpose and structure between task and therapeutic groups were explained; key concepts were covered, including group composition, norms, roles, cohesion, interaction patterns, and leadership. Highlights illustrated the nature of various therapeutic groups, including psychoeducational, support, self-help, growth, and therapy groups. Specialized techniques for group facilitation were also discussed. This chapter ended by touching on the value of group supervision in supporting the self-care of social workers.

KEY TERMS

Brainstorming	Group cohesion	Leader-centered versus group-centered
Dialectic perspective	Homogenous versus	interaction
Etic and emic approaches	heterogenous groups	Leadership grid
Group building and maintenance roles	Individual roles	Nominal group technique

Norms	Synergy	Therapeutic groups
Open versus closed groups	Task groups	
Shared leadership	Task-oriented roles	

DISCUSSION QUESTIONS

1. How would you go about promoting cohesion in a task or therapeutic group?

2. Review the taxonomy of group roles presented above. Which roles do you tend to assume in a task or therapeutic group?

3. Which of the six thinking hats do you typically wear when approaching group decision-making? When do you change hats, if ever?

SKILL DEVELOPMENT ACTIVITIES

1. With permission from the facilitator and participants, observe a task or therapeutic group. What overt and covert norms were apparent? What roles were carried out? To what extent did the group appear to be cohesive?

2. Interview a group work practitioner to learn about how they approach the development of trust, teamwork, and cohesion.

3. Watch the documentary *The Color of Fear* directed by Lee Mun Wah (1995). (The film can be found in many college libraries). In what ways does the group documented provide a good illustration of the dialectic perspective on multicultural group work?

REFERENCES

12-Step Drug Rehabilitation and Addiction Treatment Programs. (2018). American Addiction Centers. Retrieved from https://americanaddictioncenters.org/rehab-guide/12-step

Aime, F., Humphrey, S., DeRue, D., & Paul, J. (2013). The riddle of heterarchy: Power transitions in cross-functional teams. *Academy of Management Journal*, 57(2), 327–352. doi.org/10.5465/amj.2011.0756

Allen, T., & Williams, L. D. (2012). An approach to life skills group work with youth in transition to independent living: Theoretical, practice, and operational considerations. *Residential Treatment for Children and Youth, 29*, 324–342.

Anderson, D. (2007). Multicultural group work: A force for developing and healing. *Journal for Specialists in Group Work, 32*, 224–244.

Benne, K. D., & Sheats, P. (1948). Functional roles of group members. *Journal of Social Issues, 4*, 41–49.

Bergman, J. Z., Rentsch, J. R., Small, E. E., Davenport, S. W., & Bergman, S. M. (2012). The shared leadership process in decision-making teams. *Journal of Social Psychology, 152*, 17–42.

Chemers, M. M., & Ayman, R. (Eds.). (1993). *Leadership theory and research: Perspectives and directions*. San Diego, CA: Academic Press.

Cioffi, J. S. (2017). Collaborative care: Using the six thinking hats for decision-making. *International Journal of Nursing Practice, 23*, 1–7.

Cohesion. (n.d.). In *Merriam-Webster's* online dictionary. Retrieved from https://www.merriam-webster.com/dictionary/cohesion

Corey, M. S., Corey, G., & Corey, C. (2018). *Groups: Process and Practice* (10th ed.). Boston, MA: Cengage Learning.

Cox, K., & Steiner, S. (2013). *Self-care in social work: A guide for practitioners, supervisors, and administrators*. Washington, DC: NASW Press.

Davis, D. R., & Jansen, G. G. (1998). Making meaning of Alcoholics Anonymous for social workers: Myths, metaphors, and realities. *Social Work, 43*, 169–182.

De Bono, E. (1999). *Six thinking hats*. New York, NY: Back Bay Books, Little Brown.

Delbecq, A. L., Van den Ven, A. H., & Gustafson, D. H. (1975). *Group techniques for program planning*. Glenview, IL: Scott, Foresman.

Drescher, M. A., Korsgaard, M. A., Welpe, I. M., Picot, A., & Wigand, R. T. (2014). The dynamics of shared leadership: Building trust and enhancing performance. *Journal of Applied Psychology, 99*, 771–783.

Dworsky, A. (2008). The transition to adulthood among youth "aging out" of care: What have we learned? In D. Lindsey & A. Shlonsky (Eds.), *Child welfare research: Advances for practices and policy* (pp. 125–148). New York, NY: Oxford University Press.

Engleberg, I. N., & Wynn, D. R. (2010). *Working in groups* (5th ed.). Boston, MA: Allyn & Bacon.

Fiedler, F. E. (1981). Leadership effectiveness. *American Behavioral Scientist, 24*, 619–632.

Forsyth, D. R. (1999). *Group dynamics* (3rd ed.) Belmont, CA: Wadsworth.

Hersey, P., & Blanchard, K. (1982). *Management of organizational behavior* (4th ed.). Englewood Cliffs, NJ: Prentice-Hall.

Kadushin, A. & Harkness, D. (2002). *Supervision in social work*. New York, NY: Columbia University Press.

Nelson, B. (2011). Setting up a mindfulness meditation group. Retrieved from https://www.mindful.org/setting-up-a-mindfulness-meditation-group/

Osborn, A. F. (1957). *Applied imagination*. New York, NY: Scribner's.

Pike, K. L. (1954). Language in relation to a unified theory of the structure of human behavior. Glendale, CA: Summer Institute of Linguistics.

Patre, S. (2016). Six thinking hats approach to HR analytics. *Southeast Asian Journal of Human Resources, 3*, 107–108.

Shulman, L. (2016). *The skills of helping individuals, families, groups, and communities* (8th ed.). Boston, MA: Cengage Learning.

Sue, D. W. (2016). Race talk and facilitating difficult racial dialogues. *Counseling Today, 58*, 42–47.

Synergy. (n.d.). In *Merriam-Webster*'s online dictionary (11th ed.). Retrieved from https://www.merriam-webster.com/dictionary/synergy

Toseland, R. W., & Rivas, R.F. (2009). *An introduction to group work practice* (6th ed.). Boston, MA: Pearson.

Wang, D., Waldman, D. A., & Zhang, Z. (2014). A meta-analysis of shared leadership and team effectiveness. *Journal of Applied Psychology, 99*, 181–198.

Yalom, I. D. (2005). *Theory and practice of group psychotherapy*. New York, NY: Basic Books.

CREDITS

CHAPTER 8

Social Work Practice with Families

If you cannot get rid of the family skeleton, you may as well make him dance.—GEORGE BERNARD SHAW

O NE OF THE defining features of social work is its focus on helping families. This emphasis has been traced to Mary Richmond, who "built a case for social work serving families in her landmark book, *Social Diagnosis*" (Briar-Lawson & Naccarato, 2016, p. 2). Her Charity Organization Societies (COS) provided outreach and home-based services to families who were victims of poverty caused by the rapid influx of European immigrants into urban areas during the Industrial Revolution. Over subsequent decades, family-centered practitioners in the United States have seen continued struggles with poverty, structural changes in families, and rapidly expanding diversity as it relates to family composition.

According to the Pew Research Center (2015) the "traditional" family (children living with two biological parents on their first marriage) is no longer dominant in the United States, as it was up through the 1960s. Today, 25% of children under the age of 18 live in a single-parent household; 16% live in a blended family (household with a stepparent and step or half siblings). Multipartner fertility has increased substantially (parents who have biological children with more than one partner) (Carlson & Furstenberg, 2006), as has the number of same-gendered couples who are raising children (Mallon, 2013).

Another aspect of diversity relates to the varied ways in which family is defined. While the dominant Anglo-American definition centers on the nuclear family, this is not the case for many other ethnic groups. For example, African Americans typically view family as inclusive of kin and other members of their community; Asians often embrace their ancestors as valued members of their family (McGoldrick, Giordano, & Garcia-Preto, 2005). Children raised in the foster care system may consider biological and/ or foster parents as their primary family. Therefore, practitioners should invite their clients to indicate what family means to them. Next steps in family practice include a focus on identifying family strengths and resiliency.

Family Resiliency

As discussed in Chapter 4, the term *resiliency* refers to one's ability to rebound from adversity. Families embody resilience to the extent that they "absorb the shock of problems and discover strategies to solve them while finding ways to meet the needs of family members and the family unit" (Van Hook, 2016, p. 15). Research has shown that the key components of family resiliency fall into one of three primary categories: belief systems, organizational patterns, and coping processes (p. 17). What follows is a discussion of key elements in all three categories.

Belief Systems

Family beliefs and perceptions influence the manner in which members respond to life events, loss, and stressful circumstances. Beliefs that contribute to resiliency include those that contribute to family cohesion, such as "we deal with hard times together." Such relational beliefs strengthen families by providing a sense of closeness and unity (Beavers & Hampson, 1990; Walsh, 2006). Other perceptions that serve to protect families are the following: "we can trust each other," "we have hope for our future," "we persevere to overcome problems" (Van Hook, 2016). When families lack unity, trust, and hope, intervention may focus on creating the changes needed to shift those perceptions.

Organizational Patterns

Effective family functioning is also furthered by organizational patterns that buffer families from stress and assist members in "bouncing forward, rebounding and reorganizing adaptively to fit new challenges or changed conditions" (Walsh, 2006, p. 85). Consistent rituals and routines provide a stable foundation for families during difficult times. Strong leadership is "crucial for nurturance, protection, and guidance of children, as well as for caring for elders and family members with special needs" (p. 86). Flexibility in response to changing needs also contributes to family resiliency. For example, when one family member is no longer able to fulfill their role and responsibilities due to illness or injury, other members step up and fill in. Ideally, families are able to balance stability with a flexible response to new demands (Van Hook, 2016).

Coping Responses

When faced with a crisis or challenge, resilient families utilize effective coping responses. Those include the mobilization of social supports and resources to manage stress and meet family needs. Clear communication and collaborative problem solving are also important indicators of family strength (Orthner, Jones-Sanpei, & Williamson, 2004). Additionally, a commitment to spending quality time with family provides an important foundation for successful coping. This may take the form of regularly scheduled family activities or everyday moments of quality interaction (Kremer-Sadlik & Paugh, 2007). Families under stress might be encouraged to devote time each day or week to pleasurable family connection.

Family Systems and Structure

The family can be regarded as a system with component parts (subsystems) that interact as they perform critical functions and preserve family balance, or **homeostasis**. When the system is disrupted, it seeks to restore equilibrium and bring the family back to a steady state. For example, in dealing with a family member's mental illness, the system makes adjustments to promote healing and maintain cohesion. The particular ways in which a family problem solves and copes with stress are influenced by family rules, boundaries, and multigenerational transmission of patterns and expectations. Each provide an important focus for family assessment and intervention.

Family Rules

Families establish norms, or **rules**, that "prescribe the rights, duties, and range of appropriate behaviors within the family" (Hepworth, Rooney, Rooney, Strom-Gottfried, & Larsen, 2010, p. 239). Simply put, rules dictate how members should interact and behave. Some rules are *overt* and explicitly stated, such as "smoking, cursing, or hitting are not allowed." Others are *covert*—they may not be clearly communicated, yet they are implicitly understood. Examples of covert rules are "if your father says 'no,' ask your mother," "win every argument," or "always take the blame."

When working with families, it can be important to understand their overt and covert rules. For instance, if there are limited explicit rules governing the behavior of adolescent children, intervention may focus on increasing structure and limit setting in the home. Or, if overt rules are rigidly applied, the family may need assistance in assuming a more flexible approach to changing needs and circumstances. Implicit rules may be surmised by observing the ways in which family members interact. This is of foremost importance when unspoken rules reinforce shame, inferiority, and self-blame.

Renowned expert on family systems and addictive disorders Claudia Black (1981) has shed light on several unspoken rules that support alcoholism and other addictions within families:

- <u>Don't talk</u>: Members understand that they should never talk about family problems with each other or outsiders, thus the secret of dysfunctional behavior is preserved.
- <u>Don't trust</u>: Members learn that they can't trust others inside or outside of the family to keep them safe and free from harm.
- <u>Don't feel</u>: Children learn that they should repress difficult emotions and numb or distract themselves from pain.

Black has devoted her behavioral health treatment and educational seminars to helping young adults recognize such early life messages and begin the process of healing from the trauma associated with living in a substance-abusing family. Go to https://www.claudiablack.com/treatment/claudia-black-young-adult-center/ for further information on her work.

NARRATIVE APPLICATION: Covert Family Rules

Kendall was a 20-year-old college student who did well in her courses but struggled socially. She felt different from others her age and mistrustful of young men, in particular. She had tried dating but had a hard time conversing, especially when asked about her upbringing or family of origin. When upset, Kendall tended to distract herself with solitary activities, such as reading or working out. Eventually the social isolation began to bother her, so she sought services at the campus counseling center.

Kendall's counselor helped her discover the roots of her difficulties connecting with others. She learned that her family had certain unspoken rules that she had internalized—don't trust others, don't talk about your family, push away pain. She reflected on the fact that her father was addicted to pain killers and his behavior was extremely erratic. She and her mother had learned to stay out of his way and avoid talking about his troubles. They just pretended like everything was OK—nothing was worth causing him upset.

Through counseling, Kendall gained insight into her emotional challenges and learned that they are common in families of addiction. At her counselor's suggestion, she began attending an Al-Anon group on campus, a 12-step group for individuals who had been negatively affected by the addiction of a close friend or family member. There she found companionship with others who had similar backgrounds.

Family Boundaries

The concept of **boundaries** refers to the invisible lines of demarcation between the family and its environment, as well as between subsystems within the family unit. *External boundaries* regulate transactions between the family unit and other systems, such as schools, workplace, neighborhood, social services, law enforcement, and other protective services. When these boundaries are solid and impermeable, efforts by outsiders to enter the system are rebuked. For instance, a newly immigrated family may resist external influences that are seen as a threat to their cultural traditions and values. Conversely, when boundaries are permeable, information and resources are more freely exchanged with other systems.

Family practice often focuses on the *internal boundaries* between subsystems of the family (e.g., parental, sibling, grandparenting subsystems). These boundaries also vary in their flexibility and permeability. Founder of structural family therapy Salvador Minuchin (1974) believed that internal family boundaries lie upon a continuum ranging from **diffuse** to **rigid**. Diffuse boundaries allow for a great deal of involvement across subsystems (e.g., parent and child), which, when extreme, can lead to enmeshment and emotional dependency. The focus of intervention with an enmeshed family might be to clarify boundaries and allow for an age-appropriate level of autonomy and independence. At the other extreme, rigid boundaries may lead to disengagement among family members and isolation. Intervention to address rigid boundaries might include efforts to enhance communication and connection across subsystems.

It is important to recognize however, that cultures vary widely with regard to expectations concerning subsystem boundaries. In some cultural groups, diffuse or rigid boundaries are not considered problematic. This point is underscored by efforts to reframe the function of the "parentified" child in diverse families. This term has traditionally been used in referring to children who have entered the parental system by taking on excessive responsibilities in the home. It is now understood that, in some cultural and socioeconomic groups, parental responsibilities are delegated to children out of necessity. This should be considered functional unless the assumption of responsibility poses a threat to the child's health, safety, and development (Hepworth et al., 2010).

NARRATIVE APPLICATION: Restructuring Family Boundaries

Tyler grew up in a middle-class household with very strict parents. He rebelled against their rules from an early age and has had a strained relationship with them ever since. He began using drugs as a teen and "hanging with the wrong crowd." For the past several months, he has been residing in a work release facility following a conviction for drug sales and violation of probation. Tyler has a 13-year-old son, Jake, who lives with his mother and maternal grandmother. Distressed by reports that Jake had begun engaging in delinquent behavior (truancy and stealing), Tyler asked to be included in his son's family counseling.

Upon meeting the counselor, Tyler acknowledged that he had always been a disengaged parent. He was permissive with Jake, as he didn't want to adopt the kind of rigid rules that had been imposed upon him as a youth. Tyler wanted to strengthen his role as a parent, even though contact between he and Jake was limited, at least for the time being. Structural family work focused on increasing communication between Tyler and Jake through visits and phone calls. Tyler was also provided the opportunity to move into the parental subsystem, along with Jake's mother and grandmother. He participated in creating family rules and consequences for his son, and consistently praised Jake when he complied. Based on these efforts, a foundation of trust was established between father and son; Jake responded favorably to his father's increased involvement.

Multigenerational Transmission of Family Patterns

Another approach to family structure uses a multigenerational lens that recognizes family risk and protective factors that have been passed from one generation to the text. Gathering information about these factors is facilitated through the use of a **genogram**, a graphic representation of the extended family over time. Developed by McGoldrick and colleagues (1999), the genogram is rooted in systems theory and views family relationships as "highly reciprocal, patterned, and repetitive" (p. 7). The graphic tool clarifies the position a person holds within the family system, how their role is intertwined with family dynamics, and how it guides patterns that are re-created in subsequent generations. The genogram is said to "reveal aspects of the family that have been hidden from family members-secrets of their history" (p. 4).

McGoldrick's approach uses varying shapes and lines to represent family members and their connection to others, including non-blood kin. Males are represented by squares and females by circles; an X is placed inside the symbol to indicate that a family member is deceased. Additional information can be added to the family tree, including ages, dates, medical or behavioral health problems, occupations, strengths, and the nature of emotional relationships among family members. Genograms can become very complex when all partnerships, divorces, separations, remarriages, and children are included. Thus, for the sake of clarity, choices must be made as to the level of detail needed within each diagram.

Genograms serve a variety of purposes in social work practice. When created with family members, they provide a unique method for joining and engagement. They are also utilized to elicit cultural stories and to help families recognize the historical context of their current strengths and struggles. Genograms are often incorporated into case presentations, as they provide a visual reference as to who is who within the family and their connection to other members.

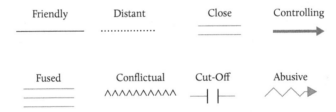

FIGURE 8.1. Relationship Lines Used in the Genogram.

NARRATIVE APPLICATION: Use of the Genogram in Family Practice

The Carter household includes two parents (Harry and Kristen) and three children (Jenny, Melody, and Rachel). This nuclear family is connected to the extended family of each parent. Harry's father (construction worker) and grandfather (logger) died from alcoholism; his mother and grandmother were both very artistic; his sister struggles with alcohol abuse. Kristen has a conflicted relationship with her mother and is emotionally cut off from her sister. She has a close relationship with her father, who divorced Kristen's mother 10 years ago and married his new wife 5 years ago.

Kristen and Harry are in conflict over their differing approaches to parenting. Harry spends a lot of time with the girls, and Kristen feels left out. She is also angry with Harry for allowing his sister to visit when she is intoxicated. With help from their family counselor, Harry and Kristen created the genogram below. It depicts the transmission of alcoholism, family strengths, and strained mother-daughter relationships. Kristen is determined to reverse this latter pattern in her relationships with her daughters. Harry began to understand the co-dependency pattern he picked up from his family and how it contributes to his difficulty setting limits with his sister. They both saw the passage of strengths from their extended family members to their children, assets they wanted to nurture.

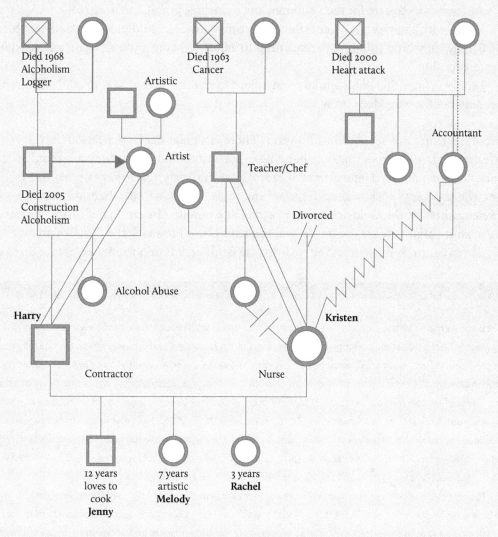

FIGURE 8.2. Carter Family Genogram Example.

Family Life Cycle

Families go through developmental stages, just as individuals do. Thus, knowing which stage a family occupies can provide useful guidance for family practitioners. Carter and McGoldrick (1988) theorized that families move through six development stages, each of which involves particular tasks and challenges:

- <u>Unattached young adult</u>: the individual seeks to establish independence from family of origin and establish a differentiated sense of self

- <u>New couple</u>: they must realign relationships with their family of origin and learn how to compromise and care for one another
- <u>Family with young children</u>: the couple needs to make adjustments in their management of time and resources to care for their children and to include grandparenting roles
- <u>Family with adolescents</u>: parents must accommodate their children's increased need for autonomy
- <u>Family launching children</u>: parents need to adjust to being a couple again and renegotiate their relationship
- <u>Family in later life</u>: older adults must adjust to multiple losses and to adult children being the center of the extended family

These stages are not set in stone, however. There is a great deal of variation in the progression of the life cycle in families today due to changing expectations and norms for young adults, couples, and parents, and older adults (Hepworth et al., 2010). Cultural groups also vary in the "timing of life cycle phases, the tasks appropriate at each phase, and their traditions, rituals, and ceremonies that mark life cycle traditions" (McGoldrick, 1992, p. 437). For example, the timing of births, norms regarding when/if adult children leave the home, and the rituals used to mark the death of an older adult vary widely across cultures. When working with diverse families, it is important to embrace these variations.

HIGHLIGHT 8.1: The Transition to Adulthood for Homeless Youth

Most cultures mark the transition from childhood to adulthood with recognition, acknowledgement, and celebration (e.g., high school graduation, coming-of-age ceremonies). Yet homeless and runaway youth are typically not afforded this privilege. In fact, most are ill-equipped to navigate the tasks associated with their phase of the family life cycle. While they may have asserted their independence from their foster, adoptive, or biological family, most struggle with the process of establishing a solid sense of identity. Moreover, many become legal adults without having achieved the developmental milestones of adolescence (Zajac, Sheidow, & Davis, 2015). Homeless young adults are often plagued by serious mental health disorders yet fall through the cracks of the public mental health system. Research has shown that utilization of mental health services drops by almost half when youth reach the age of 18 or 19; rates remain low up to the age of 25 years (Pottick, Bilder, Vander Stoep, Warner, & Alvarez, 2008).

To address this challenge, Substance Abuse and Mental Health Services Administration (SAMHSA) (2014) launched the Emerging Adults Initiative of 2009; it is aimed at supporting transition-aged youth who have a serious mental health disorder. Grants are provided to assist states in providing needed supports and services for these vulnerable young adults. The overall goal is to transform the system so that it meets the developmental needs of this population. There are three main areas for development:

- Collaboration between adult- and child-serving systems
- Policy development that is system wide and sustains youth-in-transition services
- Adoption of research-informed practice that may include trauma-informed care, peer support, and supported housing, education, and employment

This initiative recognizes the importance of blending direct services with a macro-level focus on policy development and system change. Go to: https://www.samhsa.gov/samhsaNewsLetter/Volume_22_Number_3/successful_transition/ for further information.

Family Communication

When family conflict and other presenting problems are rooted in ineffective patterns of interaction, a focus on family communication is warranted. Prominent social work clinician and communications researcher Virginia Satir (1972) theorized that family members utilize unclear and incongruent communication as a way of masking their fear of rejection. She argued that when under stress, troubled families send double-level messages wherein their words are inconsistent with their nonverbal communication. For example, a person's tone of voice and body language might negate the stated message, "I don't mind." Satir's work was devoted to helping families communicate more congruently without blaming, placating, or distracting in response to family challenges or conflict. Her work continues to guide family practice today.

The first step in communications work with families is to explore the nature of their interactions and how they convey meaning to one another. Some of the following questions may be helpful in this regard:

- How do you let one another know when you are happy with something they have done?
- How do you let each other know when you are angry? Do you raise your voice? Throw things or hit? Use derogatory names? State clearly what is bothering you without blaming?
- How do you communicate emotions, such as sadness or disappointment?
- How do you use humor with one another? Is it used to hurt or to help?

Observing families interact may also provide clues as to the barriers that interfere with healthy communication. When asked to discuss an emotionally charged issue, family members may interrupt one another, react defensively to feedback, and blame each other for family problems. When and if they are open to learning new strategies for communication, the social worker may assist them in practice skills in active listening, assertive communication, and validation.

Teaching Validation

One of the most powerful and effective communication skills is that of **validation.** This skill goes beyond active listening or reflection of a family member's words—it conveys a genuine understanding of why that person feels, thinks, and behaves the way they do, given their circumstances. The use of validation does not require one to approve of the behavior of the other person; it does, however, require recognition of the validity of their experience. For example, a mother may not agree with her daughter's choice to leave school without permission, but she may understand why her daughter did so, given the anxiety she felt about an upcoming class presentation. This mother can relay both her concern about the truancy and her appreciation for the reasons behind it. As a result, her daughter will be more inclined to take her mother's concern seriously because she feels heard and understood.

Marsha Linehan (1997) has identified six levels of validation:

- Listening, observing, engaging in reciprocal interaction
- Accurately reflecting the person's thoughts, feelings, and assumptions
- Articulating the unverbalized meanings and emotions
- Understanding the person's behavior in light of their history and biology
- Recognizing behavior as reasonable in the moment, even when it's not effective
- Radical genuineness, the recognizing and confirming the worth of the person as they are

NARRATIVE APPLICATION: Promoting Validation Among Family Members

Alex worked at a group home for teenage boys who had problems related to substance abuse. Over the last 3 months, he had been counseling Andrew, who had a history of heavy drinking and drug use to ease stress and cope with his anger related to his turbulent upbringing. His father left the home when Andrew was 5 years of age. Since that time, his mother, Cindy, has had a string of boyfriends, few of whom Andrew liked. The last one (Justin) had been physically abusive to both Andrew and Cindy, prompting the teen to run away and live for a period of time on the streets before being placed in the group home. Andrew wanted to reunify with his mother but was apprehensive; although Justin was long gone, Andrew worried that his mother would take him back.

Alex prepared Andrew to talk to his mother about his concerns in a calm manner, while also validating her stress as a single mother. Prior to the family session, Alex met with Cindy to prepare her for this conversation, as well. He listened to her concerns about Andrew returning home and suggested that she relay those to her son in their meeting. Alex explained that it would be important for her to hear Andrew's worries as well, even when it became hard to do so. He assured Cindy that he would support her in this process and then helped her understand the skill of validation.

The tension was obvious as the family session began, so Alex used a bit of humor to lighten the mood; he also acknowledged both Andrew and Cindy for taking an interest in improving their relationship and stated that it was clear that they both cared about each other. Alex created some structure for their conversation about things they liked about each other and concerns they had about living together again. When Andrew began talking about his anger related to Justin, he and Cindy both became defensive.

> Andrew: "Mom, I know you tried hard, but I hated Justin. He was an ass and mean to both of us. I would stay away so I wouldn't have to look at him. I couldn't take it when he beat on you. Now he is out of jail, and I am the one living in a group home. How could you let that happen?"
>
> Cindy: "You are in a group home because you started using drugs and took off. That's not my fault. I am terrified that you will start using again and ruin your life."
>
> Alex knew that he had to interrupt and redirect their conversation.
>
> Alex: "I know this is difficult to talk about, so let's revisit validation and think of ways we can use the skill to better understand each other. Cindy, what did you pick up on about how Alex felt when Justin was in the home? Please talk directly to him."
>
> Cindy took a long deep breath and faced her son.
>
> Cindy: "I know you were upset at the way he treated us, and it hurt you to see him hurt me. I am sorry about that. I am not happy that you ran away, but I understand why you did."
>
> Tears came to Andrew's eyes and he nodded his head.
>
> Alex: "Now it's your turn, Andrew. What is your mom worried about and why? Please talk to her about this."
>
> Andrew: "You are worried that I will keep using drugs and end up a deadbeat, like my dad."
>
> Cindy: "Yes, your dad had some good points, but he was an addict and I am afraid that you will go down that path too. I want you to have a happy life."
>
> Alex: "You both did a great job validating. Now, what can we put in place to help manage your worries?"

In this narrative, we see that Alex not only explained validation to Andrew and Cindy but coached them in applying this skill. He was fairly directive in his approach so as to prevent arguing and defensiveness. Over the following month, he continued to help them practice this critical communication skill as they prepared for and began the reunification process.

Parenting Style

When practitioners are working with families with children, the parenting style of the caregiver(s) may also be an important area of focus and intervention. To guide such efforts, Diana Baumrind (1966) articulated three styles of parenting: permissive, authoritarian, and authoritative. **Permissive parents** are described as indulgent in response to their child's impulses and desires. They are very accepting of their children but make few demands for responsible behavior or compliance with household rules. Conversely, **authoritarian parents** enforce obedience to a rigid set of standards for behavior (often through the use of punishment). The preservation of order is valued to a greater extent than negotiation or warmth in the parent-child relationship. **Authoritative parenting** is considered by Baumrind as the ideal. When using this style, the caregiver enforces reasonable standards for behavior, shares the reasoning behind rules, and allows for verbal give and take while maintaining a healthy bond and connection with their children.

Studies have revealed the impact that parenting styles have on child behavior and development. Children of permissive parents are often sociable but may exhibit poor impulse control and low academic performance (Pattock-Peckam & Morgan-Lopez, 2006). Youth raised by authoritarian parents tend to have low self-confidence and higher rates of aggressive behavior and substance abuse (Slicker, 1998) or they may engage in hostile withdrawal or rebelliousness (Baumrind, 1966). Finally, children of authoritative parents have the most favorable adjustment, socially, academically, and behaviorally (Slicker, 1998).

Some parents respond well to education about the effects of these varying styles of parenting. Others may need to see positive results from a shift in parenting style before they are willing to commit to long-term change. Shifts encouraged for permissive parents typically involve increasing structure and discipline in the household. Interventions applied with the authoritarian parent may focus on strengthening the parent-child relationship and practicing firm yet flexible approaches to discipline. Authoritative parenting skills are recognized, supported, and reinforced.

NARRATIVE APPLICATION: Addressing Parenting Style

Genie is the single parent of 8-year-old Sam. She struggles with parenting, as her ex-husband (Sam's father) was the primary disciplinarian before their divorce. Genie is concerned about Sam's increased noncompliance in her home. For several months, he has been refusing to do chores or complete his homework, despite her repeated requests and lectures. His constant arguing began taking a toll on Genie, so she adopted a permissive approach, letting him have his way and do as he pleased. Her counselor, Lynne, was helping Genie learn how to set effective limits with her son. They explored rewards Genie could offer to encourage responsible behavior, but Genie had little extra income for anything tangible. Yet, she realized that Sam had constant access to his video games—he played them for hours each day. Lynne encouraged her to require Sam to complete his homework before he would be allowed to play his games.

Next session, Genie looked forlorn. She had set the limit for Sam that they had discussed, but the intensity of his arguing had increased! She seriously doubted that this plan would work. Lynne explained to her how an **extinction burst** operates. Genie learned that when a rule is enforced for the first time, it is common for the child to test the newly imposed limit; therefore, problematic behavior often gets worse before it gets better. She realized that she would have to wait it out until Sam's intense arguing and noncompliance was extinguished.

One week later, Genie began to see positive results from her shift in parenting practices. Sam had discovered that his previous attempts at wearing down his mother with defiance were no longer effective. He began doing his homework in the afternoons and then requesting (not demanding) use of his video games. This small change gave Genie the confidence to enforce rules related to household chores, as well.

Family Culture

Every family can be said to have its own unique culture based on the intersecting identities of family members. These identities shape the way families operate, make meaning of life events, and resolve challenges. As discussed above, some family patterns are grounded in beliefs and expectations that have been passed from one generation to the next. Ethnic heritage may guide family roles, customs, and traditions. Language barriers or experiences with discrimination can influence the family's comfort level in communicating with outsiders to access needed supports and services.

It is a mistake, however, to assume that a family embraces certain attitudes and beliefs based on their ethnic affiliation, as each cultural group is very diverse. For example, a newly immigrated Hispanic family may have very different views and values than one with the same heritage that has resided in the United States for several decades. One family with same-gendered parents may have adopted children, while another might include the biological children of one parent from a previous relationship. Despite the immense within-group variations, some guidelines can be helpful in preparing social workers to work effectively with diverse families. This section will cover ways in which various cultural groups may cope with stress, define family roles, understand illness, and approach the healing process.

Stress and Coping

All families encounter stress, but those who belong to a cultural group that has been marginalized have a particularly heavy load to manage. Poverty exists for many Latino, African American, Native American, and rural families (Delgado, 2007; Conger, et al., 2002; Conger & Elder, 1994; Yellow Bird, 2001). Historical trauma has plagued Native people of America, most of whom have suffered from many years of cultural degradation. Some Asian American and Hispanic families have endured war-related trauma in their home country prior to immigrating to the United States. Acculturation stress is experienced by many of these immigrant families as they struggle to navigate between their traditional culture and the American way of life. Institutional racism is a significant threat to African American families (Chambers, 2011); stigma, as well as the lack of legal legitimacy poses on-going difficulty for gay and lesbian couples.

Coping strategies adopted in response to these stressors provide a window into the cultural assets that contribute to family resilience. Strong kinship bonds and extended family connections are valuable sources of support for many African American and Latino families (Hines & Boyd-Franklin, 2005). For most Asian Americans, the value of family is evident in the obligation to care for elders and the reverence devoted to ancestors "going back to the beginning of time" (McGoldrick et al., 2005, p. 24). Social support accessed through family, peers, and significant others is valued by many LGBT families and has been found to decrease distress in adolescents living in these households (McConnell, Birkett, & Mustanski, 2016).

Religion is another significant source of support for many marginalized families. Many Latino families rely upon the Catholic church for spiritual and social support; others belong to evangelical and Pentecostal religious communities (Shorkey, Garcia, & Windsor, 2010). While African-Americans belong to a variety of religious groups, the largest affiliation is with the Baptist church (Hines & Boyd-Franklin, 2005). This connection offers a strong spiritual base and social activities for family members of all ages. Depending on their country of origin, Asian families may practice Buddhism, Hinduism, Christianity, Taoism, or Islamic faith. Many Native Americans find strength through their spiritual connection to Mother Earth. Understanding these associations is vital for the family practitioner, as they may be central to a family's cultural identity.

Family Roles

Family roles can be thought of as the parts members play as they contribute to family structure and functioning. Culture influences the expectations the family has for certain role assignments. For example, in the traditional Anglo-American family, the male is expected to be the primary breadwinner and devote himself to maximizing the family's financial status; it is assumed that the female will care for the children and household. These norms have shifted over the last several decades, however, as more women have sought work outside the home. African American women, on the other hand, have historically worked outside the home and grandparents have played an important role in parenting the children (Hines & Boyd-Franklin, 2005). In the traditional Latino family, mothers tend to establish strong bonds with their children, while fathers assume a more authoritarian role (Van Hook, 2016). Asian American children are expected to honor their parents and bring pride versus shame to the family; older adults are charged with passing on their history and language to the younger generation, thus preserving culturally based values (Strumpf, Gicksman, Goldenberg-Glen, Fox, & Logue, 2001). Military families of all ethnicities must adopt flexible roles to accommodate the deployment of an active duty parent. These are just a few illustrations of varying role assignments across diverse families.

Illness and Healing

Families of differing cultural groups may also have divergent views about the causes of illness, as well as the steps that must be taken to advance healing. The **disease-explanatory model** adopted by mainstream U.S. medicine views the human body as a machine that must be repaired when it malfunctions (Fee, 2018). Lab tests and imaging techniques are used to detect pathology; treatment is prescribed that might include surgery, physical therapy, or medication.

Other cultures abide by an explanatory model that views *illness as the product of imbalance.* For instance, traditional Chinese medicine seeks to preserve equilibrium between yin (cold) and yang (hot) forces. Treatment is focused on restoring this balance through the use of select foods, herbal remedies, acupuncture, or meditation. Similarly, the traditional Mexican heath care system classifies an illness as hot or cold. A hot illness, such as diabetes, needs a cold treatment to restore balance, such as cold food and herbs (Fee, 2018). The Mexican approach to healing also assumes that a traumatic experience can cause *susto*, or loss of the soul. Treatment is provided by a *curandero* who conducts healing rituals that include the use of fresh herbs, massage, prayer, and the channeling of supernatural agents (Torres & Sawyer, 2005).

When working with a family that embraces indigenous healing practices, it is important that the social worker demonstrate respect for the client's holistic approach to healthcare. Sue, Rasheed, and Rasheed (2015) further contend that practitioners must avoid "equating difference with deviance" (p. 331) and should recognize the value in partnering with indigenous healers when serving diverse families. Spirituality is increasingly understood as a legitimate and essential focus in multicultural social work practice.

HIGHLIGHT 8.2: Family Practice with African Americans

When working with African Americans, social workers must appreciate the historical and systemic factors that contribute to the stress faced by family members. According to the U.S. Census Bureau (Fontenot, Semega, & Kollar, 2018), 21.2% of African American men, women, and children live below the poverty level, compared to just 10.7% of Caucasian Americans. Economic strain can take a huge toll on family stability, marital relationships, and parenting (Van Hook, 2016, p. 120). Another challenge concerns the negative stereotypes about Americans of African descent that have persisted past the end of slavery, along with blatant and more subtle instances of racism and discrimination. Given these factors, it is understandable that Black family members may harbor mistrust of White providers of health, mental health, and social services. To counteract this concern, a non-Black practitioner should display a great deal of respect for the resiliency of African American families.

While some Black individuals view mental health services as intended for "crazy people," that perception is beginning to change. According to Hines and Boyd-Franklin (2005), African Americans are now utilizing these services in greater numbers than ever before, with the most common presenting problems being "poor school adjustment, acting-out behavior, depression, 'nervous breakdown' or psychotic behaviors, drug addiction, and alcoholism" (p. 96). These authors recommend a multisystems approach to addressing these challenges, one that begins with problem solving related to the presenting concern. The practitioner then explores the family's connection to individuals and groups within their social network, such as extended family, non-blood kin and friends, church and community resources, and social services agencies. Genograms are often used to gather information about extended family members. Next, the family is encouraged to critically examine their broad social network to identify its strengths and the contributions it makes to presenting problems. Boyd-Franklin (1989) cautions, however, that an alliance of trust must be established before doing this work; otherwise, the family may feel that the practitioner is "prying into their business" (p. 143). Once information is obtained at all multisystem levels, interventions are used help the family mobilize needed resources and supports.

HIGHLIGHT 8.3: Family-Focused Practice with LGBTQ Youth

Lesbian, gay, bisexual, transgender, and questioning/queer (LGBTQ) youth are disproportionately represented in the foster care system. Some enter out-of-home care after running away from home or being forced to leave their families of origin due to conflicts concerning their sexual orientation or gender identity (National Center for Lesbian Rights, 2006). Rejection from parents predicts poor mental health outcomes for lesbian, gay, and bisexual youth—they are 5.9 times more likely to report high levels of depression and 5.4 times more likely to disclose suicide attempts than peers who received parental acceptance (Ryan, Huebner, Diaz, & Sanchez, 2009).

Family-focused practice with youth who are coming out as LGBTQ may serve to further family preservation, mental health, and well-being. A practice guide offered by the Minnesota Department of Human Services (2013) recommends that practitioners aid these families by doing the following:

- Acknowledging that the struggle family members experience with the coming out process is normal
- Assuring parents that it often takes time to reach full acceptance of this new information
- Exploring the main concern of parents with respect to the child's orientation and identity

- Educating parents that sexual orientation and gender identity are not a choice or indication of a mental disorder; conversion therapy that is intended to change sexual orientation is not successful and often results in psychological harm (American Academy of Child & Adolescent Psychiatry, 2018).
- Discussing parents' religious or moral objections to their child's orientation/identity; if possible, they may be linked to LGBTQ-friendly resources in their religious community
- Encouraging families to access support from their local chapter of Parents, Friends, and Families of Lesbians and Gays (PFLAG)

This guide can be found at the Minnesota Department of Human Services website (https://edocs.dhs.state.mn.us/lfserver/Public/DHS-6500-ENG). Family videos can be purchased from the Family Acceptance Project at San Francisco State University (https://familyproject.sfsu.edu/family-videos).

Self-Care for the Family Practitioner

A common challenge faced by social workers engaged in family practice is countertransference. It emerges as the practitioner projects their own emotions and unresolved conflicts onto their client and responds to them with either avoidance or over-involvement. Self-care involves accessing supervisory support to process these reactions and consider ways to manage bias that may result from this dynamic. With supervisory guidance, countertransference can become a useful tool for enhancing the self-awareness of the social worker.

NARRATIVE APPLICATION: Countertransference and Self-Care

Megan was a clinical social worker at a community counseling center. She had been providing individual counseling to her 15-year-old client, Misty, who was depressed and had a great deal of anger toward her mother, Pam. Megan set up a family session that included both mother and daughter to explore the roots of their conflicted relationship. When they arrived for the session, uneasiness filled the meeting room. Pam did most of the talking, while Misty appeared cut off and withdrawn. What troubled Megan the most was that Pam was quite critical of her daughter and seemed to have limited understanding of her emotional struggles. When Megan asked her what she liked about Misty, Pam redirected the conversation back to her own distress and plight as a single mother.

Following the family session, Megan sought out support from her supervisor and shared her extreme dislike for Pam and resistance to setting up another family session. The supervisor asked her to consider why this mother triggered such strong emotions in her. After some thought, Megan was able to put the pieces together. She realized that the dynamics between Pam and Misty were strikingly similar to those that existed between her and her own mother. Consequently, she had sympathy for Megan and intense anger toward Pam. Her supervisor was very supportive and suggested that she include a co-therapist in the next session to help manage her countertransference. Megan accepted the offer and was grateful for the time given to process her emotions. From that point on, she made an increased effort to connect with Pam and help her improve her relationship with Misty. She also decided it was time to let go of her resentment toward her own mother, as it was no longer serving her.

SUMMARY

This chapter introduces basic concepts and techniques for direct practice with families. It presented theories defining various aspects of family functioning, include resiliency, systems, life cycle, communication, parenting style, and culture. Material was also offered related to family rules, boundaries, and the use of genograms to assess family structure. Illustrations and applications highlighted variations in family beliefs, stressors, roles, healing practices, and coping strategies often seen in diverse cultural groups. Self-care for the family practitioner was devoted to the management of countertransference, a dynamic that frequently emerges in family practice. This chapter, along with Chapters 6 and 7, provide a foundation for the focus on specialized practice models to follow.

KEY TERMS

Disease-explanatory model

Extinction burst

Family boundaries (diffuse and rigid)

Family roles

Family rules

Genogram

Homeostasis

Parenting style (permissive, authoritarian, authoritative)

Validation

DISCUSSION QUESTIONS

1. Why is it important to begin family work with a focus on resiliency?

2. What overt and covert rules were adopted by your family(ies) of origin?

3. How might you go about teaching validation skills to a family?

SKILL DEVELOPMENT ACTIVITIES

1. Create a genogram of your extended family (three generations).

2. Watch the training webinar entitled *Cultural Beliefs and Practices,* as moderated by Caroline Fee and sponsored by San Jose State University and the Stanford Geriatric Training Center (http://www.sjsu.edu/at/atn/webcasting/events/gerontology/index.html). Share what you have learned that you found most interesting and informative.

3. Read the practice guide for working with LGBTQ youth produced by the Minnesota Department of Human Services (https://edocs.dhs.state.mn.us/lfserver/Public/DHS-6500-ENG). What did you learn that you will incorporate into your practice?

REFERENCES

American Academy of Child & Adolescent Psychiatry (2018). Conversion therapy. Retrieved from https://www.aacap.org/AACAP/Policy_Statements/2018/Conversion_Therapy.aspx

Beavers, W., & Hampson, R. (1990). *Successful families: Assessment and interventions.* New York, NY: Norton.

Briar-Lawson, K., & Naccarato, T. (2013). Family services. In *Encyclopedia of Social Work.* Retrieved from http://socialwork.oxfordre.com

Baumrind, D. (1966). Effects of authoritarian parental control on child behavior. *Child Development, 37,* 887–907.

Black, C. (1981). *It will never happen to me.* New York, NY: Random House.

Boyd-Franklin, N. (1989). *Black families in therapy: A multisystems approach.* New York, NY: Guilford Press.

Carlson, M. J., & Furstenberg, F. F. (2006). The prevalence and correlates of multi-partnered fidelity among urban U.S. parents. *Journal of Marriage & Family, 68,* 718–732.

Carter, B., & McGoldrick, M. (Eds.). (1988). *The changing life cycle: A framework for family therapy* (2nd ed.). New York, NY: Gardner Press.

Chambers, C. L. (2011). *Drug laws and institutional racism: The story told by the Congressional record.* El Paso, TX: LFB Scholarly.

Conger, R., & Elder, G. (1994). *Families in troubled times: Adapting to change in rural America.* New York, NY: Aldine de Gruyter.

Conger, R., Wallace, L., Sun, Y., Simons, R., McLoyd, V., & Brody, G. (2002). Economic pressure in African-American families: A replication and extension of the model. *Developmental Psychology, 38,* 179-193.

Delgado, M. (2007). *Social work with Latinos: A cultural assets paradigm.* New York, NY: Oxford University Press.

Fee, C. (2018). Cultural health beliefs and practices. [Webinar]. In *Cultural Competence when Working with Older Adults* series. Retrieved from http://www.sjsu.edu/at/atn/webcasting/events/gerontology/index.html

Fontenot, K., Semega, J., & Kollar, M. (2018). *U.S. Census Bureau, Current Population Reports* (P60-263). Income and Poverty in the United States: 2017, U.S. Government Printing Office, Washington, DC.

Hepworth, D. H., Rooney, R. H., Rooney, G. D., Strom-Gottfried, K., & Larsen, J. (2010). *Direct social work practice: Theory and skills.* Belmont, CA: Brooks/Cole, Cengage Learning.

Hines, P. M., & Boyd-Franklin, N. (2005). African American families. In M. McGoldrick, J. Giordano, & N. Garcia-Preto (2005). *Ethnicity and family therapy* (pp. 87-100). New York, NY: Guilford Press.

Kremer-Sadlik, T., & Paugh, A. L. (2007). Everyday moments: Finding "quality time" in American working families. *Time and Society, 16,* 287-308.

Linehan, M. M. (1997). Validation and psychotherapy. In A. Bohart & L. Greenberg (Eds.), *Empathy reconsidered: New directions in psychotherapy.* Washington, DC: American Psychological Association.

Mallon, G. P. (2013). Lesbian, gay, bisexual, and transgender (LGBT) families and partnering. In *Encyclopedia of Social Work.* Retrieved from http://socialwork.oxfordre.com/

McConnell, E. A., Birkett, M., & Mustanski, B. (2016). Families matter: Social support and mental health trajectories among lesbian, gay, bisexual and transgender youth. *Journal of Adolescent Health, 59,* 674-680.

McGoldrick, M. (1992). Ethnicity and the family life cycle. *Family Business Review, 5,* 437-459.

McGoldrick, M., Gerson, R., & Shellenberger, S. (1999). *Genograms: Assessment and Intervention* (2nd ed.). New York, NY: W. W. Norton.

McGoldrick, M., Giordano, J., & Garcia-Preto, N. (2005). *Ethnicity and family therapy.* New York, NY: Guilford Press.

Minnesota Department of Human Services. (2013). *Working with lesbian, gay, bisexual, transgender, and questioning/queer youth.* (DHS-6500-ENG). Retrieved from https://edocs.dhs.state.mn.us/lfserver/Public/DHS-6500-ENG

Minuchin, S. (1974). *Families and family therapy.* Cambridge, MA: Harvard University Press.

National Center for Lesbian Rights. (2006). *LGBTQ youth in the foster care system.* Retrieved from http://www.nclrights.org/wp-content/uploads/2013/07/LGBTQ_Youth_In_Foster_Care_System.pdf

Orthner, D. K., Jones-Sanpei, H., & Williamson, S. (2004). The resilience and strengths of low-income families. *Family Relations, 53,* 159-167.

Pattock-Peckam, J. A., & Morgan-Lopez, A. A. (2006). College drinking behaviors: Mediational links between parenting styles, impulse control, and alcohol-related outcomes. *Psychology of Addictive Behaviors, 20,* 117-125.

Pew Research Center. (2015). *Parenting in America: Outlook, worries, aspirations are strongly linked to financial situation.* Retrieved from http://www.pewresearch.com

Pottick, K. J., Bilder, S., Vander Stoep, A., Warner, L. A., & Alvarez, M. F. (2008). U.S. patterns of mental health service utilization for transition age youth and young adults. *Journal of Behavioral Health Services and Research, 35,* 373-389.

Ryan, C., Huebner, D., Diaz, R.M., & Sanchez, D. (2009). Family rejection as a predictor of negative health outcomes in white and Latino gay and bisexual young adults. *Pediatrics, 123,* 346-352.

Satir, V. (1972). *Peoplemaking.* Palo Alto, CA: Science and Behavior Books.

Shorkey, C., Garcia, E., & Windsor, I. (2010). Spirituality as a strength in the Latino community. In R. Furman & N. Negi (Eds.), *Social work practice with Latinos: Key issues and emerging themes* (pp. 85-101). Chicago, IL: Lyceum Books.

Slicker, E. K. (1998). Relationship of parenting style to behavioral adjustment in graduating high school seniors. *Journal of Youth and Adolescence, 27,* 345-372.

Strumpf, N. E., Gicksman, A., Goldenberg-Glen, R. S., Fox, R., & Logue, E. H. (2001). Caregiver and elder experiences of Cambodian, Vietnamese, Soviet Jewish, and Ukrainian refugees. *International Journal on Aging and Human Development, 53,* 233-252.

Substance Abuse and Mental Health Services Administration. (2014). From youth to adulthood: Offering hope. *SAMSHA News, 22.* Retrieved from https://www.samhsa.gov/samhsaNewsLetter/Volume_22_Number_3/successful_transition/

Sue, D. W., Rasheed, M. N., & Rasheed, J. M. (2015). *Multicultural social work practice: A competency-based approach to diversity and social justice.* Hoboken, NJ: John Wiley & Sons.

Torres, E. C., & Sawyer, T. L. (2005). *Curandero: A life in American folk healing.* Albuquerque: University of New Mexico Press.

Van Hook, M. P. (2016). *Social work practice with families: A resiliency-based approach.* New York, NY: Oxford University Press.

Walsh, F. (2006). *Strengthening family resilience* (2nd ed.). New York, NY: Guilford Press.

Yellow Bird, M. (2001). Critical values and first Nations People. In R. Fong & S. Puruto (Eds.), *Culturally competent practice: Skills, interventions, and evaluations* (pp. 61-74). Boston, MA: Allyn & Bacon.

Zajac, K. I., Sheidow, A. J., & Davis, M. (2015). Juvenile justice, mental health, and the transition to adulthood: A review of service system involvement and unmet needs. *Child and Youth Services Review, 56,* 139-148.

CHAPTER 9

Models of Practice and Specialized Skills

Change is the end result of all true learning. —LEO BUSCAGLIA

Social work embraces a variety of evidence-based models of intervention, defined as those that have been empirically validated (Chambless, 1999). These research-supported approaches are consistent with social work values and have been adopted across a wide range of human services settings. Because they represent divergence from practice based on tradition, common sense, or "gut level" reactions to client needs, their use requires thorough training and coaching in the application of principles and techniques. This chapter will introduce several of the most commonly used evidence-based change strategies: motivational interviewing, solution-focused practice, the narrative approach, and cognitive-behavioral intervention.

Motivational Interviewing

The motivational interviewing (MI) model was born out of the recognition that many clients seen by social workers are not ready to admit to problems, much less tackle the process of making change. Some have been mandated by the courts to receive services due to difficulties associated with addiction or other problematic behaviors. Many more wrestle with a great deal of ambivalence about giving up old habits or troubled relationships. The use of motivational interviewing allows the social worker to avoid power struggles with these so-called resistant clients by conveying compassion and a genuine appreciation for their absolute worth as human beings. The underlying spirit of this model is devoted to partnership, acceptance, and honoring each person's autonomy. In alignment with these values, the practitioner strives to evoke strengths that are already present in the individual, as opposed to "installing something that is missing" (Miller & Rollnick, 2013, p. 24).

The seeds of this approach were planted in the 1970s when a study of treatments provided to problem drinkers yielded unexpected results. Psychology researcher William Miller devoted his dissertation research to examining the outcomes of therapies that varied in intensity. Findings revealed that the most intensive treatment for alcohol abuse worked no better than the least intensive therapy or the use of a self-help manual (Miller & Munoz, 1976). A later study showed that the strongest predictor of successful outcomes for manual-guided therapies to treat excessive drinking was the level of accurate empathy displayed by the therapist (Miller & Baca, 1983). Following a period of study in Norway, Miller published a paper in which he presented an early formulation of motivational interviewing. He distinguished it from other models by emphasizing its reliance on "empathy to access an underlying natural change process during a relatively brief intervention" (Moyers, 2004, p. 294). While on sabbatical in Australia, Miller initiated a partnership with Stephen Rollnick, who had been using MI in the United Kingdom, with a special emphasis on addressing client ambivalence. Together, they wrote the first edition of the seminal text entitled *Motivational Interviewing: Preparing People to Change Addictive Behavior* (1991). Since that time, the model has continued to evolve and is now used to address behavioral problems other than substance abuse. It is widely practiced in hospitals, primary care medical centers, mental health clinics, residential programs, and criminal justice settings.

As of 2013, there were over 1,200 publications on motivational interviewing and more than 200 rigorous studies of the model's outcomes (Miller & Rollnick, 2013). Recent meta-analytic studies (statistical analyses of multiple studies) have found that MI is effective in promoting adolescent substance use behavior change (Jensen, Cushing, Aylward, Craig, & Steele, 2011), weight loss in adults with Type 2 diabetes (Ekong & Kavookjiian, 2016), and healthy lifestyle behavior in cancer patients and survivors (Spencer & Wheeler, 2016). However, the developers of the model acknowledge that there is a high degree of variability in effects across studies, sites, and clinicians. They assert that client response to MI is strongly influenced by practitioner skill in implementing the model. Thus, Miller and Rollnick recommend that aspiring motivational interviewers participate in training, coaching, and observed practice as a means of acquiring and demonstrating proficiency.

The MI Method: Four Basic Processes

Early descriptions of the motivational interviewing method delineated two phases of work: building motivation and consolidating commitment. Based on feedback from clinicians that the application of these two phases was somewhat confining, the developers of MI identified four overlapping processes that form the flow of motivational interviewing: engaging, focusing, evoking, and planning. Each of these processes is discussed below.

Engaging

As with all strength-based clinical models, engagement in MI involves the creation of a mutually respectful relationship between client and practitioner. Specific to motivational interviewing, engaging involves the avoidance of traps that interfere with sustained and effective listening, exploring, and affirmation of the client's values and goals. Those traps are said by Miller and Rollnick (2013) to include the following:

- Assessment Trap: placing the client in a one-down, inferior role by asking numerous questions to which they respond with short and simple answers
- Expert Trap: setting up the expectation that the practitioner is in control and has the answers to the client's dilemma
- Premature focus trap: pressing too quickly on what is seen by the practitioner as the "real problem" and setting up a plan prior to understanding the client's concerns
- Labeling trap: using labels that carry stigma and evoke discord ("alcoholic," "addict")
- Blaming trap: focusing on who is at fault for the client's problems
- Chat trap: participating in excessive "small talk" to the exclusion of meaningful exploration of client concerns (pp. 40–45)

Engagement in MI is further guided through the application of the acronym **OARS**: Open Questions, Affirming, Reflecting, and Summarizing. *Open questions*, as discussed in chapter 3 of this text, invite the client to explore and express what is important to them. *Affirmation* involves highlighting the person's strengths and inherent worth. *Reflection* offers a guess or hypothesis about what the client is feeling or meaning as they respond to open-ended questions; *summarizing* entails tracking and reviewing what has been said over the course of the interview—similar to collecting flowers one by one and then sharing them with the client as a bouquet (Moseley, Peterson, Gonzales, & Sava, 2011).

Another important skill that is used during engagement is **rolling with resistance**. This requires that the practitioner resist the temptation to argue, warn, caution, direct, lecture, or confront the client about the importance of behavior change. Instead, they recognize and appreciate the person's reasons for avoiding the change process. For example, if a college student states that it would be very hard for them to give up the social aspect of binge drinking, the social worker would acknowledge that such a change could be difficult. Similarly, if a client states that smoking helps them manage workplace stress, the practitioner might appreciate and explore various stressors the individuals faces on the job. This strategy reduces defensiveness on the part of the client and provides important clues concerning issues that contribute to the problematic behavior.

Lastly, engagement involves an *exploration of the client's values and goals*. Open questions are used to elicit the person's hopes and dreams for the future, along with the values they cherish (e.g., family, faith, independence, freedom, humor, friendship). This inquiry provides fruitful information about what motivates the individual and may form the basis for later work aimed at highlighting inconsistencies between what the client values and how they are conducting their lives. Reflections of the client's stated goals also provide affirmation of their worthiness and potential.

Focusing

Focusing is a collaborative activity aimed at specifying a target for change that will be the topic of on-going discussion. In some cases, the change goal is clear, such as mood management for the person who has been diagnosed with bipolar disorder. Other times, multiple concerns are on the table that will need to be sorted out before a clear direction can be established. When the practitioner offers information or ideas to support the focusing process, they are advised to ask permission first ("Would it be OK with you if I share … ?"). Agenda mapping is a tool offered by Miller and Rollnick (2013) that may expedite the process of focusing. Change options are listed using language such as "we might work on" or "you could devote our time to." A visual aid may be used depicting various options for change within hand-drawn bubble shapes or boxes. This tool is often used to delineate potential objectives, prioritize goals, and find a mutually agreed-upon direction. "To move forward with the MI processes of evoking and planning it is essential to have a clear eye on the far horizon" (p. 119).

Evoking

Preparing clients for change involves recognizing and eliciting their ambivalence about taking the steps needed to resolve the primary problem. When individuals are ambivalent, they express arguments both for and against change. **Sustain talk** is the term used by motivational interviewers when referring to statements the client makes about why change would be hard or improbable. Such statements support the status quo by focusing on the person's desire to continue the target behavior, their doubts about their ability to change, and their reasons for avoiding it. **Change talk** refers to comments made in favor of change. They reflect the person's interest in the change outcome, ability to make the change, reasons to make it, and needs that support change. It should be noted that change talk doesn't necessarily indicate a commitment to change.

The role of the practitioner is to ask evocative questions to facilitate sustain and change talk, such as the following:

Sustain Talk

- What would be hard for you in making the change?
- What is it that you like about the ways things are now?
- What will you need to give up to make the change?
- What concerns do you have about making change?

Change Talk

- How do you want your life to be different?
- Why is it important that you change?
- What is the downside to the way things are now?
- What will be better when you make the change?

The social worker then makes **double-sided reflections** that highlight the client's ambivalence. For example, they might cast an eye on the client's reasons for and against change by saying, "You hate being hungover and missing work, yet you don't want to disappoint your buddies who expect you to drink with them." Another useful technique is called **heightening discrepancies.** Here the practitioner helps the client recognize the mismatch between status quo and the way they want things to be. In carrying out this strategy, the worker avoids judgmental remarks ("Don't you see that your behavior is not helping you reach your goals?") and, instead, guides the client in connecting the dots, gradually coming to the realization that their present behavior is inconsistent with their life goals and the values they hold dear. The **importance ruler** may be used to gauge the client's perceived level of importance attached to change (Moseley et al., 2011). This tool is applied by asking the client to rate the importance of change on a scale from 0 to 10, with 10 being of highest importance; follow-up questions can include: "Why are you at a ____ and not a lower number?" or "What would it take to move your score up?" Such follow-up questions can be very effective in evoking change talk.

Planning

When the client shows signs of readiness to make change, planning can begin. These signs include increased change talk, diminished sustain talk, and statements indicating that they are imagining a future in which change has occurred (Miller & Rollnick, 2013). Planning focuses on how the client will make the desired change and the specific steps they will take toward their change goals. Troubleshooting is performed to clarify how the client will manage obstacles that may arise as they begin carrying out their plan. Commitment is strengthened by addressing reluctance that comes up for the client as they approach implementation; self-efficacy is promoted by affirming client strengths and ability to succeed.

Once action has begun, change is supported through "flexible revisiting" of engagement, focusing, evoking, and planning (p. 297).

Motivational Interviewing with Native Americans

Leaders in the field of Native American behavioral health have embraced MI due to its fit with culturally based values and beliefs that honor the wisdom within every person. Funded by a grant from the National Institute on Alcohol Abuse and Alcoholism (NIAAA), Alaska Native Kamilla Venner and her colleagues (2006) created a manual for guiding the use of MI in Native American communities. This training guide infuses the elements of spirituality, community, and cultural identity into the practice of MI. It suggests the following prayer for introducing MI to Native people and for conveying the essence of this approach. *

> Guide me to be a patient companion
>
> To listen with a heart as open as the sky
>
> Grant me vision to see through (his/her) eyes
>
> And eager ears to hear his story
>
> Create a safe and open meadow in which we may walk together
>
> Make me a clear pool in which he may reflect
>
> Guide me to find in him your beauty and wisdom
>
> Knowing your desire for him to be in harmony—healthy, loving, and strong
>
> Let me honor and respect his choosing of his own path
>
> And bless him to walk it freely
>
> May I know once again that although he and I are different
>
> Yet there is a peaceful place where we are one. (p. 15)

This adaptation of MI also leverages the Native American values of spirituality and community to enhance motivation for change. For instance, the practitioner may explore ways in which intended change aligns with the client's spiritual beliefs. Or, they might ask about the individual's role in their family and community and how the target behavior has interfered with their role performance. Particularly important when working with traditional Native Americans is an inquiry into the person's cultural identity and ways that it offers protection and guidance during the change process.

The authors of this manual provide a tip sheet to support providers in making sound reflections. This tool labels sample reflections as "hot," "warm," or "cold": hot responses are said to be consistent with the MI approach, warm ones are developing or moderately effective, while cold reflections are

---

* Kamilla L. Venner, Sarah W. Feldstein, and Nadine Tafoya , "Using Prayer to Describe MI," Native American Motivational Interviewing: Weaving Native American and Western Practice, pp. 15. Copyright © 2006 by Venner, Feldstein & Tafoya.

inconsistent with the essence of MI. To illustrate, listed below are potential reflections that might be offered to a middle-aged man who was court ordered to counseling and expresses frustration about having to attend.

Hot: "You don't really want to be here." (said warmly and supportively)

Warm: "The court said to come, so I hope you do."

Cold: "Well, you'd better come back when YOU are ready for change and not just because the court sent you."

Hot: "Tell me a little bit more about that." (said warmly and supportively)

"You're wondering whether counseling can help you."

Warm: "The court said to come."

Cold: "Yeah, your PO said that you were in denial." (p. 74)

HIGHLIGHT 9.1: MI Reminder Card

Tools that help practitioners hold true to the principles of MI model are very valuable, especially given that outcomes have been shown to be greatest when interventions are closely monitored. The Center for Evidence Based Practice at Case Western University offers a free MI Reminder Card ("Am I Doing This Right?") that can be accessed through their website: www.centerforebp.case.edu/resources/tools/mi-reminder-card

This reminder card includes 11 questions intended to guide the practitioner in self-assessment:

1. Am I listening more than talking, or talking more than I am listening?
2. Do I keep myself sensitive and open to this person's issues, whatever they may be? Or am I talking about what I think the problem is?
3. Do I invite this person to talk about and explore his/her own ideas for change? Or am I jumping to conclusions and possible solutions?
4. Do I encourage this person to talk about his/her reasons for not changing? Or am I forcing him/her to talk only about change?
5. Do I ask permission to give my feedback? Or am I presuming that my ideas are what he/she really needs to hear?
6. Do I reassure this person that ambivalence to change is normal? Or am I telling him/her to take action and push ahead for a solution?
7. Do I help this person identify successes and challenges from his/her past and relate them to present change efforts? Or am I encouraging him/her to ignore or get stuck on old stories?
8. Do I seek to understand this person? Or am I spending a lot of time trying to convince him/her to understand me and my ideas?
9. Do I summarize for this person what I am hearing? Or am I just summarizing what I think?
10. Do I value this person's opinion more than my own? Or am I giving more value to my viewpoint?
11. Do I remind myself that this person is capable of making his/her own choices? Or am I assuming that he/she is not capable of making good choices?

Solution-Focused Practice

If our sense of reality is socially constructed, as was originally postulated by sociologists Berger and Luckmann (1966), then our beliefs about ourselves, our struggles, strengths, and limitations are derived though social relationships. The labels we use to define self, along with the assumptions we make about what we can achieve, are created through our interactions with others. This is the philosophy of **social constructionism**, a theoretical framework that provides a foundation for solution-focused practice. It guides the social worker in the use of relationship and language so as to create an expectancy of positive change. This section will begin with a brief history of the model and findings of effectiveness research before delving into the particular skills used by solution-focused practitioners.

The solution-focused model was developed by Steve de Shazer and Insoo Kim Berg in the 1980s as an alternative to the problem-solving approach. They designed strategies aimed at helping clients create a positive vision for their future and gain a "deeper understanding of the strengths and resources [they] can use in turning that vision into reality" (De Jong & Berg, 2002, p. ix). They viewed the client as the expert in their own lives and asserted that helping professionals need to assume a "not knowing" stance as they explore their client's frame of reference. This was quite a departure from the prevailing paradigm that prized the practitioner's ability to diagnose and treat psychosocial problems.

The designation of solution-focused practice as an evidence-based approach is based on research conducted over the last several decades. A systematic review of studies performed from 1990–2010 produced preliminary support for this model, as used in treating children with externalizing and internalizing behavior problems, it was found to be particularly effective as an early intervention (Bond, Woods, Humphrey, Symes, & Green, 2013). Findings from a recent meta-analysis showed that solution-focused practice is effective for a wide range of psychological and behavioral problems, particularly for depression in adults (Gingerich & Peterson, 2012). A nation-wide study of 4,559 public child welfare cases found that those with a high level of adherence to the solution-based approach had significantly better outcomes than other cases in areas of safety, permanency, and family well-being (Antle, Christensen, van Zyl, & Barbee, 2012).

Conducting a Solution-Focused Interview

Solution-focused practice requires effective listening on the part of the social worker. In fact, Insoo Kim Berg (De Jong & Berg, 2002) suggested that the most accomplished practitioners of this model listen to the client with *"solution-building ears"*; by this she meant that they hear the client's story without "filtering it through their own frame of reference" (p. 21). Instead of reacting to what the client communicates, the practitioner tunes into the "hints of possibility" that are reflected in the person's words. For instance, if a teen calls his mother names as he describes his anger about her curfew, the social worker would resist the temptation to redirect him and instead would listen for what is important to that adolescent, that is, freedom and parental trust. This information becomes important throughout the interview.

A second important interviewing skill involves formulating open questions that demonstrate genuine curiosity about what the client wants. Paraphrasing is then used to make clear that the client has been heard and **reality-based compliments** are given to draw attention to client successes and strength. Client meanings are explored in depth, and solution talk is highlighted. Questions that are unique to this model are discussed below.

Miracle Question

The **miracle question** is the bread and butter of solution-building practice. It moves beyond simply asking the client to wave a magic wand and discuss what they would like to make happen. The magic wand technique usually generates broad fantasies and unrealistic notions of what could happen in a make-believe world (e.g., "I would win 10 million dollars in the lottery"). Conversely, the miracle question makes use of a narrative that prompts clients to identify specific and concrete changes they would like to see occur in their day-to-day life. De Shazer (1988) suggests the following:

> *Now, I want to ask you a strange question. Suppose that while you are sleeping tonight and the entire house is quiet, a miracle happens. The miracle is that the problem which brought you here is solved. However, because you are sleeping, you don't know that the miracle has happened. So, when you wake up tomorrow morning, what will be different that will tell you that a miracle has happened and the problem which brought you here is solved?* (p. 5)

Follow-up questions are used to elicit specific changes the client expects to feel, observe, or hear that will indicate that their problem has been resolved.

Exception Finding

Interviewing for exceptions involves asking the client about times when the problem might have been expected to occur but did not. For example, if the presenting problem is arguing between spouses, they might be asked to talk about a time when they disagreed but didn't argue. "Tell me about a time when you two disagreed but didn't end up arguing? What was different about that time?" This type of questioning draws the client's attention away from conflict and toward strengths and possible solutions. In another interview, a mother may share concern about her daughter's irresponsible behavior, as evidenced by her failure to complete chores. This parent might be asked to discuss a time in the recent past when her daughter did her chores, or at least some of them. Details would be requested about this exception to the problem to shed light on what made it different. Suppose that the mother states that her daughter did do most of her chores on a day when she had the house all to herself and could decide when to complete them. This questioning allows the client to gain insight about a potential solution to her problem: allow her daughter to decide when to complete chores over a limited period of time.

Coping Questions

Coping questions are used to shift the client's focus from pain and hopelessness to their capabilities with regard to surviving overwhelming conditions. This tool is built on the recognition that even when individuals are severely troubled by hardship, they have survived some aspect of their plight. Consider a single parent who is depressed about her divorce, traumatized by her ex-husband's abuse, and overwhelmed with the responsibility of caring for her children while working a full-time job. The social worker might acknowledge the large amount of stress and responsibility that she is carrying and ask, "How have you managed to cope as well as you have with all that going on?" This type of question is often met with a pause as the client considers their response. Within a few moments, they are usually able to identify some asset (e.g., faith, relationships, hardiness) that brings them strength or fortitude. Responses to coping questions are typically followed by compliments through which the practitioner acknowledges the client's inherent strength.

Scaling Questions

Scaling questions are utilized to reinforce small steps toward enhanced coping. As suggested by De Jong and Berg (2002), the client is asked to scale their coping at present in relation to their state when the problem was at its worse. "On a scale of 0 to 10, where 10 means you are coping with your situation as well as anyone could and 0 means your coping is at its worst, how would you rate your coping right now?" Clients usually select a number that is higher than 0; let's say 3. This allows the social worker to ask, "How have managed to get from 0 to 3?" As with the use of coping questions, this inquiry focuses the client's attention on their progress toward change, however small. Another follow-up question asks the client to consider what would need to happen for them to move from a 3 to 6, prompting them to develop next steps in overcoming their challenge. Scaling questions can also be used to measure client progress and confidence over time.

Building Solutions in Child Welfare

In 2000, Insoo Kim Berg partnered with child welfare administrator Susan Kelly to promote a new paradigm for public child welfare agencies, one that embraces the culture of empowerment. In their co-authored book, they encourage child protection services (CPS) workers to acquire the skills needed to build egalitarian relationships. They advocate for an approach in which CPS workers cooperate *with* clients rather than insisting on cooperation *from* them. Berg and Kelly (2000) adapted solution-focused strategies to child welfare work and offered sample questions, as shown below:

Coping questions are aimed at acknowledging the difficulty in the client's situation:

"Wow, how do you do it? It must have been very tough just to get through the week."

"How come it's not worse, given all the things you are going through?"

"How did you manage to stay sober for a whole week?" (pp. 97–98)

Scaling questions are used to gauge the client's confidence, safety issues, and motivation:

"On a scale of 1 to 10, where 10 stands for how confident any parent could be in making sure their child is safe and 1 stands for you are not sure at all, that is you feel very shaky about your child's safety, where would you put yourself between 1 to 10 right now?"

"On a scale of 1 to 10, where 10 stands for as determined as anybody could be in your circumstances to get your daughter back, how close would you say you are to 10 right now?" (p. 110)

Exception finding is focused on acquiring details with regard to small successes:

"Tell me about the times in recent days when you could have hit [your son] but somehow managed to handle it differently?"

"In what other situations have you been able to manage your temper in such a as way that you did not regret it later?" (p. 104)

Jacqueline Corcoran (1999) also applied the solution-focused approach to child protection work and stressed the importance of CPS workers using language in a way that creates **expectancy for change**.

For example, instead of asking the client "*If* you are taking care of your children, what will the judge say?" the worker would ask, "*When* you are taking care of your children, what will the judge say." The simple substitution of the word *if* with *when* communicates the expectation that the client will make needed change.

Another fairly recent development has been the infusion of a solutions-oriented approach into the process for conducting investigations of suspected child abuse or neglect. Turnell and Edwards (1999) introduced the **signs of safety** framework that expands risk assessment to include evidence of safety and strength in the home. Like solution-focused practice, this approach is built on partnership and collaboration with families served. The signs of safety model has been widely adopted by child welfare agencies across North America, Europe, and Australia. See https://www.signsofsafety.net/ for further information.

Narrative Approach

Another model of practice that is rooted in social constructionism is the narrative approach to social work. It was originally developed by Michael White, Cheryl White, and David Epstein, leaders in the field of family therapy in Australia and New Zealand. Michael founded the Dulwich Centre, now considered the primary home of narrative practice. He and his colleagues collaborated in the development of a practice model that understood the importance of meaning making through language and life stories. They asserted that individuals and families construct life stories that help them make sense of their past and guide them in knowing what to expect in the future (Van Hook, 2016). When a person's life story is "problem-saturated," they keep "repeating old problematic patterns" (p. 248). Such cases call for narrative strategies that help the client reconstruct their story so as to achieve liberation from negative and confining themes.

The evidence base supporting narrative practice is rapidly expanding. Over the last decade, empirical research has demonstrated its effectiveness in increasing self- and social awareness and responsible decision-making in children (Beaudoin, Moersch, & Evare, 2016), reducing psychological distress in youth diagnosed with autism (Cashin, Browne, Bradbury, & Mulder, 2013), improving school behavior in children with symptoms of attention deficit-hyperactivity disorder (Looyeh, Kamali, & Shafieian, 2012), and reducing symptoms of depression in adults (Lopes et al., 2014; Vromans & Schweitzer, 2010).

A qualitative study of group narrative therapy with diverse older adults produced several important thematic findings. Upon interview, participants spoke to the value they placed on mutual aid and peer support that they received during group sessions. Group members also voiced appreciation for the externalization of problems, a technique described below. These aspects of the therapy allowed clients to separate themselves from guilt associated with problems related to depression and/or misuse of substances (Poolea, Gardner, Flower, & Cooper, 2009).

The Narrative Practice Process

The social worker begins the narrative process by establishing a collaborative relationship with their client and by listening to how they discuss their problem. Particular attention is paid to the themes of the problem-based story and the meaning that the client has made of troubling circumstances. Once the problem-saturated account is understood, a variety of techniques are used that will culminate in the creation of an alternative narrative.

Externalizing the Problem

An important goal of the narrative practitioner is to separate the client's identity from their presenting problem. This is done through the use of **externalizing conversations** in which "problems are spoken of as separate from people" (Morgan, 2000, p. 18). The client might be asked to name the problem; children may be encouraged to draw it. As an example, a person struggling with depression might name their problem the "dark cloud." Next, questions are asked to further personify the problem.

"When does the dark cloud show up?"

"What does the dark cloud try to convince you about yourself?"

"What kind of voice does it use?"

"What type of tricks does it use to bring you down?"

"When does it go away?"

Conversations of this kind "begin to disempower the effects of labelling, pathologizing, and diagnosing" that are experienced by many clients (p. 24).

Tracing the Influence of the Problem

Once the problem has been externalized, the social worker will ask questions aimed at specifying the influence that the problem has had over time. This serves two primary purposes; first, it makes clear that the impact of the problem is not fixed—there are times when its influence is greater than others. Second, it allows the practitioner to ascertain the impact of the problem on various aspects of the person's life. The client may be asked how the problem has affected their health, relationships, work, or sense of self. Discussions of this type demonstrate that the practitioner has an interest in understanding the client's distress related to the primary problem.

Discovering Unique Outcomes

The next line of questioning seeks to identify times in the recent past when the client has fought back and successfully resisted the problem's influence and control. The **unique outcome**, sometimes referred to as a "sparkling event," can be anything that doesn't align with the problem-saturated story, "a plan, action, feeling, statement, quality, desire, dream, thought, belief, ability, or commitment" (Morgan, 2000, p. 52). With careful listening, the practitioner may notice a unique outcome as the client tells their story. If so, they inquire further to elicit more detail, often using "who," "what," "when," "where," and "how" questions. This helps the client appreciate the significance of this exception to the rule and increases the likelihood that they will identify additional unique outcomes.

Alternative Story Development

New themes are created when the meaning of the unique outcomes is explored. To assist the client in understanding the significance of these unique events, questions such as the following may be asked:

"What does it say about you that you were able to resist the dark cloud that day?"

"How were you able to take charge and avoid dark cloud this morning?"

"Who would be least surprised to hear about you taking control?"

As unique outcomes are further developed, they form the basis for an alternative life story line. To begin this new narrative, the client is asked to come up with a title that reflects its departure from the problem-based account (e.g., overcoming loss, winning my fight with depression). The practitioner may then ask about others who have knowledge of the client's ability to resist the problem. With the client's permission, these individuals may be contacted in order to obtain rich detail that is used to thicken the new plot. As the reauthored life story unfolds, the client may be encouraged to share it with supportive and significant others. Therapeutic documentation is used (e.g., photos, letters, certificates, diagrams) to record the emerging themes, along with the client's commitment to their newly constructed narrative.

Tree of Life Metaphor

A creative adaptation of the narrative approach uses the tree of life as a metaphor to guide the client in exploring their life story. Individuals are asked to draw their tree, with the understanding that its parts represent differing aspects of their life. They then note their personal information within each corresponding segment of the drawing. As described by Weller (n.d.), the metaphor is specified as follows:

- *Roots* represent where the person came from and the culture they grew up in
- *Ground* signifies things they do daily to nurture themselves
- *Trunk* represents their skills and values
- *Branches* depict their hopes, dreams, and wishes
- *Leaves* are assigned to the people that are important to them in a positive way
- *Fruits* signify attributes that have been passed onto them by the leaves
- *Flowers* represent the legacy they wish to leave to others

NARRATIVE APPLICATION: Applying the Tree of Life Metaphor

Olivia was a 12-year-old girl who was removed from her biological mother at 7 years of age. Since that time, she has lived in three different foster homes. Her first foster family was not a good fit, and her stay ended after 6 months. The second placement lasted 2 years, and Olivia bonded with the foster mother (Linda) and foster grandmother (Mary). This placement ended when Linda died following a year-long bout of breast cancer. Olivia's third placement has been with a couple (Sue and JoAnn) who are considering adoption but have concerns about Olivia's anxiety and difficulty attaching.

In her most recent counseling session, Olivia's social worker (Tyler) asked her to draw a tree on a large piece of paper, including its roots, trunk, branches, and leaves. He then suggested that they could think about this tree as a symbol of Olivia's life. Tyler guided the girl in exploring each segment of her tree. Next to the roots, Olivia noted where she came from: "My mom, Carmen. She came here from Mexico with her boyfriend before she was arrested and sent to prison." In the trunk, she listed her skills in art and her best subject, English. Within the branches, she noted her dream to "belong somewhere" and "be part of a family." When asked about people that have been important to her, Olivia immediately said "Linda and Mary" and entered their names on the leaves closest to the trunk. She thought for a moment, then added Carmen, Sue, and JoAnn's names on leaves further out on the branches.

Next, Olivia was asked to consider what she has learned from the people listed in the leaves. She was then prompted to draw some brightly colored fruits next to the leaves, as they would represent all that Linda, Mary, Carmen, Sue, and JoAnn have passed on to her that is good. Olivia said that from Linda she learned to be strong; from Mary, she learned how to give really good hugs. "I learned some Spanish words from my mom. I still know them." She entered this information onto the colorful fruits. Olivia had a harder time identifying things she has learned from Sue and JoAnn, so she and Tyler decided to get back to that later. As for her legacy, Olivia said she wanted to pass on her strength to others and then noted that ambition in a flower that she drew next to Linda's leaf.

Discussion then focused on how Olivia was currently using the strength that had been passed to her:

"I am not as afraid as I was when I first moved into my new foster home. I like them, but they will probably give up on me and leave like everyone else."

"I know your wish is to be a part of a family. What would need to happen for Sue and JoAnn's leaves to move closer to your trunk?"

"I don't know. Maybe after a while I can start to trust them more," Olivia said tentatively.

"Yes, especially as you get better and better at keeping anxiety away," Tyler suggested.

They then decided that anxiety was an insect that tries to nibble on Olivia's leaves, fruit, and flowers. They agreed to work on some tools Olivia could use to keep that annoying pest away.

Cognitive-Behavioral Intervention

Cognitive-behavioral intervention, otherwise known as cognitive behavioral therapy (CBT) is based on the assumption that a person's cognitions (thoughts and beliefs) influence how they respond to various life circumstances. When using CBT, the social worker is focused on identifying and restructuring irrational beliefs or thinking patterns that contribute to their client's emotional or behavioral challenges. This approach is rooted in cognitive theory, as advanced by Aaron Beck and discussed in Chapter 4. Since the 1960s, CBT has been used successfully to address a wide range of socioemotional problems and mental health conditions.

Cognitive-behavioral intervention enjoys a solid research base that supports its overall effectiveness. Most recently, a comprehensive review of 269 meta-analyses was conducted to examine the intervention's efficacy across a broad range of study populations and presenting problems (Hofmann, Asnaani, Vonk, Sawyer, & Fang, 2012). The strongest positive effects were found when CBT was used to address general stress, insomnia, anxiety disorders in children and adults, bulimia, somatoform disorders, and anger control problems. A systematic review of controlled studies of CBT group intervention revealed its positive impact on adolescents with depression (Keles, & Idsoe, 2018). Another meta-analysis showed that CBT is an effective intervention for attention-deficit disorder and oppositional defiant disorder in youth (Battagliese et al., 2015).

Research has also examined the effectiveness of culturally specific adaptations of CBT. For example, a systematic review of culturally adapted CBT used with Latino immigrants revealed the model's promise in treating depressive symptoms (Pineros-Leano, Liechty, & Piedra, 2017). Another study focused on the benefits of culturally adapted CBT group counseling as compared with standard CBT group counseling for depressed, low-income, African American women. The adapted approach contextualized the intervention to address African American family issues, female identity, and spirituality; anecdotes from African American literature were used to clarify concepts. Results demonstrated that the women who received the adapted protocol exhibited a reduction in depressive symptoms that was twice the magnitude of that displayed by women who participated in the standard CBT group (Kohn, Oden, Munoz, Robinson & Leavitt, 2002). Studies of this kind demonstrate the importance of adapting this intervention to the cultural identity of clients served.

Implementing Cognitive Behavioral Interventions

CBT is not about telling a client that their thinking is faulty or disordered. It is about guiding them through an exploration of their automatic thoughts or core beliefs and helping them decide for themselves the extent to which these cognitions are supporting or hindering their progress toward growth or goal attainment. Before engaging in this work, the social worker must establish a trusting relationship with the client. This allows the service recipient to disclose their cognitions with limited fear of negative judgement. The process of cognitive behavioral intervention is fairly structured, and is typically focused on (1) helping the client understand the connection between thoughts and emotions, (2) uncovering thoughts that are unhelpful to them, and then (3) defusing or disputing negative thinking.

Introducing Cognitive Theory

The approach that a social worker uses to introduce cognitive theory depends upon the developmental stage of the client and their level of comprehension. Some adults are readily able to grasp the role of negative thinking in their lives. Other adults, children, and adolescents are likely to benefit from diagrams that illustrate the mediating effect of beliefs on a person's response to stressors. The A-B-C model was first used by Albert Ellis (1957) to illustrate the pathway from triggering event (antecedent) to automatic thoughts about the event (belief), finally leading to emotional and behavioral response (consequence). Applying this model to hypothetical events can help drive the point home—what a person believes about a set of circumstances has a significant impact on how they cope (see Highlight 9.2).

HIGHLIGHT 9.2: Hypothetical Events for Teaching Cognitive Theory

- Imagine two people who have been laid off from their job at the same company. One person decides that they were laid off because they are a loser; they are concerned that they will not find another job anytime soon. The second person decides that they were laid off because the company is having financial troubles but believes they will find something better. How will they each respond to this event? Clearly, the first person will be much more distressed than the second.
- Imagine a teen who has entered the mall and sees a group of peers in the food court who were laughing as they notice his arrival. He might assume they are laughing at him. In this case, how will he feel? What will he do? On the other hand, the teen might decide that the peers could have been laughing at a joke that had nothing to do with him. How will he feel? What will he do?

A	B	C
Antecedent ⟶	**Belief** ⟶	**Consequences**
(Triggering Event)	(Automatic Thought)	(Emotional & Behavioral Response)

FIGURE 9.1. A-B-C Diagram.

Uncovering the Client's Unhelpful Thoughts

The process of exploring client cognitions can take a variety of forms. One approach is to simply ask a client to discuss a recent situation that was upsetting to them. Next, they would be guided in recalling how their body felt at the time, what thoughts they were having, the emotions they experienced, and how they responded behaviorally. Based on one or more reviewed real-life scenarios, some of the client's negative beliefs about self, the world, or the future will become clear. An adolescent may, for example, report feelings of anxiety and self-doubt that they had at a school-based event. Their automatic thought was that they will look foolish if they try to socialize with a peer. Their core belief might be "no one likes me." As a result of these cognitions, the teen left the event early, fears upcoming social situations, and avoids opportunities to make friends.

Worksheets completed as a homework assignment can be helpful in elucidating thoughts that occur in response to specific situations, as they arise. The Center for Clinical Interventions offers a thought diary that can be found on their website (https://www.cci.health.wa.gov.au). It provides space for the client to record (1) activating event/situation, mental picture, or physical trigger, (2) beliefs or self-statements and a rating of the extent to which the thoughts are believed, and (3) consequences, or how they felt in response to the activating event and a rating of intensity of that feeling (0 to 100). When a client completes a worksheet of this kind over the course of several days or a week, rich data is provided that may be used to guide the cognitive-behavioral intervention.

Diffusing and Disputing Unhelpful Beliefs

Cognitive restructuring involves efforts to disempower negative or unhelpful beliefs. One strategy is to ask the client to imagine the unhelpful thought as a bully or unwelcome intruder. They then visualize themselves resisting the intruder's influence and fighting it off with positive affirmations. Strategic *use of metaphor* and imagination is an effective tool for diffusing troubling thoughts.

Socratic questions, as discussed in Chapter 3, are also used to guide the client in assessing the accuracy of their negative beliefs. The individual may be asked to consider evidence that supports a self-defeating thought as well as evidence that contradicts it. For example, if a male client believes that he is not capable of controlling his violent behavior, he might be asked about the basis for this belief along with times when he managed his aggression even when angry or times when he responded to an anger-provoking situation with less aggression that usual. The evidence disputing the original belief is highlighted to aid the client in adopting a more balanced perspective.

The **thought record** is another CBT tool aimed at tracking thinking patterns over a short period of time. Greenberger and Padesky (1995) share a commonly used format that includes seven columns within which the client records the following:

- Situation triggering stress
- Moods (name them and rate intensity on scale 0 to 100)
- Automatic thoughts (in response to a trigger)
- Evidence that supports the distressing thought ("hot thought")
- Evidence that does not support the hot thought
- Alternative, more balanced thought
- Follow-up rating of mood intensity (0 to 100)

The thought record is then reviewed with the social worker to further process thoughts and emotions and solidify adaptive thinking. Research has shown that this tool has a positive impact on anxiety-related beliefs and behavior (McManus, Van Doom, & Yiend, 2011).

HIGHLIGHT 9.3: Thought Record

Some clients will respond to evidence that disputes a negative thought with "yes, but" thinking in which they further justify the unhelpful core belief. A unique adaptation of the thought record was developed to counter this type of "yes, but" thinking and is referred to as *trial-based thought record* (TBTR) (Reis de Oliveira, 2016). Using this technique, the social worker suggests a judicial process in which the negative core belief is "on trial." This image is used as the client considers all the evidence when completing the thought record. The "trial" may also be simulated using an empty chair technique in which the client plays one or more courtroom inspired roles: defendant, prosecutor, defense attorney, jury member (Delavechia, Velasques, Duran, Matsumoto, & Reis de Oliveira 2016). Studies have shown this tool to be effective in weakening unhealthy cognitions and their associated emotions (p. 32).

Self-Care: Cognitive Coping for the Social Worker

An essential component of self-care entails thinking about one's own thinking with regard to clients, self, and service systems. It is not uncommon for practitioners to become bogged down with thoughts of lack and limitation when faced with stressful circumstances on the job. In fact, social workers often adopt misguided beliefs and unrealistic assumptions about their own capabilities. In his article entitled "How to Deal with Your Most Difficult Client—You," Albert Ellis (1984) discussed five **musturbations**, defined as "irrational things that therapists and other helping professionals tell themselves about what they *must* do or what *should* occur" during their practice (as cited in Cox & Steiner, 2013, p. 79). They are as follows:

1. The belief that the practitioner must be successful with clients almost all of the time
2. The expectation that they must be one of the most outstanding practitioners
3. The assumption that they must be liked and respected by all of their clients
4. The belief that since they work hard, their clients should be equally hard working
5. The assumption that they must be able to enjoy their work almost all of the time

Catching cognitions of this kind is a suggested strategy for self-care aimed at enhancing the self-efficacy of the practitioner (Cox & Steiner, 2013, p. 81). When the social worker recognizes that they have adopted musturbations or other irrational beliefs about their work, it is important that they consider the accuracy of these thoughts. The likelihood that a social worker will be the best in the world, have successful outcomes with almost all of their clients, be liked by all, and enjoy their work almost all of the time, is extremely slim. The anecdote to musturbations is the adoption of more realistic appraisals:

- I will do the best that I can with all of my clients
- I will engage in lifelong learning as it relates to my practice
- Some of my clients will have a hard time working toward goals
- Work won't always be easy and enjoyable
- I will celebrate successes, however small

SUMMARY

This chapter provides an overview of four commonly used, evidenced-based models for direct practice in social work: motivational interviewing, solution-focused practice, the narrative approach, and cognitive-behavioral intervention. For each model, a brief history was shared, along with recent research supporting its effectiveness. Specific strategies and skills were described, along with unique adaptations of each practice framework. Finally, a cognitive approach to self-care was suggested that is aimed at strengthening the self-efficacy of the social worker. The author's hope is that the material provided in this chapter will pique the reader's interest in pursuing hands-on-training in one or more of the models discussed.

KEY TERMS

Change talk

Coping questions

Double-sided reflections

Expectancy for change

Externalizing conversations

Heightening discrepancies

Importance ruler

Interviewing for exceptions

Miracle question

Musturbations

OARS

Reality-based compliments

Rolling with resistance

Scaling questions

Signs of safety

Social constructionism

Sustain talk

Thought record

Unique outcomes

DISCUSSION QUESTIONS

1. Why is it important to roll with resistance when conducting a motivational interview? How would you go about using this technique with a client who is ambivalent about making change?

2. How does the philosophy of social constructionism inform solution-focused and narrative practices?

3. Which of Ellis's musturbations have you adopted at some point in your work? How can you adopt a more realistic appraisal of your capabilities?

SKILL DEVELOPMENT ACTIVITIES

1. Explore one of the websites below and share what you learned.

   https://motivationalinterviewing.org/

   https://solutionfocused.net/what-is-solution-focused-therapy/

   https://dulwichcentre.com.au/

   https://beckinstitute.org/get-informed/what-is-cognitive-therapy/

2. Create your own tree of life, as described above. What did you learn about yourself from conducting this exercise?

3. Track your own thinking patterns by maintaining a thought record for 1 week. What connections did you discover between your "hot thoughts" and emotions?

REFERENCES

Antle, B. F., Christensen, D. N., van Zyl, M. A., & Barbee, A. P. (2012). The impact of the solution-based casework (SBC) practice model on federal outcomes in public child welfare. *Child Abuse & Neglect, 36*, 342–353.

Battagliese, G., Caccetta, M., Luppino, O. I., Baglioni, C., Cardi, V., Mancini, F., & Buonanno, C. (2015). Cognitive behavioral therapy for externalizing disorders: A meta-analysis of treatment effectiveness. *Behaviour Research and Therapy, 75*, 60–71.

Beaudoin, M., Muersch, M., & Evare, B. S. (2016). The effectiveness of narrative therapy with children's social and emotional skill development: An empirical study of 813 problem-solving stories. *Journal of Systemic Therapies, 35*, 42–59.

Berg, I. K., & Kelly, S. (2000). *Building solutions in child protective services.* New York, NY: W.W. Norton.

Berger, P. L., & Luckmann, T. (1966). *Social construction of reality: A treatise in the sociology of knowledge.* Garden City, NY: Doubleday.

Bond, C., Woods, K., Humphrey, N., Symes, W., & Green, L. (2013). Practitioner review: The effectiveness of solution-focused brief therapy with children and adolescents: A systematic and critical evaluation of the literature from 1990–2010. *Journal of Child Psychology and Psychiatry, 54*, 707–723.

Cashin, A., Browne, G., Bradbury, J., & Mulder, A. M. (2013). The effectiveness of narrative therapy with young people with autism. *Mental Health Nursing, 26*, 32–41.

Chambless, D. L. (1999). Empirically validated treatments: What now? *Applied and Preventive Psychology, 8*, 281–284.

Corcoran, J. (1999). Solution-focused interviewing with child protective services clients. *Child Welfare, 78*, 461–479.

Cox, K., & Steiner, S. (2013). *Self-care in social work: A guide for practitioners, supervisors, and administrators.* Washington, DC: NASW Press.

De Jong, P. & Berg, I. K. (2002). *Interviewing for solutions* (2nd. ed.). Pacific Grove, CA: Brooks/Cole.

Delavechia, T. R., Velasques, M. L., Duran, E., Matsumoto, L. S., & Reis de Oliveira, I. (2016). Changing negative core beliefs with trial-based thought record. *Archives of Clinical Psychiatry, 43*, 31–33.

De Shazer, S. (1988). *Clues: Investigating solutions in brief therapy.* New York, NY: Norton.

Ekong, G., & Kavookjian, J. (2016). Motivational interviewing and outcomes in adults with Type 2 diabetes: A systematic review. *Patient Education and Counseling, 99*, 944–952.

Ellis, A. (1957). Rational psychotherapy and individual psychology. *Journal of Individual Psychology, 13*, 38–44.

Ellis, A. (1984). How to deal with your most difficult client—you. *Psychotherapy in Private Practice, 2*, 25–35.

Gingerich, N. J., & Peterson, L. T. (2012). Effectiveness of solution-focused brief therapy: A systematic review of controlled outcome studies. *Research on Social Work Practice, 23*, 266–283.

Greenberger, D., & Padesky, C. A. (1995). *Mind over mood: Change how you feel by changing the way you think.* New York, NY: Guilford Press.

Hofmann, S. G., Asnaani, A., Vonk, I. J. J., Sawyer, A. T., & Fang, A. (2012). The efficacy of cognitive behavioral therapy: A review of meta-analyses. *Cognitive Therapy and Research, 36*, 427–440.

Jensen, C. D., Cushing, C. C., Aylward, B. S., Craig, D. M., & Steele, R. G. (2011). Effectiveness of motivational interviewing interventions for adolescent substance use behavior change. *Journal of Consulting and Clinical Psychology, 79*, 433–440.

Keles, S., & Idsoe, T. (2018). A meta-analysis of group cognitive behavioral therapy (CBT) interventions for adolescents with depression. *Journal of Adolescence, 67*, 129–139.

Kohn, L. P., Oden, T., Munoz, R. F., Robinson, A., & Leavitt, D. (2002). Brief report: Adapted cognitive behavioral group therapy for depressed low income African American women. *Community Mental Health, 38*, 497–504.

Looyeh, M. Y., Kamali, K., & Shafieian, R. (2012). An exploratory study of the effectiveness of group narrative therapy on the school behavior of girls with attention-deficit/hyperactivity symptoms. *Archives of Psychiatric Nursing, 26*, 404–410.

Lopes, R. T., Goncalves, M. M., Machado, P., Sinai, D., Bento, T., & Salgado, J. (2014). Narrative therapy vs. cognitive-behavioral therapy for moderate depression: Empirical evidence from a controlled clinical trial. *Psychotherapy Research, 24*, 662–674.

McManus, F., Van Doom, K., & Yiend, J. (2012). Examining the effects of thought records and behavioral experiments in instigating belief change. *Journal of Behavior Therapy and Experimental Psychiatry, 43*, 540–547.

Miller, W. R., & Baca, L. M. (1983). Two-year follow-up of bibliotherapy and therapist-directed controlled drinking training for problem drinkers. *Behavior Therapy, 14*, 441–448.

Miller, W. R., & Munoz, R. F. (1976). *How to control your drinking.* Englewood Cliffs, NJ: Prentice-Hall.

Miller, W. R., & Rollnick, S. (1991). *Motivational interviewing: Preparing people to change addictive behavior.* New York, NY: Guilford Press.

Miller, W. R., & Rollnick, S. (2013). *Motivational interviewing: Helping people change* (3rd ed.). New York, NY: Guilford Press.

Morgan, A. (2000). *What is narrative therapy? An easy-to-read introduction.* Adelaide, South Australia: Dulwich Centre Publications.

Moseley, A., Peterson, T., Gonzales, A., & Sava, S. (2011). Motivational interviewing for better health outcomes. [Power Point slides]. Retrieved from https://www.thenationalcouncil.org/webinars/motivational-interviewing-for-better-health-outcomes/

Moyers, T. B. (2004). History and happenstance: How motivational interviewing got its start. *Journal of Cognitive Psychotherapy, 18*, 291–298.

Pineros-Leano, M., Liechty, J. M., & Piedra, L. M. (2017). Latino immigrants, depressive symptoms, and cognitive behavioral therapy: A systematic review. *Journal of Affective Disorders, 208,* 567–576.

Poolea, J., Gardner, P., Flower, M. C., & Cooper, C. (2009). Narrative therapy, older adults, and group work: Practice, research, and recommendations. *Social Work with Groups, 32,* 288–302.

Reis de Oliveira, I. R. (2011). Trial-based thought record (TBTR): Preliminary data on a strategy to deal with core beliefs by combining sentence reversion and the use of an analogy to a trial. *Revista Brasileira de Psiquiatria, 30,* 12–18.

Spencer, J. C., & Wheeler, S. B. (2016). A systematic review of Motivational Interviewing interventions in cancer patients and survivors. *Patient Education and Counseling, 99,* 1099–1105.

Turnell, A. and Edwards, S. (1999). *Signs of Safety: A safety and solution oriented approach to child protection casework.* New York: WW Norton.

Van Hook, M. P. (2016). *Social work practice with families: A resiliency-based approach* (2nd ed.). New York, NY: Oxford University Press.

Venner, K. L, Feldstein, S. W., & Tafoya, N. (2006). Native American motivational interviewing: Weaving Native American and Western practice. [Power Point slides] Retrieved from https://www.integration.samhsa.gov/clinical-practice/Native_American_MI_Manual.pdf

Vromans, L. P., & Schweitzer, R. D. (2010. Narrative therapy for adults with a major depressive disorder: Improved symptoms and interpersonal outcomes. *Psychotherapy Research, 21,* 4–15.

Weller, N. B. (n.d.). The tree of life: A simple exercise for reclaiming your identity. Retrieved from http://nathanbweller.com/tree-life-simple-exercise-reclaiming-identity-direction-life-story/

CREDIT

CHAPTER 10

Endings and Evaluations

So comes snow after fire, and even dragons have their ending!—J. R. R. TOLKIEN

THE ENDING OF social work services ideally marks the client's passage from a place of self-doubt, distress, or despair to one of enhanced skill, mastery, and self-confidence. It is a transition from the safety found in the professional helping relationship to a new phase of personal development that is self-guided or supported by informal or other formal helpers. When handled effectively, the ending stage consolidates all that was learned and prepares the client for change maintenance. This chapter will provide an overview of various types of endings, activities that comprise this transition period, and theoretical approaches to the ending process. It will conclude with discussion of differing methods used for evaluating services performed over the course of the helping relationship.

Types of Endings

Direct services end for a host of reasons. Sometimes the ending is planned to coincide with time limits imposed by the agency or by the departure of the practitioner from the service setting. Other times, it is unplanned and occurs at the request of the client or the social worker. Each type requires attention to differing issues, as shown below.

Unplanned Endings

An **unplanned ending** of social work services takes place when a client discontinues their participation in the intervention process. This may occur if the individual believes they have made adequate progress or is unsatisfied with the services received. Or, it may be the result of inadequate resources or chaotic conditions that limit the client's ability to follow through with scheduled appointments. Treatment drop-out is not uncommon. According to the American Psychological Association, at least 20% of the clients receiving clinical services end treatment prematurely (Chamberlin, 2015). Drop-out rates in college counseling centers range from 25% to 50% (Walsh, 2016); they are also high in child welfare settings and "lead to high rates of removal of children from their families and to eventual termination of parental rights" (Dawson & Berry, 2002, p. 293). Effective engagement strategies and broadly focused case management services are recommended as a means of reversing this trend (p. 299).

When a client ends services unexpectedly, the social worker may reach out to them by phone, email, or letter and encourage them to participate in a closing session (Hepworth, Rooney, Rooney, Strom-Gottfried, & Larsen 2010). If the client agrees to a final meeting, the additional time might be used to discuss barriers interfering with attendance, goals underway or attained, risks associated with premature ending, and options for resuming services. Through whatever means are possible, the social worker should demonstrate a genuine interest in receiving the client's feedback about services received, including what worked for them and what didn't. By conveying this interest, they model a nondefensive approach to hearing constructive criticism.

Unplanned endings also occur at the initiation of the social worker, who may determine that a client needs a higher level of care (e.g., residential or hospital-based care) than what is provided at the current service setting. Other times, the practitioner leaves their practice unexpectedly or become ill and unable to continue serving. Or they may decide to end services due to boundary violations on the part of the client, such as repeatedly calling the helping professional after hours or persisting in a quest for personal information about them (Walsh, 2016). The social worker could also request termination of services if, after repeated warnings, the client engages in disruptive, aggressive, or offensive behavior during individual, group, or family sessions. In circumstances of this kind, it is prudent for the social worker to suggest alternative sources of assistance for the client. In fact, social workers, supervisors, and administrators must understand their ethical obligations when any client is terminated prematurely. The NASW Code of Ethics (National Association of Social Workers, 2017) states the following:

> Social workers should take reasonable steps to avoid abandoning clients who are still in need of services. Social workers should withdraw services precipitously only under unusual circumstances, giving careful consideration to all factors in the situation and taking care to minimize possible adverse effects. Social workers should assist in making appropriate arrangements for continuation of services when necessary. (p. 17)

Planned Endings

Planned endings are always preferable, as they allow for a mutually understood process, review of work completed, and a seamless transition to a new practitioner, as needed. Often the time limits imposed by the agency or funding source are well known in advance of the ending and can be planned for proactively. In many of these cases, the client will have achieved some, if not all, of their treatment goals at termination yet may still benefit by referrals to other types of services, such as low-income housing, employment services, or education supports. If the social worker has planned a departure from the agency, they must consider the needs of their clients with respect to continued services with another provider. When a referral is made, best practice involves a transfer of case-related information to the new provider, ideally through a meeting that includes the client as well as the referring and receiving practitioner. If records are requested by the new provider, the client must sign a consent for release of information for that to occur in an ethically responsible manner. In some settings, such as hospice agencies, services end with the death of the client. Referrals for family members may be indicated if they opt for on-going grief and loss services or supports.

Activities of the Ending Phase

Effectively timed, planned, and executed endings increase the likelihood that clients will sustain gains that were made over the course of service delivery. In the best of circumstances, agency time limits and ending criteria are explained during the first meeting with the client. As the ending phase nears, the practitioner will, ideally, partner with the client in carrying out activities aimed at solidifying progress and creating closure (Walsh, 2016). Each of those activities are discussed below.

Review Gains Made

Client confidence in their ability to successfully transition from social work services is buttressed through a review of progress they have made during the service delivery period. This review may focus on the steps taken, skills acquired, and movement made toward their treatment goals. Clients are typically asked to reflect on changes and achievements, however small; practitioners often offer their own perspective on shifts in client thinking and behavior that have been observed. Even when clients continue to struggle with presenting problems, they may embrace the suggestion that resiliency is a process that evolves over time. For example, at the end of her stay in a shelter, a survivor of domestic violence may remain highly ambivalent about leaving her abusive partner. Nonetheless, she could be recognized for her success in registering for college, obtaining financial aid, and becoming more independent.

Create Change Maintenance Plan

Planning for the maintenance of change often begins with consideration of ways to taper services so that there is greater and greater time between meetings as the end nears. This allows the client to gradually experience some of the stressors that are likely to occur once services have ended completely. Whenever possible, future challenges should be anticipated, with a focus on how the client will cope and utilize newly acquired skills. If the client is recovering from a mental health or substance abuse disorder, planning should include efforts to identify triggers (people, places, circumstances that increase the likelihood of relapse) and how they will be managed. Or, if the client suffers from post-traumatic stress disorder, planning would focus on the management of symptoms related to trauma reminders. Sources of informal support (provided by family, friends, neighbors) are often explored as alternatives or supplements to professional services.

Address Continuing Needs

Even after problems are resolved, underlying needs must be met for clients to function optimally following discharge from services. Referrals may be needed for concrete resources, such as stable housing, transportation, and child or elder care. Safety planning is imperative for high-risk clients, along with prearranged appointments for psychiatric care or on-going therapy. Many clients benefit by engagement in social and recreational programs, or those that offer peer support. For those seeking employment or education, the focus may be on completing applications for colleges, adult education, or job search assistance programs. A well-rounded plan for addressing on-going needs is vital to change maintenance.

Process Client Reactions to Ending

Client reactions to the ending of services are multifaceted. When outcomes have been positive, the individual will likely display pride in their achievements and excitement about moving forward. They may also reveal increased confidence in their ability to establish healthy and productive relationships as a result of the caring, professional partnership they experienced with the social worker. At the same time, the client may feel sadness at the loss of this relationship, and anxiety about a future without the support of professional services. These emotions should be recognized and validated. On the other hand, some clients experience relief when they have completed a rehabilitation or treatment program, whether their participation was voluntary or involuntary. Others react to the end of services by ignoring it and avoiding discussion of its relevance. If avoidance is an on-going interpersonal pattern for the client, the practitioner might ask gently probing questions to facilitate mutual recognition of the ending.

Conduct Ending Rituals and Celebrations

Successful endings often include rituals or celebrations that acknowledge the client's graduation from services. Whenever possible, these rituals should incorporate the client's cultural traditions as they relate to ending relationships. Physical reminders of the learning attained are commonly used, such as certificates of completion or good-bye cards. When the client is transitioning from a therapeutic group, it is customary for the participants to hold a party and share their fond memories of the departing group member.

Creative Social Worker, a blog developed by Social Work Helper (2019) for sharing social work interventions, offers a variety of creative activities that may be used to end the therapeutic relationship. They each make use of a metaphor for helping youth understand service endings.

- Ready to Set Sail: A toy boat is used to represent the voyage the client will take as they transition from services. The youth is asked to complete small cards on which they note what they will take with them as they depart (lessons learned, skills acquired, etc.). These cards are then placed inside the boat that the youth will take home at the close of services.
- Treasure Chest: A small wooden "treasure" box is decorated by the client and filled with color-coded, jewel-adorned cards on which the youth notes their treasures (strengths, supportive people, self-care activities, etc.).
- Suitcase: A small plastic or cardboard suitcase is decorated by the client. Similar to the above activities, the youth is asked to complete cards on which they note what they have learned and what they will take with them on their journey. The suitcase is then filled with the cards and taken home.

Supplies for these exercises are readily available in most craft stores and easily applied. The resulting exercises provide an opportunity for clients to process their ending and leave services with a transitional object, one that offers comfort, while symbolizing their attachment to those who helped facilitate their growth.

Self-Care: Addressing Practitioner Reactions to Endings

In addition to satisfaction and fulfillment, social workers may feel sadness or unease during the ending process, particularly if the professional relationship with their client was mutually gratifying. These reactions can be due, in part, to the practitioner's understanding that they will most likely never know what the future holds for the individuals they have served. Letting go can be hard at times. If the ending occurred with poor outcomes, the social worker may experience feelings of guilt or anger. Supervision is an important vehicle for processing and resolving these commonly experienced emotional reactions. It is a sign of strength versus weakness to access supervision for the purpose of coping with reactions to service endings.

Self-care for the social worker during or following endings may also be furthered though participation in self-soothing activities. For some, this involves spending time with friends and family. For others, connecting with nature provides comfort and perspective. Many find that hobbies or recreational activities help reduce stress, and that "unplugging" from technology, for a period of time, provides needed respite. Mindfulness exercises or meditation may rekindle awareness that all things have a beginning and an end. By recognizing emotions and accepting loss, practitioners reduce overall suffering and sustain their commitment to the helping profession.

NARRATIVE APPLICATION: Ending Internship

Kirk was a social work student doing his internship at an adult day program that served individuals with developmental disabilities. He had worked closely with Reggie, a 35-year-old with Down syndrome. As the end of his internship neared, Kirk became increasing concerned about how Reggie might react to his departure. He discussed his concerns with his supervisor, and they created a plan for the transition of services to another worker, Ray. Kirk took Reggie on an outing, and with his agreement, included Ray. As they ran errands, Kirk acknowledged how much progress Reggie had made in learning how to socialize and use good boundaries. He asked Reggie to tell Ray about his increased comfort level in public. Reggie complied and also told Ray about his favorite activities. By the end of the trip, it was clear that they had forged a connection. The next day, Kirk reminded Reggie that his time at the center would be ending soon and suggested that Ray was someone he could count on when he needed help. Reggie agreed and said with a smile, "I like him." On Kirk's last day, a good-bye party was held in his honor.

Several staff members spoke to the attendees (including participants, family members, and employees) about how hard it was to say good-bye, and went on to say that they were very glad to have had the opportunity to work with Kirk. With Ray at his side, Reggie presented Kirk with a gift—a framed photo of the day-program group, signed by all. Kirk's concerns about Reggie were alleviated, and he left the program with some very fond memories.

Practice Model Perspectives on Endings

As was shown in the previous chapter, varying practice models approach the early and middle stages of intervention quite differently, although similarities clearly exist as well. This also holds true for the ending phase of service delivery—each model approaches it in a manner that is consistent with its tenets, although some elements are shared. The chapter now turns to discussion of ending principles and procedures that have been specified for solution-focused interviewing, narrative practice, and cognitive-behavioral intervention. It will be apparent that some of these guidelines are shared across these three models, while others are quite unique.

Solution-Focused Interviewing

When using a solution-focused approach, the social worker begins to focus on the ending of services in the goal-setting stage, when targets for change are specified and prioritized. This paves the road for an on-going process of progress monitoring and later decisions about when services are no longer needed.

Ending sessions are often begun by asking the client, "What's better?" (De Jong & Berg, 2002). This question is very different from the ill-advised "Is anything better since our last session?" The latter communicates doubts about client progress, while the former relays confidence in the client's ability to make change. When the client responds to "What's better?" with exceptions to the problem, these are explored and amplified. A follow-up question might be, "What else is better?" (p. 143), with further exceptions handled in a similar fashion. Scaling questions are also used to highlight progress made and gauge the client's confidence in their ability to persist with their plan after services have ended. "What number on our scale of 1 to 10 would you need to be for our work to be done?" This line of inquiry opens the door for the development of strategies needed to enhance confidence and sustain change. O'Connell (2005) suggests the following questions for use in the ending phase:

- What will you need to help you stay on track? What support will you need to continue making change?
- What will be the first thing you will do if the problem returns?
- When you know something does not work, how will you help yourself from doing it again?
- How will you remind yourself about the things that you now know help? (p. 92)

Answers to these inquiries form the basis for a change maintenance plan.

NARRATIVE APPLICATION: Solution-Focused Approach to Ending

Ginger was a 75-year-old woman who had been seeing a social worker (Wendy) for home-based counseling to address her social isolation and severe depression. Ginger lived in an active adult community but stayed primarily to herself due to her depressed moods, apathy, and fatigue. She had been married to her ex-husband for 20 years, but they divorced the previous year after it became clear that he had reunited with his high school sweetheart.

As a result of her counseling with Wendy, Ginger's mood, energy level, and self-worth had improved. The social worker had used the miracle question and exception finding to help Ginger recognize her strengths, social skills and interest in pursuing new relationships. Ginger joined a bridge club in her community and looked forward to weekly games with her new acquaintances. As their counseling sessions were coming to a close, Wendy asked her the following:

Social Worker: "What's better?"

Ginger: "I wake up feeling good."

Social Worker: "Feeling good how?"

Ginger: "I have energy now to face the day."

Social Worker: "Wow, you have come long way since we first met. What else is better?"

Ginger: "I am not afraid of going out of my house. I like my new friends."

Social Worker: "You are happier when you have something social to look forward to."

Ginger: "Yes, I am."

Social Worker: "So Ginger, on our scale of 1 to 10, how confident do you feel about continuing this progress as services end?"

Ginger: "I am feeling pretty confident. I would say about an 8."

Social Worker: "You are much more confident than before! What will need to happen to bring your score up to a 9?"

Ginger: "I think I just need to do it and see that I can."

Social Worker: "I have every confidence in you. What is the first thing you will do if your depression returns?"

Ginger: "I will remind myself that ex-husband can't hold me back from having new people in my life. Being around them will help. If that doesn't work, I will call you and see if you can come out again."

Social Worker: "That's always an option. Let's plan on checking in again in a couple of weeks."

Ginger: "Yes, that would be good."

Narrative Practice

Consistent with its focus on the client's life story, a narrative approach views the ending of services as a natural transition into a new and more hopeful chapter in life. In fact, the narrative model rejects the notion of termination as loss and instead views it as a rite of passage; adoption of this metaphor helps clients move from "problematic statuses to unproblematic ones" (Epston & White, 1995, p. 342). In ending sessions, the practitioner consults with the client as they conduct a historical review of the service delivery process and the thematic shifts that have occurred. Therapeutic documents are revisited (notes, letters, drawings) and the social worker may offer an additional letter that shares their perceptions of the client's growth (see Highlight 10.1) and/or a certificate that recognizes the client's success. "Unique redescription questions" are asked that prompt the client to reflect upon insights they have attained; "unique possibility questions" explore how the future may unfold, based on all that the client has learned (pp. 348–349).

The "definitional ceremony," developed by White (2007), is another process that occurs in the ending phase of narrative work. A structured forum is held in which the client shares aspects of their life story that depict its evolution. An audience is present that may include family members, friends, and/or community members who have engaged in their own narrative work. After the client has shared, participants discuss what they have learned from the presentation and how it relates to their own life experiences (Van Hook, 2014). The primary purpose of this meeting is to affirm and solidify the client's newly framed life story.

HIGHLIGHT 10.1: Sample Letter from Social Worker to Client

Dear Hannah,

I am honored to have had the opportunity to work with you over the last several months. When we started, you saw yourself as a victim due to all the situations in which you were degraded and mistreated. You were having a hard time resisting the influence of Black Hole, who had convinced you that you were worthless. You did the hard work of tracing the effects he had on your health and relationships. Then, something important happened. You remembered several sparkling moments in which you refused to listen to Black Hole and allowed Joy into your life. This showed that you have the strength to stand up for yourself and claim your self-worth. Your new life story is so powerful—it shows that you are a survivor and uniquely capable of helping others who struggle with Black Hole. Thank you for allowing me to be part your journey.

Sincerely, S. W.

Cognitive-Behavioral Intervention

Like practitioners of solution-focused practice, those utilizing cognitive-behavioral intervention begin to anticipate endings at the onset of service delivery, when desired end behaviors are identified. As treatment progresses, the client is prepared to apply problem-solving and coping skills in their natural environment, without the direct support of the social worker. In fact, "the ultimate goal of the cognitive-behavioral therapist is to work himself out of a job by teaching the client the skills needed to solve problems on his/her own" (Nelson & Politano, 1993, p. 255). One method of promoting the generalization of skills across settings and situations involves the use of homework assignments. As discussed in the previous chapter, self-monitoring through the completion of thought records and rating scales is encouraged in this approach to change. The ultimate goal is to enhance the client's self-efficacy, or sense of competence in managing, thoughts, emotions, and behavior.

When service completion nears, the practitioner will explore the client's thoughts about ending services. They will also reduce the frequency of sessions and support the client in creating a relapse prevention plan that identifies risks and how they will be managed. In some cases, a "self-therapy" program is developed toward the maintenance of "healthy cognitive practices" (Walsh, 2016, p. 90). The plan might include regular practice of controlled breathing, journaling, or recording thoughts, and relaxation or mindfulness activities. Booster sessions are often scheduled to allow the client to return once or twice after a period of time (1–3 months) post termination.

Types of Evaluation

Service ending also involves the completion of efforts to evaluate services provided. While evaluation may begin well before case closure, it is typically finalized at termination. Both process and outcome evaluations provide a wealth of information that may be used to recognize strengths and design needed improvements for service delivery programs. They promote accountability on the part of the social worker and their agency, and further their compliance with ethical standards for the profession. The NASW Code of Ethics states that "social workers should monitor and evaluate policies, the implementation of programs, and practice interventions" (National Association of Social Workers, 2017, Section 5.02).

Process Evaluation

Process evaluation is a systematic inquiry into the nature of services provided and the extent to which interventions were delivered as planned. It may include a focus on who was served, how often, and how, along with clients' level of satisfaction with the process. Methods used for this type of evaluation are quite varied. Records may be reviewed to gather data regarding the focus of services delivered. Survey questionnaires or scales may be administered to clients to ascertain their perspective on the process and the degree to which it was helpful. Qualitative research methods are often used, including client interviews or focus groups with program participants. Recordings (video or audio) are also used to assess implementation; participant observation or shadowing of practitioners during client sessions, are particularly valuable methods for evaluating their process.

A special type of process evaluation is referred to as **fidelity assessment**. It evaluates the extent to which services adhered to the principles of the evidence-based practice model adopted. This type of evaluation is increasingly understood to be vital in demonstrating accountability for practice that is faithful to the program's core components. "It allows for feedback and improvement, as well as opportunities for quality assurance and continuous quality improvement" (U.S. Department of Health and Human Services, n.d., p. 2).

Fidelity can be monitored using one or more of the following methods:

- Semi-structured interviews with service providers, clients, and others involved in service delivery
- Surveys administered to clients, practitioners, and other program stakeholders

- Documentation review using tools for measuring adherence to essential practices
- Observation rating scales employed by external evaluators during client sessions, groups, or family and team meetings

Brenda was a recent college graduate who had thrived in her research courses. Upon finishing the BSW program, she accepted a job on the evaluation team at a large nonprofit organization serving high-risk youth and families. Her first assignment was to participate in fidelity assessment for the agency's wraparound program (see Chapter 4 for an introduction to the wraparound process). She received intensive training in the use of the Team Observation Form (TOM), developed by the Wraparound Fidelity Evaluation and Research Team based at the University of Washington. She was then responsible for observing wraparound team meetings and recoding whether or not indicators of high-fidelity practice were evident. The tool includes 36 items that are organized around seven categories: full meeting attendance, effective teamwork, driven by strengths and family, based on priority needs, use of natural and community supports, outcomes-based process, and skilled facilitation. Following the meetings, she calculated scores for each category, produced a total fidelity score for the meeting, and shared the results with the facilitator before submitting them to the program director.

Brenda was confident in her ratings and scoring but was anxious about discussing results with wraparound facilitators. On one occasion in particular, she worried about the reaction of the facilitator due to low scores in domains related to attendance and use of natural and community supports. She tried to soften the negative feedback when meeting with facilitator, Rob.

Brenda: "Rob, you received really high scores for your facilitation skills. It's clear you know how to run a team meeting."

Rob: "Thanks Brenda, but I see there are low scores in a couple of areas too, and it's pretty frustrating."

Brenda: "Remember that this assessment is not intended to find fault. It's to identify strengths and areas where improvement might help you and the team get better results."

Rob: "Yeah, and I know I am not the only one having a hard time getting agency reps and natural supports to the table."

Brenda: "Yes, I have seen that across the board, and I know it's hard for many wraparound programs to score high in these areas."

Rob: "OK, I'll try not to take it personally. I think our wrap team needs to come up with some solutions to address this issue."

This narrative illustrates the benefits of fidelity assessment, when results are utilized for on-going quality improvement. Ratings should be shared in a supportive and collaborate manner, with the understanding that fidelity to any model of practice evolves over time.

Outcome Evaluation

Outcomes are the product of participation in an intervention process. **Outcome evaluations** provide evidence of change as a result of services rendered—they measure or gather qualitative data about the extent to which clients attained their treatment goals. On a programmatic level, they provide information to support the agency's mission and justify funding received from donors, grants, or state and federal agencies. Data is typically focused on the following:

- Demographics of Client's Served: age, gender, presenting problems
- Client Change: symptom reduction; improvements in physical, psychological, and social functioning; increased access to resources
- Client Satisfaction: consumer views on the strengths and limitations of services received
- Agency Mandates: reduction of recidivism, prevention of hospitalizations or placement in residential care, stability of housing or independent living
- Cost Effectiveness/Cost-Benefit: cost of services in relation to outcomes

Methods for Assessing Client Change

Data concerning client change can be assessed through the use of questionnaires that include closed- and open-ended questions tapping attitudes, knowledge, or self-reported benefits of services received. Such surveys are fairly easy to implement and can be tailored to the characteristics of the program under study. However, self-reported assessments of change do not always offer an accurate account of progress toward service delivery goals. The use of existing **scales** may be a more viable source of data if the instrument has demonstrated adequate **validity** and **reliability.** Validity refers to the tool's ability to measure what is intended; reliability is the consistency with which it does so. Many standardized instruments are available to measure behavioral health symptoms and levels of psychological functioning. Go to the Substance Abuse and Mental Health Service Administration (SAMHSA) website (www.integration.samhsa .gov/clinical-practice/screening-tools) for information about commonly used scales. A select few that are widely used in the mental health field are as follows:

- *Patient Health Questionnaire* (PHQ-9), a nine-item tool for assessing levels of depression (Kroenke, Spitzer, & Williams, 2001)
- *Mood Disorders Questionnaire* (MDQ), a set of 13 questions related to symptoms of bipolar disorder (Hirschfeld et al., 2000)
- *GAD-7*, a seven-item tool for identifying symptoms of generalized anxiety disorder (Spitzer, Kroenke, Williams, & Lowe, 2006)
- *PTSD Checklist*, a 20-item measure of symptoms related to post-traumatic stress disorder (Weathers, Litz, Herman, Huska, & Keane, 1993)
- *Children's Global Assessment Scale* (CGAS), used by clinicians to rate the functioning of children and adolescents (Shaffer et al., 1983)

A unique instrument, the empowerment scale, was developed by Rogers and colleagues (1997). It measures the personal empowerment of mental health consumers using 28 items across five domains: self-esteem, power/powerlessness, community activism and autonomy, optimism and control over the future, and righteous anger. It was created through **participatory action research**, a method in which the researcher assists a disadvantaged group to "define their problems, define the remedies desired, and take the lead in designing the research that will help them realize their aims" (Rubin & Babbie, 2016, p. 309). In this case, the researchers constructed the scale based on input from a consumer research advisory board because they believed that "for evaluation to be meaningful and credible, constituents of that research must be involved" (Rogers, Chamberlin, Ellison, & Crean, 1997, p. 1043). The resulting scale has demonstrated excellent reliability and validity (Rogers, Ralph, & Salzer, 2010).

The Family Empowerment Scale (Koren, DeChillo, & Friesen, 1992) is a 34-item measure of empowerment in parents or other family caregivers of children with emotional, behavioral, or developmental disorders. It assesses caregiver attitudes, knowledge, and behavior consistent with empowerment at the family, service system, and community/political level. It has also shown very good validity and reliability and has been rated as a high-quality empowerment scale (Cyril, Smith, & Renzaho, 2016).

Direct observation also serves as a valuable source of data for measuring client change. For example, home-health practitioners may track client performance with regard to activities of daily living (ADLs). School-based service providers may record information concerning student attendance and behavior in the classroom (e.g., number of outbursts, aggressive incidents, attending behaviors, disciplinary referrals). In some cases, direct observations are guided through the use of a coding system.

A well-studied and validated observational coding system is used in evidence-based treatment programs for children with behavioral problems, such as Parent-Child Interaction Therapy [PCIT] and Incredible Years. The Dyadic Parent-Child Interaction Coding System (DPICS) (Eyberg, Nelson, Ginn, Bhuiyan, & Boggs, 2013) measures the frequency and quality of parent-child interactions during play sessions. More specifically, it guides the recording of both parent behavior (e.g., use of praise, reflections, commands) and child behavior (e.g., compliance, noncompliance). While time consuming to administer, tools of this kind allow for a structured and relatively objective measurement of target behaviors over time.

Assessing Client Satisfaction

Questionnaires measuring satisfaction with services involve clients/consumers in the process of program evaluation. These tools may be devoted to collecting both process and outcome data. A frequently adopted measure, CSQ-8 (Attkisson & Greenfield, 2004) was designed for use in the field of mental health. It includes eight items that rate satisfaction with the amount and quality of services received and whether the respondent would use the service again, if needed. Standardized satisfaction scales used in child welfare include the Parents with Children in Foster Care Satisfaction Scale (Harris, Poertner, & Joe, 2000) and the Parent Satisfaction with Foster Care Services Scale (Kapp & Vela, 2004). A revised version of the Consumer Satisfaction Rating Scale (Con-Sat-R) (Norlander, Ivarsson, Anderson, & Norden, 2016) is now commonly used with clients receiving psychiatric and/or social services. To assess patient satisfaction with medical social work services, the Mayo Foundation for Medical Evaluation and Research (O'Brien & Stewart, 2009) developed a survey that includes seven questions relating to the social worker's communication and responsiveness to patient needs (see Highlight 10.2).

Satisfaction surveys and scales allow clients to offer their perspective about the extent to which services met their expectations. However, these measures are limited by social desirability bias—the tendency to generate responses that present the respondent in a favorable light. This bias has been referred to as the "thank you effect" by Fraser and Wu (2015), who assert that clients typically report high levels of satisfaction due to their appreciation for "even minimal amounts of attention" (p. 771). These authors also suggest that clients may be reluctant to give negative feedback due to fear that it may be held against them when/if they need to access services in the future. It is important that these measures are administered in an anonymous fashion in order to alleviate this concern.

HIGHLIGHT 10.2: Mayo Clinic Satisfaction Scale

Overall, how satisfied were you with your experience with the social worker?

Very	Somewhat		Somewhat	Very
1 ☐ satisfied	2 ☐ satisfied	3 ☐ Neither	4 ☐ dissatisfied	5 ☐ dissatisfied

How helpful were the services provided to you by the social worker?

1 ☐ Very helpful   2 ☐ Somewhat helpful   3 ☐ Not at all helpful

How willing was the social worker to spend time with you?

1 ☐ Very willing   2 ☐ Somewhat willing   3 ☐ Not willing

Did you have issues that would have been difficult to handle without the help of a social worker?

1 ☐ No   2 ☐ Yes

Did the help from the social worker make it easier for you to complete your radiation therapy?

1 ☐ No   2 ☐ Yes

How did the social worker help you with your radiation therapy?

_____

_____

_____

Thank you, you are finished.

FIGURE 10.1. Mayo Clinic Satisfaction Scale.

A commonly used qualitative method for assessing client satisfaction is the **focus group interview**. It allows the evaluator to gain information on a single topic from multiple individuals simultaneously. According to Vaughn and colleagues (1996), focus group membership should range from 6–12, and discussion should be moderated by a skilled facilitator who ensures adequate structure within an atmosphere that is participatory and relaxed. In the field of healthcare, focus group interviews are becoming the norm for soliciting opinions, perceptions, thoughts, and experiences of service users. A study of the use of focus groups in the field of community mental health (Zupančič, Pahor & Kogovšek, 2018) found that they are a useful tool for engaging consumers in evaluating the quality of mental health services. Caution must be exercised in interpreting the results of focus group data, however, as they may not generalize to other groups or programs.

Agency Outcome Reporting: Where Macro Meets Micro

The documentation that direct service practitioners complete for their public or private organization forms the basis for reports that must be submitted for the agency to comply with legislation and funding requirements. A prime example is seen in the field of public child welfare. The U.S. Department of Health and Human Services (HSS) creates an annual child welfare outcome report in order to meet the requirements of the Adoption and Safe Families Act of 1997. It compiles data provided by state and local agencies that covers seven outcome categories:

- Reduction of the reoccurrence of child abuse
- Reduction of the incidence of child abuse or neglect in foster care
- Increased permanency for children in foster care
- Reduction of time in foster care to reunification without reentry into the system
- Reduction of time in foster care to adoption
- Increased placement stability
- Reduced placements of young children in group homes or institutions

Such clearly articulated outcomes provide guidance for social workers in understanding the ultimate aims of their services. Go to the HSS website at https://www.acf.hhs.gov/ for more detailed information on these reported outcomes.

Cost Evaluation

Cost evaluation is carried out with differing types of data and analyses. Cost comparisons simply offer detailed accounts of the costs related to two or more programs. **Cost-effectiveness analysis** compares the efficiency of treatment alternatives in achieving desired outcomes that are measured in nonmonetary units. An example is seen in a study that focused on the cost effectiveness of multisystemic therapy (MST), an intensive, community-based treatment for juvenile offenders (Sheidow, Jayawardhana, Bradford, Henggeler, & Shapiro, 2012). The researchers calculated cost-effectiveness ratios for this treatment and for usual community services, as provided to substance-abusing youth participating in family or drug court. These ratios were based on average cost per case over outcomes of substance use and criminal activity. Results showed that multisystemic therapy was more cost effective than usual community services, particularly in reducing alcohol and poly-drug substance use in youth.

Cost-benefit analysis involves the placement of a monetary value on each outcome of an evaluation. The overall financial benefit of the program is calculated based on the value of the combined outcomes after accounting for costs related to service delivery. An illustration of this type of analysis compared the cost/benefit of multisystemic therapy with that of individual therapy provided to juvenile offenders (Klietz, Borduin, & Schaeffer, 2010). The value of crime reduction was based on estimated savings with respect to law enforcement services, court processing, community supervision, and potential losses for crime victims. Results showed that while the cost for MST services was much higher than the cost of individual therapy, its financial benefit was substantially greater due its success in preventing the costs associated with crime. This type of information is quite valuable to agency staff and administrators who are considering investment in the adoption of an evidence-based treatment.

Reflexive Practice/Feedback-Informed Treatment

In addition to formal evaluations conducted on an agency-wide level, reflexive intervention may be carried out by the practicing social worker who systematically monitors the success of their own practice (DePoy & Gilson, 2003, p. 142). Using this approach, the practitioner reviews each session to ascertain what happened and how, what worked well, and what needs to be done differently. The evidence from this assessment is then used to inform future practice decisions.

Feedback-informed treatment (FIT) is the term utilized in the field of behavioral health for treatment guided by the practitioner's own on-going evaluation. It involves the use of self-report measures, provided routinely to clients to solicit their feedback about the therapeutic relationship as well their progress toward improved personal, interpersonal, and social functioning. This method originated with the introduction of a new paradigm in the mid-1990s: "*patient-focused research*—that is concerned with the monitoring of an individual's progress over the course of treatment and the feedback of this information to the practitioner, supervisor, or case manager" (Howard, Moras, Brill, Martinovich, & Lutz, 1996, p. 1059). Early instruments used to monitor progress were very lengthy, prompting Miller and Duncan to develop scales that are brief (just four items each) and easy to administer: Outcome Rating Scale (ORS) and Session Rating Scale (SRS) (Miller & Duncan, 2000). These measures are designed for implementation on a session-by-session basis and are now the most commonly used feedback-informed treatment tools. Both have demonstrated good reliability and validity when compared with longer FIT scales (Campbell & Hemsley, 2009).

Research has shown that treatment outcomes are enhanced through the adoption of FIT measures. For example, a study performed with clients served at a university-based counseling clinic revealed that those who received feedback-informed treatment made significantly greater gains than those who received treatment as usual (no feedback) (Reese, Norsworthy, & Rowlands, 2009). Research conducted with couples receiving therapy at a community counseling center showed that those who participated in FIT made significantly greater improvement than those in treatment as usual, and displayed almost four times the rates of clinically significant change (Anker, Duncan, & Sparks, 2009). A recent review of research conducted on the impact of FIT showed that in over half of the studies examined, clients receiving FIT made significantly greater gains on at least one outcome. Clients who were not on track benefitted most from feedback to their clinician (Gondek, Edbrooke-Childs, Deighton, & Wolpert, 2016). Similarly, another meta-analysis showed that off-track clients who received feedback-informed treatment had three times the odds of attaining clinically significant improvement than those who received treatment as usual (Lambert & Shimokana, 2011). This approach to reflexive practice is very promising, particularly when adopted with clients who are making limited progress.

HIGHLIGHT 10.3: Feedback-Informed Treatment Scales

Outcome Rating Scale (ORS)

Looking back over the last week (or since your last visit), including today, help us understand how you have been feeling by rating how well you have been doing in the following areas of your life, where marks to the left represent low levels and marks to the right represent high levels.

Overall
(General sense of well-being)
Low _____ High

Individually
(Personal well-being)
Low _____ High

Interpersonally
(Family, close relationships)
Low _____ High

Socially
(Work, school, friendships)
Low _____ High

Session Rating Scale (SRS)

Please rate today's session by placing a hash mark on the line nearest to the description that best fits your experience.

Relationship

| I did not feel heard, under-stood and respected | _____ | I feel heard, understood and respected |

Goals and Topics

| We did not work on or talk about what I wanted to work on or talk about | _____ | We worked on or talked about what I wanted to work on and talk about |

Approach or Method

| The therapist's approach is not a good fit for me | _____ | The therapist's approach is a good fit for me |

Overall

| There was something missing in today's session | _____ | Overall, today's session was right for me |

As with any assessment tool, the effectiveness of FIT scales depends upon the style of administration. When asking clients to complete a routine session or outcome measure, it is important that social workers communicate a genuine desire to learn from the information requested. This allows the service recipient to feel safe offering their perceptions of the strengths and limitations of services rendered. Furthermore, FIT empowers clients to use their voice and allows the service provider to self-correct any aspects of their approach that is not working well or achieving intended results. The social worker's hunger for feedback is key to professional growth, an assertion that will be explored further in the upcoming chapter. Another benefit of on-going feedback is that it allows for a deeper understanding of evaluation data provided at case closure.

SUMMARY

This chapter focuses on the process involved with ending social work services. The differing types of endings were discussed, along with activities that promote a smooth transition and the maintenance of change following termination of services. Self-care was addressed as it relates to practitioner reactions to endings. Perspectives on termination/transition were also offered, as advanced by differing practice models: solution-focused interviewing, narrative approach, and cognitive-behavioral intervention. Evaluation methods, as used to monitor process and measure outcomes, were also covered. The chapter ended by highlighting the value of reflexive practice and feedback-informed treatment.

KEY TERMS

Cost-benefit analysis

Cost-effectiveness analysis

Direct observation

Feedback-informed treatment

Fidelity assessment

Focus group interview

Outcome evaluation

Participatory action research

Planned endings

Process evaluation

Reflexive intervention

Scales (validity and reliability)

Unplanned endings

DISCUSSION QUESTIONS

1. What ending rituals and ceremonies might you use with your clients?

2. What reactions to endings will be important for you to process with a trusted colleague or supervisor?

3. How will you incorporate reflexive intervention into your practice?

SKILL DEVELOPMENT ACTIVITIES

1. As an experiment in self-care, unplug completely from technology for one day. Describe your experience.

2. Explore the website for the National Wraparound Implementation Center (NWIC; https://www.nwic.org). What does NWIC offer, and why is it important?

3. Interview a manager or administrator for an agency that provides social work services. Ask about outcome reporting that is done to meet legislative and/or funding requirements.

REFERENCES

Anker, M., Duncan, B., & Sparks, J. (2009). Using client feedback to improve couple therapy outcomes. *Journal of Consulting and Clinical Psychology, 77*, 693–704.

Attkisson, C. C., & Greenfield, T. K. (2004). The UCSF Client Satisfaction Scales: The Client Satisfaction Questionnaire-8. In M. Maruish (Ed.), *The use of psychological testing for treatment planning and outcome assessment* (3rd. ed.). Mahwah, NJ: Lawrence Erlbaum.

Campbell, A., & Hemsley, S. (2009). Outcome rating scale and session rating scale in psychological practice: Clinical utility of ultra-brief measures. *Clinical Psychologist, 13*, 1–9.

Chamberlin, J. (2015). Are your clients leaving too soon? *Monitor on Psychology, 46*. Retrieved from http://www.apa.org/monitor/2015/04/clients.aspx

Cyril, S., Smith, B. J., & Renzaho, A. M. (2016). Systematic review of empowerment measures in health promotion. *Health Promotion International, 31*, 809–826.

Dawson, K., & Berry, M. (2002). Engaging families in child welfare services: An evidence-based approach to best practice. *Child Welfare, 81*, 293–317.

De Jong, P., & Berg, I. K. (2002). *Interviewing for solutions* (2nd ed.). Pacific Grove, CA: Brooks/Cole-Thomson Learning.

DePoy, E., & Gilson, S. F. (2003). *Evaluation practice: Thinking and action principles for social work practice*. Pacific Grove, CA: Brooks/Cole-Thomson Learning.

Epston, D., & White, M. (1995). Termination as a rite of passage: Questioning strategies for a therapy of inclusion. In R. A. Nielmeyer & M. J. Mahoney (Eds.), *Constructivism in psychotherapy* (pp. 277–313). New York, NY: Guilford Press.

Eyberg, S. M., Nelson, M. M., Ginn, N. C., Bhuiyan, N., & Boggs, S. R. (2013). *Dyadic parent-child interaction coding system: Comprehensive manual for research and training* (4th ed.). Gainesville, FL: PCIT International.

Fraser, M. W., & Wu, S. (2016). Measures of consumer satisfaction in social welfare and behavioral health: A systematic review. *Research on Social Work Practice, 26*, 762–776.

Gondek, D., Edbrooke-Childs, J., Deighton, J., & Wolpert, M. (2016). Feedback from outcome measures and treatment effectiveness, treatment efficiency, and collaborative practice: A systematic review. *Administration and Policy in Mental Health and Mental Health Services Research, 43*, 325–343.

Harris, G., Poertner, J., & Joe, S. (2000). The parents with children in foster care satisfaction scale. *Administration in Social Work, 24*, 15–27.

Hepworth, D. H., Rooney, R. H., Rooney, G. D., Strom-Gottfried, K., & Larsen, J. (2010). *Direct social work practice: Theory and skills*. Belmont, CA: Brooks/Cole, Cengage Learning.

Hirschfeld, R. M., Williams, J. B., Spitzer, R. L., Calabrese, J. R., Flynn, L., Keck, P.E., Jr., ... Zajecka, J. (2000). Development and validation of a screening instrument for bipolar spectrum disorder: The Mood Disorder Questionnaire. *American Journal of Psychiatry, 157*, 1873–1875.

Howard, K. I., Moras, K., Brill, P. L., Martinovich, Z., & Lutz, W. (1996). Evaluation of psychotherapy: Efficacy, effectiveness, and patient progress. *American Psychologist, 51*, 1059–1064.

Kapp, S. A., Vela, R. H. (2004). The parent satisfaction with foster care services scale. *Child Welfare, 83*, 263–287.

Klietz, S. J., Borduin, C. M., & Schaeffer, C. M. (2010). Cost-benefit analysis of multisystemic therapy with serious and violent juvenile offenders. *Journal of Family Psychology, 24*, 657–666.

Koren, P. E., DeChillo, N., & Friesen, B. J. (1992). Measuring empowerment in families whose children have emotional disabilities: A brief questionnaire. *Rehabilitation Psychology, 37*, 305–321.

Kroenke, K., Spitzer, R. L., & Williams, J. B. (2001). The PHQ-9: Validity of a brief depression severity measure. *Journal of General Internal Medicine, 16*(9), 606–613.

Lambert, M. J., & Shimokana, K. (2011). Collecting client feedback. *Psychotherapy, 48*, 72–79.

Miller, S. D., & Duncan, B. L. (2000). *The outcome and session rating scales*. Chicago, IL: International Center for Clinical Excellence.

Nelson, W. M., & Politano, P. M. (1995). The goal is to say "goodbye" and have the treatment effects generalize and maintain. *Journal of Cognitive Psychotherapy, 7*, 251–263.

Norlander, T., Ivarsson, B., Andersson, J., & Norden, T. (2016). Consumer satisfaction rating scale: Revised for use in both psychiatric care and social services. *Social Behavior and Personality, 44*, 931–942.

National Association of Social Workers. (2017). *Code of ethics of the National Association of Social Workers*. Washington, DC: NASW Press.

O'Brien, M. W., & Stewart, S. J. (2009). Measuring satisfaction with social work services. *Social Work in Health Care, 48*, 105–118.

O'Connell, B. (2005). *Solution-focused therapy*. Thousand Oaks, CA: SAGE.

Reese, R. J., Norsworthy, L. A., & Rowlands, S. R. (2009). Does a continuous feedback system improve psychotherapy outcomes? *Psychotherapy: Theory, Research, Practice, Training, 46*, 418–43.

Rogers, E. S., Chamberlin, J., Ellison, H. L., & Crean, T. (1997). A consumer-constructed scale to measure empowerment among users of mental health services. *Psychiatric Services, 48*, 1042–1047.

Rogers, E. S., Ralph, R. O., & Salzer, M. S. (2010). Validating the empowerment scale with a multisite sample of consumers of mental health services. *Psychiatric Services, 61*, 933–936.

Rubin, A., & Babbie, E. (2016). *Essential research methods for social work* (4th ed.). Boston, MA: Cengage Learning.

Shaffer, D., Gould, M. S., Brasic, J., Ambrosini, P., Fisher, P., Bird, H., & Aluwahlia, S. (1983). A children's global assessment scale (CGAS). *Archives of General Psychiatry, 40*, 1228–31.

Sheidow, A., Jayawardhana, J., Bradford, W. D., Henggeler, S. W., & Shapiro, S. B. (2012). Money matters: Cost-effectiveness of juvenile drug court with and without evidence-based treatments. *Journal of Child & Adolescent Substance Abuse, 21*, 69–90.

Social Work Helper. (2019). Ending the therapeutic relationship: Creative termination activities. Retrieved from https://www.socialworkhelper.com/2014/04/02/ending-therapeutic-relationship-creative-termination-activities/

Spitzer, R. L., Kroenke, K., Williams, J. B., & Lowe, B. (2006). A brief measure for assessing generalized anxiety disorder: The GAD-7. *Archives of Internal Medicine, 166*(10), 1092–1097.

U.S. Department of Health and Human Service. (n.d.). *Fidelity monitoring tip sheet.* Retrieved from www.acf.hhs.gov/sites/default/files/fysb/prep-fidelity-monitoring-ts.pdf

U.S. Department of Health and Human Services, Administration for Children and Families. (2019). *Child Welfare Outcomes 2015: Report to Congress.* Retrieved from https://www.acf.hhs.gov/cb/resource/cwo-2015

Van Hook, M. P. (2014). *Social work practice with families: A resiliency-based approach* (2nd ed.). Chicago, IL: Lyceum Books.

Vaughn, S., Shay Schumm, J., & Sinagub, J. M. (1996). *Focus group interviews in education and psychology.* Thousand Oaks: SAGE.

Walsh, J. (2016). *Endings in clinical practice: Effective closure in diverse settings* (2nd ed.) New York, NY: Oxford University Press.

Weathers, F., Litz, B., Herman, D., Huska, J., & Keane, T. (1993, October). *The PTSD checklist (PCL): Reliability, validity, and diagnostic utility.* Paper presented at the Annual Convention of the International Society for Traumatic Stress Studies, San Antonio, TX.

White, M. (2007). *Maps of narrative practice.* New York, NY: W. W. Norton

Zupančič, V., Pahor, M., & Kogovšek, T. (2018). Focus group in community mental health research: Need for adaption. *Community Mental Health Journal*, 1–12.

CREDITS

CHAPTER 11

Supervision and Lifelong Learning

I am always doing that which I cannot do, in order that I may learn how to do it.—PABLO PICASSO

T HE TERM *RISK* takes on a negative connotation in social work when it is applied to client factors, such as poverty or oppression, that are associated with adverse conditions. Risky behavior on the part of an individual may be seen as an indication of poor judgement or inadequate impulse control. Conversely, *risk taking* by the social worker is thought to be an essential component of professional growth and goal attainment when it is executed with care and deliberation. This chapter is devoted to ways that practitioners may take healthy risks during supervision and, thereby, set the stage for a lifelong process of learning. The chapter will begin with a focus on the purpose of supervision, followed by ways that the social worker can make maximum use of this vital resource. It will continue with discussion of the meaning of lifelong learning and strategies for furthering it throughout one's career.

Purpose of Supervision

The field of social work is evolving toward a deepened appreciation for the value of supervision as a vehicle for enhancing the professional development of social work employees and students. Supervision provides critical support, education, and guidance for practitioners, and ensures that they are doing what's needed to protect clients and maintain ethical and other professional standards. As stated by Kadushin and Harkness (2002), modern social work supervision can be thought of as a "three-legged stool" that includes a focus on administration, education, and support of social workers. At its best, supervision is built on a relationship of trust, respect, confidentiality, and empathy between supervisor and supervisee (National Association of Social Workers, 2013). This allows for emotional safety as the supervisee assumes a critical lens in viewing their practice and recognizing areas for growth. Both parties in the supervisory relationship bear responsibility for sustaining a trusting and collaborative partnership.

Social exchange theory, as proposed by Blau (1964), offers insight into the development of a strong supervisory relationship. This theory suggests that an interpersonal connection is valued to the extent that one's efforts and investment are balanced by benefits and rewards. As applied to supervision, benefits can include job satisfaction and enhanced effectiveness (Kadushin & Harkness, 2002). Additionally, effective supervision "is known to serve as a buffer against stressful work conditions, to provide protection from unreasonable job demands, to offer emotional and social support during difficult times, and to guide workers in negotiating the challenges of the job and the organizational context" (Mor Barak, Travis, Pyun, & Xie, 2009, p. 4).

In a review of 27 studies of supervision conducted between 1990 and 2007 across child welfare, social work, and mental health settings, Mor Barak et al., (2009) and colleagues found that the supervisory dimensions of task assistance, socioemotional support, and interpersonal interaction were positively associated with favorable outcomes for supervisees.

Task assistance encompasses instruction, training, and coaching in the completion of assigned duties. *Social and emotional support* includes listening to supervisees as they share work-related stress and providing supportive comments and perspectives. *Supervisory interpersonal interaction* refers to the worker's perception of the overall quality of their experience with supervision. Based on these findings, the researchers developed a conceptual framework that guides understanding of the pathways from these dimensions to either detrimental or beneficial outcomes for workers. Detrimental outcomes of poor supervision include burnout, anxiety, and job-related stress, while beneficial outcomes of effective supervision are job satisfaction and worker well-being, effectiveness, and commitment to the organization (see Figure 11.1). When social workers need help in any one of these dimensions, it is important that they find a way to ask for what they need. If the primary supervisor is unavailable or unprepared to provide needed assistance, the social worker is advised to seek out strong mentors in the workplace who can provide task assistance and support or engage in constructive and instructive conversation. In fact, mentoring by colleagues can be a valuable supplement to guidance provided by even the most involved and effective supervisor.

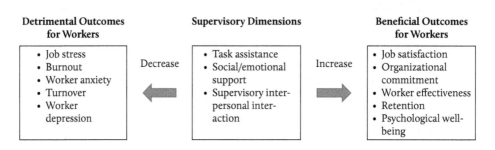

FIGURE 11.1. Mor Borak's Conceptual Model of the Effects of Supervision.

Adapted from Mor Barak, Travis, Pyun, & Xie (2009).

Learning Objectives

It is rare and improbable that any entry level social worker will have all of the knowledge and skill they will need to attain superior performance. In fact, the primary responsibility of the early career social worker is to learn through observation, inquiry, and action aimed at building competency. It is also important that they understand the learning or performance objectives that they are working toward to demonstrate effectiveness on the job; these are ideally developed in collaboration with the supervisor. Performance objectives generally fall into one of several categories: knowledge, skill, relationship building, and multicultural awareness.

Knowledge

Knowledge is obtained through critical thinking as it relates to human behavior theories that have relevance to the population being served—many have been discussed and applied in this text. The acquisition of knowledge also entails staying current on research data and evaluation reports that explain client and community needs, risk and resiliency factors, and the benefits of various approaches to intervention. Learning as it pertains to community resources is also beneficial across all service settings.

Foundational social work knowledge also includes information specific to the practitioner's subfield of practice. For example, child protection services (CPS) workers need to understand the role of social work in the various stages of the CPS process: intake, investigations, on-going child protection. They also need knowledge as it pertains to risk assessment, signs of safety, court reporting, and the importance of permanency in supporting healthy child development. Social workers in the behavioral health field need knowledge of diagnostic categories, as defined by the *Diagnostic and Statistical Manual of Mental Disorders* (*DSM*) (American Psychiatric Association, 2013), risk factors for suicide and harm to others, and criteria for admission to various levels of care, such as outpatient, inpatient, and partial hospitalization programs. Practitioners who work with older adults must acquire knowledge related to healthy aging, activities of daily living (ADL), and various forms of cognitive impairment, including vascular dementia and Alzheimer's disease. Following completion of a social work degree, continuing education is vital, as new knowledge is constantly emerging across all subfields of practice.

Skill

Skill embodies a wide range of abilities needed to meet job requirements and expectations. Most social work positions require skill in engagement, crisis intervention, assessment, goal setting, intervention, and documentation. Use of technology is an area of skill development that is increasingly important across all subfields of social work—it contributes to successful networking, data collection, grant writing, and research. Effective verbal and written communication is needed to carry out assignments involving education, outreach, counseling, report writing, and record keeping; bilingual and bicultural skills are highly valued in the profession. Organizational and time management skill is required by most, if not all, social work positions.

Some areas of skill development are specific to the mission of the organization. For instance, workers in the field of behavioral health need skill in conducting recovery plans to prevent relapse in clients served. Medical social workers require skill as it relates to discharge planning and short-term grief and loss support counseling. Practitioners in domestic violence programs are expected to be skilled in advocacy, safety planning, and case management. Finally, workers in veteran services must recognize symptoms of post-traumatic stress disorder and utilize evidence-based approaches to treat this condition. These are just a few examples of specialized skills required by various agencies that employ social workers.

Relationship Building

Of paramount importance in the profession of social work is successful relationship building with colleagues, co-workers, supervisors, clients, and interagency or interdisciplinary partners. Key to effective work relationships are trust, consideration, honesty, tact, and valuing the opinions of others (Tallia, Lanham, McDaniel, & Crabtree, 2006). When conflicts or disputes occur, one is advised to go directly to the other person involved as opposed to complaining and gossiping about the issue with others. When meeting to discuss differing views, the social worker must be prepared to understand the perspective of the other individuals who have a stake in resolving the problem.

Emotional intelligence (EQ) is an essential ingredient of healthy professional relationships. It facilitates interaction between colleagues and co-workers that is genuine, nonjudgmental, and respectful. As discussed by Goleman (1998), the emotionally intelligent individual has a high degree of self-awareness, self-regulation, motivation, empathy, and social skill. "*Self-awareness* means having a deep understanding of one's emotions, strengths, weaknesses, needs, and drives" (p. 95). People who are self-aware understand how their feelings and moods affect others, themselves, and their own work performance. *Self-regulation* is the ability to master one's emotions and impulses. Individuals with the capacity to self-regulate tend to be thoughtful and calm under pressure—they also cope well with change and ambiguity. *Motivation* is the drive to succeed beyond expectations. This drive is aimed at achieving for the sake of achievement versus toward some external recognition or reward. *Empathy* allows one to recognize the emotions of others, appreciate their viewpoints, and offer feedback in a caring and considerate manner. *Social skill* includes the ability to build bonds, establish rapport, and utilize persuasion effectively.

One or more domains of emotional intelligence may form the basis for a professional goal or objective. While many practitioners take pride in their ability to empathize with others, some may benefit by improved self-awareness or self-regulation. Others may need to focus on enhancing motivation as it relates to particular aspects of their assigned responsibilities. Social skill development may be devoted to new assignments involving networking or team leadership.

The profession of social work offers many opportunities to build EQ and model its use for clients and colleagues.

Multicultural Awareness

As discussed in previous chapters, multicultural awareness begins with an understanding of one's own culture and built-in biases. It is furthered with a humble approach to learning about the cultural identity of others. Knowledge of the cultural groups served by one's organization supports effective engagement. Yet, many social service agencies serve cultural groups disproportionally; outreach to underserved, at-risk populations may be needed to reverse this trend. Social workers should also embrace cultural differences with their colleagues based on race, ethnicity, primary language, gender identity, or generation (baby boomers, Generation X, Y, Z). In doing so, they support their organization's movement beyond diverse hiring practices to the creation of an **inclusive environment** (Cox & Steiner, 2013). An inclusive workplace is one in which people of diverse cultural groups are embraced and integrated across all levels of the organization.

HIGHLIGHT 11.1: Multigenerational Workforce

In recent years, increased attention has been devoted to the impact of multigenerational diversity in the workplace. The implications of shifting demographics for the profession of social work is discussed by NASW Senior Practice Associate Torrico Meruvia (2013), who contends that each generation has differing orientations toward work, authority, leadership, and communication, as shown below. Collegial relationships may be enhanced through an understanding of these differences.

Views	Traditionalists (Born before 1945)	Baby Boomers (1946–1965)	Gen X (1966–1980)	Gen Y (Mid-80s to mid-90s)
General Outlook	Practical, Conservative	Optimistic	Cynical	Hopeful
Work Ethic	Committed	Ambition, high achievers	Balanced	Eager
Authority	Respectful	Love/hate	Unimpressed	Equality
Leadership	Hierarchy	Consensus	Competence	Collaboration
Communication Preferences	Personal interaction, letters, memos	Phone calls, personal interactions	Email, text messages	Email, text messages
Relationships	Personal sacrifice	Personal gratification	Reluctance to commit	Inclusive

Adapted from Torrico Meruvia, 2013.

Generation Z is now entering the workforce; these employees have strong technological skills, are open to change, and have a desire for challenge (Heery & Noon, 2017).

Preparing for Supervision

It is the responsibility of the supervisee to prepare for supervision so as to demonstrate accountability and receptivity to feedback and learning. If, instead, the social worker attends supervision sessions unprepared, the use of time may be of limited benefit. The supervisee might ask their supervisor how to best prepare for time spent together. What follows are suggestions suited to supervisory process across many types of service settings:

- Be prepared to share something that has been working well on the job.
- Be prepared to report on your progress toward learning objectives.
- Bring questions and concerns about new agency policies, specifically how they will impact your work.
- Bring solutions to barriers toward effective service delivery and/or compliance with agency protocols.
- Bring ethical dilemmas encountered, and your thoughts about ethical decision-making.
- Be prepared to selectively share emotions related to your work, along with coping skills that you are using.
- Bring notes and/or diagrams that illustrate case-related successes and challenges. Be sure to request feedback about situations in which you feel stuck engaging, assessing, or intervening with clients.

Learning Style and Supervision

It is widely accepted that people learn in different ways. Understanding one's own preferences with regard to learning can assist social workers in acquiring needed knowledge and skill to perform effectively. As proposed by Fleming (1995), the V.A.R.K. model identifies four primary learning styles that reflect an individual's preferred manner of collecting, processing, and storing information. **Visual learners** are said to prefer modes of instruction that include images, charts, and diagrams, while **auditory learners** learn best by listening to lectures, stories, or verbal instructions. Others prefer reading material and writing about it (**read/write learners**). Lastly, **kinesthetic learners** prefer experiential modes of instruction and opportunities to learn by doing. Many inventories and questionnaires are available online to help one in determining their primarily style of learning.

Social workers might consider sharing their dominant learning style with their supervisor so that some learning activities may be tailored to their preferred mode of acquiring knowledge. Visually oriented learners might utilize genograms in supervision when discussing the strengths and difficulties of an individual client or family. Using various symbols and labels, these diagrams depict the intergenerational relationships between family members. Visual learners may also gravitate toward the use of flowcharts or other tools to graphically represent concepts under discussion. Auditory learners may be drawn to verbal instruction, lectures, and podcasts that discuss issues related to social work practice, while those with a reading/writing preference may be motivated to share a favorite article from class with colleagues or supervisors. Workers who learn kinesthetically are likely to benefit by role plays, simulations, or other activities that allow them to practice new skills. They tend to seek out opportunities to learn through "concrete and multi-sensory experiences," and master theory through its application (Fleming, 1995, p. 2).

It is unrealistic to expect that all learning activities will be geared toward the supervisee's dominant style, and many people do well with blended modes of instruction. Moreover, learning preferences can change based on the time and circumstances (Kapadia, 2008). That said, building on one's strengths with respect to learning can enhance the supervisory experience and the social worker's success in attaining performance objectives.

Personality and Supervision

The personality styles of both supervisor and supervisee have a significant impact on the supervisory relationship. Some aspects of personality have been found to have greater bearing on this relationship than others. This is illustrated in a study conducted by Dettlaff (2005) of the effects of personality style on social work student and field instructor perceptions of the supervisory relationship. Results showed that the quality of this relationship was rated significantly higher when the supervisor and supervisee had similar personality types with respect to extroversion versus introversion and sensing versus intuition. The extroversion/introversion dimension concerns where individuals seek energy, with extroverts obtaining it through interaction with other people and introverts finding it through reflection and internal processing. The sensing/intuition realm concerns differing ways of processing information, with "sensors" seeking practical facts that may be obtained through the use of their five senses and "intuitives" relying upon insight and abstract thinking. These findings have important implications for relationship building in supervision.

When an introverted supervisee is matched with an extroverted supervisor, the former may need to verbalize their need for reflection before discussing new material in supervision. This clarification can prevent the supervisor from misunderstanding this preference as an indication of inattention or lack of understanding. The introverted supervisee may also need to mentally prepare for the process of receiving feedback and understand its value in guiding practice. In some cases, they may need to take action and/or make client contact sooner than they would prefer and before they have thoroughly processed all relevant information. In contrast, an extroverted supervisee who is supervised by an introvert may need to voice their need for active engagement in discussion and learning. They may also benefit by participation in group supervision as a supplement to individual meetings with the supervisor.

Differences between the supervisor and supervisee on the sensing versus intuition dimension are also important to consider. Sensing supervisees prefer hands on experiences and direct observation before conceptualizing cases. They also lean toward conventional approaches that have proven success. This inclination may need to be discussed with an intuitive supervisor who prefers the use intuition and creative problem solving. On the other hand, the intuitive supervisee "prefers to understand the big picture and theory behind their actions before delving into the details of new information" (Dettlaff, 2005, p. 82). They are also interested in exploring possibilities and thinking outside of the box. When such personality differences are understood to be learning preferences as opposed to personal limitations, the effectiveness of supervision is enhanced.

NARRATIVE APPLICATION: Adapting Supervision to Personality Differences

Tatum was a social work student who had started her internship at a public behavioral health center. She was bubbly and extroverted, excited to learn as much as she could about mental health treatment. Her field instructor, Gayle, was reserved and introverted—she approached her role as supervisor very methodically. She set up an orientation schedule for Tatum that involved meeting employees and shadowing them as they worked with consumers in individual and group sessions. She also asked Tatum to review charts and the agency policies and procedures manual. When it was time to meet for supervision, she asked Tatum if she had completed all assigned activities. Tatum reported the activities she had completed and those that were pending.

"Do you have any questions?" Gayle asked.

Tatum shared a detailed account of her experience observing a group session that didn't appear to go well. One of the group members had dominated the session, and others appeared frustrated, rolling their eyes as the dominant member spoke. The therapist had assumed a fairly passive role and did little in the way of redirection.

"How would you handle a situation like this?" Tatum asked.

"It would depend," Gayle responded. "You might talk with the therapist about the group. Some of those group members can be challenging."

"OK."

Later in the conversation, Tatum asked Gayle about why she chose to work in the behavioral health field.

"I was offered this position five years ago, and it just felt right. I like the variety. The work is never boring."

"I can see that!" Tatum responded.

"Let's go over some of the safety policies," Gayle said. "I want to make sure you understand them."

Over the following month, Tatum became more and more disappointed in supervision. She had hoped for a more engaging process where she and Gayle would discuss clinical issues and treatment methods. Instead, Gayle cut short conversations and referred her to others, many of whom seemed stressed and unable to take time for mentoring.

During her practicum class, Tatum shared her frustration and asked for feedback from her instructor and fellow students. "Gayle seems aloof and uninterested in me. I am not learning what I had hoped, and I still don't have any cases," she disclosed. The practicum teacher discussed personality differences and how they can affect the supervisory relationship. She encouraged all students in the course to take a brief personality test and share the results with their field instructor. "This can open the door for discussion about personality differences in the workplace."

Tatum completed the test and learned that she was an extrovert and a sensor, who was drawn toward hands-on experiences. She shared the findings with Gayle, who asked to complete the test, as well. Gayle learned that she was an introvert who values intuition. They had a fruitful discussion about how their differences affect the process of supervision. Gayle recognized the need to step up her engagement with Tatum and provide her with additional activities that would provide challenge. She was pleased to learn that Tatum was ready to jump in and take on a client for counseling and case management.

Motivation in the Workplace

Social work practitioners are motivated on the job to the extent that their needs are met through their work. Yet, the needs that drive motivation vary from person to person. Numerous theories have been advanced to explain such variations in human motivation in the workplace, including Maslow's hierarchy, Herzberg's two factor theory, and McClelland's need theory. Each will be summarized below, as applied to social work.

Maslow's Hierarchy

As discussed in Chapter 3, **Maslow's hierarchy of needs** is depicted as a pyramid that contains various primary human motivators. Basic necessities of life (e.g., food, shelter, clothing, healthcare) provide the foundation for other needs listed in ascending order: safety, social connection, esteem, and self-actualization. This model offers some insight into the various categories of need that drive motivation in the workplace. One social worker might be operating at one level of need, while others may be working to gratify needs at a different level of the pyramid. This model assumes that employees should meet their needs at the lower levels of the hierarchy before taking on new assignments aimed at attaining higher-order needs for esteem and self-actualization. However, critics of this model argue that there are many exceptions to this rule. For example, a social worker could be driven to meet social needs even before acquiring optimum salary or health care benefits that provide for basic necessities.

Herzberg's Two Factor Theory

Herzberg argued that the work environment contains two differing factors that promote productivity and job satisfaction. *Hygiene factors* include job security, good working conditions, and high salary. If they are not met, workers become very dissatisfied with their job. However, if met, they do not guarantee that the employee will be highly motivated (Weinbach & Taylor, 2015). *Motivation factors*, on the other hand, do motivate workers, as they appeal to their needs for self-actualization. "They include, for example, challenge, interesting work, freedom, responsibility, and potential for growth" (p. 207). Herzberg encouraged the incorporation of motivation factors into workplace assignments so as to further job enrichment. The direct service worker might act on this theory by requesting opportunities to attend training, take on more challenging assignments, or serve as lead for a project or multidisciplinary team.

McClelland's Need Theory

Research conducted by McClelland identified three different organizational types—those motivated by *power*, *affiliation*, or *achievement*. He suggested that people motivated by power are attracted to positions that offer control as well as influence over others and decision-making opportunities. Those motivated by affiliation have a dominant need for acceptance and interpersonal connection; they tend to avoid conflict or circumstances that might result in rejection. Finally, individuals who are motivated by achievement fear failure and have a strong desire to succeed in their work assignments. It has been pointed out that there are strengths and limitations associated with each type, and some people may behave in accordance with two or more of these motivators in differing circumstances (Weinbach & Taylor, 2015). Social workers might benefit by reflecting upon the strength of their needs across these categories and requesting corresponding learning activities. The result may be enhanced motivation and success in meeting performance goals and objectives.

HIGHLIGHT 11.2: Activities Designed for McClelland's Organizational Types

Based on your self-assessment of your needs for power, affiliation, and/or achievement, consider taking on one or more of the following activities.

If your dominant need is for

Power:

- Read about leadership traits and abilities
- Develop a full understanding of your agency's mission and vision for the future
- Interview leaders in the agency and ask about their approach to leadership
- Seek out opportunities to coordinate agency efforts and facilitate teams

Affiliation:

- Chair a social committee that circulates birthday cards for employees
- Lead workplace efforts to decorate for holidays
- Offer support to volunteers and students working for the organization
- Coordinate monthly meals that tap tastes and recipes from varying cultures

Achievement:

- Organize a contest for employees focused on fundraising or timeliness of documentation
- Write a monthly newsletter that highlights client and staff achievements
- Create a plan for your own advancement in the organization or profession
- Track your own successes in meeting client needs and mastering skills

---

Lifelong Learning

Social work education does not end on graduation day with the receipt of a BSW or MSW diploma—it should be thought of as a continuum that includes a social work degree and continues with on-going efforts to further one's professional development (Congress, 2012). This expectation is explicitly stated in the NASW Code of Ethics (National Association of Social Workers, 2017):

> *Social workers should strive to become and remain proficient in professional practice and the performance of professional functions. Social workers should critically examine and keep current*

with emerging knowledge relevant to social work. Social workers should routinely review the professional literature and participate in continuing education relevant to social work practice and social work ethics. (Section 4.01)

Social work educational programs now stress the importance of lifelong learning, typically defined as an on-going expansion of practice-based knowledge throughout one's social work career. This approach to learning is understood to be vital because "social work finds itself at the intersection of innovation, expanding knowledge, and external scrutiny" (Nissen, Pendell, Jivanjee, & Goodluck, 2014, p. 385). In fact, the Council on Social Work Education (CSWE) (2015) requires educators to build competencies in lifelong learning and commitment to a continual process of updating skills to ensure that practice is effective and relevant.

It is important to recognize, however, that lifelong learning is a personal process that is distinct from lifelong education (Billett, 2010). It moves beyond the completion of workplace training or formal courses and encompasses a "set of values and principles regarding the role of on-going acquisition, integration, and application of new knowledge throughout one's lifetime" (Nissen et al., 2014). Lifelong learning is rooted in a conscious decision to do what it takes to continually broaden one's skills and deepen one's understanding of the needs and strengths of individuals. groups, families, and communities served. Additionally, it requires receptivity to coaching by experts in new or emerging models of practice. An important key to this process is the value of humility, as it promotes awareness of the limits of ones' knowledge and the need to continually expand expertise (Cournoyer & Stanley, 2002).

Most social workers accept the need for continuing education and comply with professional standards or agency policies that require the completion of various courses or training programs. Some may not, however, fully actualize their talents or embrace new approaches that have proven success. To evolve one's practice, new skills must be integrated over time. To maximize that integration, practitioners need to value and embrace corrective feedback from practitioners who have greater training and experience. In order to stay current and relevant, they should utilize expanding resources that are available to advance expertise. Over time, their professional gifts will become easily recognized.

Embracing Corrective Feedback

Lifelong learning is enhanced when one fully utilizes constructive and corrective feedback from clients, supervisors, and mentors. Receiving feedback can be challenging, however, when it triggers the listener's fears and insecurities about not being good enough or of value to others. Thankfully, skill in accepting feedback can be learned. Human resource consultants offer some basic guidelines (Hacker, 2003):

- Make sure you understand the nature of the feedback; ask clarifying questions, as needed
- Listen attentively and avoid interruptions or distractions
- Maintain eye contact with the person giving feedback
- Paraphrase what you heard to ensure understanding

Exploring this process further, London and Smither (2002) introduce the concept of **feedback orientation**, defined as "overall receptivity to feedback including comfort with feedback, tendency to seek feedback and process it mindfully, and the like likelihood of acting on the feedback to guide behavior change and performance improvement" (p. 81). These authors assert that a strong feedback orientation is associated with

- a desire for self-awareness,
- openness to new experiences,

- beliefs that value feedback,
- a focus on attaining mastery and competence, and
- a sense of accountability to use feedback.

London and Smither (2002) suggest that one's initial and secondary thoughts and emotions related to feedback play an important role in the processing of useful information. They recommend a mindful approach to understanding the meaning of feedback and coping with negative emotions. These authors also adopt a person-in-environment approach by conceptualizing the individual's feedback orientation in relation to the feedback culture of their organization. A strong feedback culture is one in which learning is a primary value, supported by frequent coaching to improve job performance. Both individual feedback orientation and the organizations' feedback culture are said to influence how employees receive and utilize critical feedback (see Highlight 11.2).

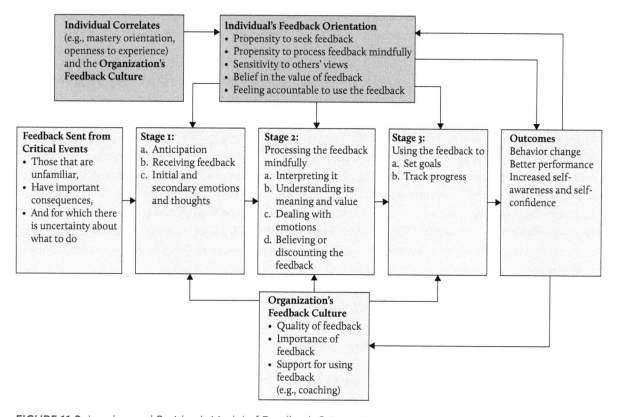

FIGURE 11.2. London and Smither's Model of Feedback Orientation.

Social workers can support their own professional development and a positive feedback culture in their agency by modeling a nondefensive approach to constructive criticism. This involves practice taking in information, considering its importance, and deciding the extent to which it has merit. Acting on viable feedback requires self-discipline and sustained attention to behavior change, which is never easy. The reward is pride and self-worth based on an evolving sense of accomplishment and professional integrity.

Commitment to Evolving Expertise

Evolving expertise as a professional social worker can be attained in a variety of ways—through reading books, journals, and websites, participating in training seminars, and utilizing coaching by experts in an evidence-based model of practice. Sources of on-going training and education are plentiful. NASW offers a range of professional development resources including the following:

- **Annual conferences** at the national and state level offer opportunities to network, and attend innovative workshops, keynote speeches by highly-regarded social workers, and award ceremonies and celebrations. Discounted rates are available to social work students.
- **Social Work Online CE Institute** offers courses in a variety of formats (webinar, podcast, webcast) that have earned NASW accreditation. Courses cover a wide range of topics, including aging, addictions, case management, child abuse, family violence, behavioral health, services to children, youth and families, spirituality, and wellness.
- **Specialty practice sessions (SPS)** are devoted to the creation of online communities focused on particular areas of social work practice. SPS also offer newsletters, webinars, and other practice-specific professional development activities.

Go to https://www.socialworkers.org/Careers/Continuing-Education for further information.

A variety of websites offer detailed information pertaining to evidence-based practice models used in social work. For instance, the Child Welfare Information Gateway of the Department of Health and Human Services provides a link to the <u>California Evidence-Based Clearinghouse for Child Welfare</u> (CEBC). The mission of the clearinghouse is to promote the use of evidence-based practices with youth and families involved with the public child welfare system. It offers a searchable database that includes a wide range of programs; descriptions include the program goals, essential components, delivery, required training, and relevant, peer-reviewed research. A scientific rating is assigned to each model based on the degree to which it is supported by rigorous research. The CEBC website (http://www.cebc4cw.org) is a valuable resource for social workers and family service agencies seeking to adopt a practice model that has proven success.

SAMSHA sponsors the online <u>Evidence-Based Practices Resources Center</u> (https://www.samhsa .gov/ebp-resource-center), which provides information and tools needed to incorporate evidence-based practices into substance abuse and mental health services. Users can search by topic area, population, or targeted audience and access articles, toolkits, treatment improvement protocols, evidence reviews, and links to practice model websites.

The <u>National Child Traumatic Stress Network</u> (https://www.nctsn.org/) provides detailed information on child trauma, trauma-informed care, and evidence-based trauma treatments. Basic and culture-specific fact sheets are offered, along with training guidelines. Practitioners can search for information based on trauma type, language, and audience.

Based at the National Council on Aging, the <u>National Chronic Disease Self-Management Educational Resource Center</u> supports the sustainability of evidence-based health promotion and disease prevention programs in communities and online. It offers learning collaboratives, best practices toolkits, success stories, and webinars on many topics, including Medicare, Medicaid, senior nutrition, economic security for older adults, senior centers, behavioral health, and aging mastery (https://ncoa.reingolddev.com/ center-for-healthy-aging/cdsme-resource-center/).

HIGHLIGHT 11.3: Learning Collaboratives and Communities

Learning collaboratives and communities have become a popular means of promoting innovation and excellence across participating organizations. They provide professionals an opportunity to engage in collaborative learning with peers from other agencies who are working toward similar goals. An example is seen in the <u>Trauma-Sensitive Schools National Learning Community</u>, sponsored by the National Council for Behavioral Health (NCBH) with the aim of supporting the implementation of trauma-sensitive educational environments (Lewis, Johnson, & Black, 2018). Core implementation teams are created at participating schools and may include teachers, social workers, school counselors, administrators, and parents. Team members are engaged in training webinars on topics related to the impact of trauma on brain development, the effects of trauma on student learning, and practices adopted by trauma-sensitive schools. They also participate in individual consult calls and cohort calls with other participating schools. In addition, they each have access to online tools, resources, and list-serve correspondence.

As stated in the NCBH National Learning Community Informational Webinar, the collaborative learning model is devoted to the following:

- Collective knowledge
- Real world experiences
- Social networking
- Widespread practice improvement
- Common and unique concerns, challenges, and needs

Go to the NCBH website at https://www.thenationalcouncil.org/ for additional information.

Unveiling Your Professional Gifts

Each and every social worker has unique gifts, some more fully actualized than others. With time and sustained practice, these talents, skills, and abilities become more apparent as the social worker's style evolves and shapes their professional identity. Along the way, these gifts can be unveiled in circumstances where they support healing, recovery, hope, and transformation. This is the ultimate reward of social work practice.

To determine your gifts, you might consider times on the job when things seemed to click into place quite easily. Perhaps you noticed that you have a natural ability to tune into another person's areas of strength and vulnerability. In addition, you may have an in-depth understanding of the values embraced by a particular culture and can connect easily with members of that cultural group. Or, you may have a unique strength when it comes to applying theoretical concepts to real life situations. The following questions are aimed at assisting social workers in defining their true gifts:

- Do you have compassion for people experiencing hardship?
- Do you have an ability to see beyond labels and stereotypes, and connect with oppressed individuals, families, communities?
- Are you fully present when conversing with another person?
- Are you able to leverage your own experiences with adversity in ways that help others?
- Do you have bicultural or bilingual abilities?
- Do you embrace theoretical concepts and apply them with ease to real life circumstances?
- Can you clearly articulate the mission of social work and your organization?

- Are you skilled in motivating others?
- Can you speak to the values of your agency in compelling ways?
- Do you have strong organizational skills, as applied to work-related responsibilities?
- Do you enjoy research, statistics, data collection, and analysis?
- Are you motivated to address social justice issues through macro-level activities?

The above list is certainly not exhaustive when it comes to recognizing the talents, skills, and abilities of social workers. The reader is encouraged to identify others that may be relevant to their field of social work practice. Please be reminded that such gifts become more valuable over time, as used with differing people, places, and presenting problems. The fine-tuning of one's skill is a key outcome of lifelong learning.

HIGHLIGHT 11.4: The Social Work Portfolio

Cournoyer and Stanley (2002) recommend that social workers create a portfolio that demonstrates their on-going growth and professional development. They view the portfolio as

A well-organized and carefully prepared collection of documents related to one's readiness for profes-sional social work practice. [It] reflects documentary evidence of an active, self-directed approach to learning and ongoing growth as a social work student or practitioner. (p. 1)

Suggested components of the portfolio include the following:

- Table of Contents
- Introductory statement that reflects one's aspirations and learning goals
- Current resumé
- Personal statement that describes one's philosophical approach to service
- Copies of academic transcripts and diplomas
- Self-assessment of strengths and weaknesses as a social worker
- Certificates of completion for training seminars
- Professional licenses
- Awards relevant to professional practice

A well-crafted social work portfolio is intended to increase one's "employability quotient," thus increasing their odds of obtaining preferred positions in the profession (p. 4).

Self-Care: Gratitude Is Gold

Gratitude can be defined as a life orientation toward "noticing and appreciating the positives in the world" (Wood, Froh, & Geraghty, 2010, p. 891). This orientation includes appreciation of others, and a focus on what one has, beauty encountered, and the positive in the present moment. Research has revealed that gratitude is linked to positive affect, well-being, and improved interpersonal relationships (Emmons & McCullough, 2003). Thus, it is a valuable tool for self-care in social work.

Gratitude can be cultivated by the following:

- Taking a gratitude walk in which one notices aspects of their environment that bring joy and beauty

- Posting gratitude quotes in the workplace or home (e.g., "put on your positive *perspectacles*"), as suggested by Social Work Community (http://www.socialworkcommunity.com/2016/06/gratitude-a-self-care-tool/)
- Writing a letter of gratitude to someone who has been helpful
- Writing a "reverse bucket list," including meaningful experiences that have already occurred (Social Work Community)
- Using an app for one's smart phone that provides regular reminders to be grateful

Social work provides many opportunities for gratitude. In reflecting upon the last year, practitioners might acknowledge insights acquired from mentors and supervisors. They may also embrace gratitude for lessons learned from clients and colleagues. Even stressful experiences can be seen for the benefits they have offered in terms of increased wisdom, confidence, and self-efficacy. Generally speaking, the social worker might thank their lucky stars that they have embarked upon a career that, while challenging, is rarely boring. Gratitude leads to satisfaction and contentment with the present, as imperfect as it may be.

SUMMARY

The aim of this chapter is to inspire social workers to take ownership of their learning throughout their career. To begin, the purpose and value of supervision was covered, along with the use of performance objectives to guide development of knowledge, skill, and successful relationships in the workplace. Next, factors that influence supervision were discussed, including learning style and personality. Lifelong learning was conceptualized, and resources for on-going professional development were shared. Finally, practitioners were encouraged to discover their unique gifts and take pride in their use across all realms of practice.

KEY TERMS

Emotional intelligence	Inclusive environment	Maslow's hierarchy of needs
Feedback orientation	Learning style (visual, auditory, read/	McClelland's need theory
Herzberg's two-factor theory	write, kinesthetic)	Social exchange theory

DISCUSSION QUESTIONS

1. What type of learning activities are most suited to your personality and learning styles?

2. Which of McClelland's organizational types is/are consistent with the factors that motivate you in social work? How so?

3. What challenges do you face in accepting corrective feedback? How can you overcome these challenges?

SKILL DEVELOPMENT ACTIVITIES

1. Interview someone who belongs do a different generational group than you do. Share with them the chart in this chapter concerning the multigenerational workforce. Inquire about the extent to which the traits listed for their generation are consistent with their orientation toward work ethic, authority, leadership, communication, and relationships. How does this information help you understand this individual in a deeper way than you did previously?

2. Explore one of the websites described in the section entitled Commitment to Evolving Expertise. What did you learn that may guide your on-going professional development?

3. Review the list of questions above aimed at helping you identify your unique professional gifts. Maintain a journal over time in which you describe experiences that reflect your assets.

REFERENCES

American Psychiatric Association (2013). *Diagnostic and statistical manual of mental disorders* (5th ed.). Washington, DC: American Psychiatric Publishing.

Billett, S. (2010). The perils of confusing lifelong learning with lifelong education. *International Journal of Lifelong Education, 29*, 401–413.

Blau, P. M. (1964). *Exchange and power in social life.* New York, NY: Wiley.

Bohlinger, A. I., Wahlig, J. L., & Trudeau-Hern, S. (2014). Teaching self-compassion to decrease performance anxiety in clinicians. In R. A. Bean, S. D. Davis, & M. P. Davey (Eds.), *Clinical supervision activities for increasing competence and self-awareness.* Hoboken, NJ: John Wiley & Sons.

Congress, E. P. (2012). Guest editorial continuing education: Lifelong learning for social work practitioners and educators. *Journal of Social Work Education, 4*, 397–401.

Council on Social Work Education. (2015). Educational, policy, and accreditation standards for baccalaureate and master's social work programs. Retrieved from https://cswe.org

Cournoyer, B. R., & Stanley, M. J. (2002). *The social work portfolio: Planning, assessing and documenting lifelong learning in a dynamic profession.* Pacific Grove, CA: Brooks/Cole.

Cox, K., & Steiner, S. (2013). *Self-care in social work: A guide for practitioners, supervisors, and administrators.* Washington, DC: NASW Press.

Dettlaff, A. (2005). The influence of personality type on the supervisory relationship in field education. *Journal of Baccalaureate Social Work, 11*, 71–86.

Emmons, R. A., & McCullough, M. E. (2003). Counting blessings versus burdens: Experimental studies of gratitude and subjective well-being in life. *Journal of Personality and Social Psychology, 84*, 377–389.

Fleming, N. D. (1995), I'm different; not dumb. Modes of presentation (VARK) in the tertiary classroom. In A. Zelmer (Ed.), Research and Development in Higher Education, *Proceedings of the 1995 Annual Conference of the Higher Education and Research Development Society of Australasia (HERDSA), HERDSA, 18*, 308–313.

Goleman, D. (1998). What makes a leader? *Harvard Business Review, 76*, 93–102.

Hacker, C. A. (2003). Maintaining positive relationships when giving and receiving critical feedback. *Information Systems Management, 20*, 77–79.

Heery, E., & Noon, M. (2017). *A dictionary of human resource management* (3rd ed.). New York, NY: Oxford University Press.

Kadushin, A., & Harkness, D. (2002). *Supervision in social work* (4th ed.). New York, NY: Columbia University Press.

Kapadia, R. (2008, November). *Teaching and learning styles in engineering education.* Paper presented at the 38th Annual Frontiers in Education Conference. doi:10.1109/FIE.2008.4720326

Lewis, S., Johnson, K., & Black, P. (2018). Trauma-sensitive schools national learning community [Webinar]. Retrieved from https://www.thenationalcouncil.org/wp-content/uploads/2014/02/National-Trauma-Sensitive-Schools-Informational-Webinar.pdf

London, M., & Smither, J. W. (2002). Feedback orientation, feedback culture, and the longitudinal performance management process. *Human Resource Management Review, 12*, 81–100.

Mor Barak, M. E., Travis, D. J., Pyun, H., & Xie, B. (2009). The impact of supervision on worker outcomes: A meta-analysis. *Social Service Review, 83*, 3–32.

National Association of Social Workers. (2013). *Best practice standards in social work supervision.* Retrieved from https://www.socialworkers.org

National Association of Social Workers, (2017). *Code of ethics of the National Association of Social Workers.* Washington, DC: NASW Press.

Nissen, L., Pendell, K., Jivanjee, P., & Goodluck, C. (2014). Lifelong learning in social work education: A review of the literature and implications for the future. *Journal of Teaching in Social Work, 34*, 384–400.

Social Work Community. (2017, January 3). *Gratitude (A self-care strategy).* Retrieved from http://www.socialworkcommunity.com/2016/06/gratitude-a-self-care-tool/

Tallia, A. F., Lanham, M. J., McDaniel, R. R., & Crabtree, B. J. (2006). 7 characteristics of successful work relationships. *Family Practice Management.* Retrieved from www.aafp.org/fpm

Torrico Meruvia, R. (2013). Navigating a multigenerational workforce in child welfare. *Practice Perspectives.* National Association of Social Workers. Retrieved from https://www.socialworkers.org/

Weinbach, R. W., & Taylor, L. M. (2015). *The social worker as manager: A practical guide to success* (7th ed.). Boston, MA: Pearson.

Wood, A. M., Froh, J., & Geraghty, A. (2010). Gratitude and well-being: A review and theoretical integration. *Clinical Psychological Review, 30*, 890–905.

CREDITS

INDEX

Lightning Source UK Ltd.
Milton Keynes UK
UKHW051114020622
403857UK00003B/53